CIVILITY, BARBARISM, AND THE EVOLUTION OF INTERNATIONAL HUMANITARIAN LAW

Efforts to moderate conflict are as old as conflict itself. Throughout the ages, restraint in warfare has been informed by religious and ethical considerations, chivalry and class, and, increasingly since the mid-nineteenth century, a body of customary and treaty law variously referred to as the laws of war, the law of armed conflict (LOAC), or international humanitarian law (IHL). As they evolved from the mid-nineteenth century, these laws were increasingly underpinned by humanitarianism, then, in the mid-twentieth century, were assumed to be universal.

But violations of these restraints are also as old as conflict itself. The history of conflict is replete with examples of exclusions from protections designed to moderate warfare. This edited volume explores the degree to which protections in modern warfare might be informed by notions of 'civility' and 'barbarism', or, to put it another way, asks if only those deemed to be civilised are afforded protections prescribed by the laws of war.

MATT KILLINGSWORTH is Senior Lecturer in International Relations at the University of Tasmania. He has held visiting fellowships at the University of Oxford's Institute for Ethics and Armed Conflict and the European University Institute. He is the co-editor of *Violence and the State* (Manchester University Press, 2016) with Matthew Sussex and Jan Pakulski, and the former Chair of the Tasmanian Red Cross International Humanitarian Law Committee.

TIM MCCORMACK is Professor of International Law at the University of Tasmania and the Special Adviser on War Crimes to the Prosecutor of the International Criminal Court in The Hague. He was the Foundation Australian Red Cross Professor of International Humanitarian Law and Founding Director of the Asia Pacific Centre for Military Law at Melbourne Law School, Charles H. Stockton Distinguished Scholar-in-Residence at the US Naval War College, and James Barr Ames Visiting Professor at Harvard Law School. He co-edited (with Suzannah Linton and Sandesh Sivakumaran) *Asia-Pacific Perspectives on International Humanitarian Law* (Cambridge University Press, 2019).

CIVILITY, BARBARISM, AND THE EVOLUTION OF INTERNATIONAL HUMANITARIAN LAW

Who Do the Laws of War Protect?

Edited by

MATT KILLINGSWORTH

University of Tasmania

TIM MCCORMACK

University of Tasmania

CAMBRIDGE
UNIVERSITY PRESS

CAMBRIDGE
UNIVERSITY PRESS

Shaftesbury Road, Cambridge CB2 8EA, United Kingdom

One Liberty Plaza, 20th Floor, New York, NY 10006, USA

477 Williamstown Road, Port Melbourne, VIC 3207, Australia

314–321, 3rd Floor, Plot 3, Splendor Forum, Jasola District Centre, New Delhi – 110025, India

103 Penang Road, #05-06/07, Visioncrest Commercial, Singapore 238467

Cambridge University Press is part of Cambridge University Press & Assessment, a department of the University of Cambridge.

We share the University's mission to contribute to society through the pursuit of education, learning and research at the highest international levels of excellence.

www.cambridge.org
Information on this title: www.cambridge.org/9781108488495

DOI: 10.1017/9781108764049

First published 2024

A catalogue record for this publication is available from the British Library.

Library of Congress Cataloging-in-Publication Data
Names: Killingsworth, Matt, editor. | McCormack, Timothy L. H., editor.
Title: Civility, barbarism, and the evolution of international humanitarian law : who do the laws of war protect? / edited by Matt Killingsworth, University of Tasmania; Tim McCormack, University of Tasmania.
Description: Cambridge, United Kingdom ; New York, NY : Cambridge University Press, 2023. | Includes bibliographical references and index.
Identifiers: LCCN 2023031155 (print) | LCCN 2023031156 (ebook) | ISBN 9781108488495 (hardback) | ISBN 9781108726450 (paperback) | ISBN 9781108764049 (ebook)
Subjects: LCSH: War (International law) | Humanitarian law. | Courtesy. | Civilization.
Classification: LCC KZ6471 .C557 2023 (print) | LCC KZ6471 (ebook) | DDC 341.6/7–dc23/eng/20230929
LC record available at https://lccn.loc.gov/2023031155
LC ebook record available at https://lccn.loc.gov/2023031156

ISBN 978-1-108-48849-5 Hardback

CONTENTS

CONTRIBUTORS

GAVIN DALY is Senior Lecturer in Modern European History at the University of Tasmania. He has published widely on Britain and France during the Napoleonic Wars, with a particular focus on the cultural history of war, and on the laws of war. His most recent book is *Storm and Sack: British Sieges, Violence and the Laws of War in the Napoleonic Era, 1799–1815* (Cambridge University Press, 2022).

RICHARD DEVETAK is Professor of the History of International Thought at The University of Queensland (UQ). He was Head of the School of Political Science and International Studies at UQ from 2013 to 2018. Richard's major contributions have been in the area of international relations theory, more specifically in the exposition and analysis of Frankfurt School Critical Theory and post-structuralism, and in international intellectual history. His writings in these areas have been published in leading journals, including *International Affairs*, *Millennium*, *History of European Ideas*, *International Theory*, and *Review of International Studies*. His books include *Critical International Theory: An Intellectual History* (Oxford University Press, 2018); as lead editor, *An Introduction to International Relations* (Cambridge University Press, 2017, 3rd edition); and, as co-editor with Jacqui True, *Theories of International Relations* (Bloomsbury, 6th edition, 2022). He currently co-edits *The Review of International Studies.*

SIOBHAIN GALEA is a Migration Lawyer with Carina Ford Lawyers in Melbourne and a member of both the Australian Red Cross Victoria Youth Advisory and the International Humanitarian Law Advisory Committees. She graduated from the University of Tasmania with BA/LLB and 1st class honours in Law in 2018 and was the Legal Assistant to the Special Adviser on International Humanitarian Law to the Prosecutor of the International Criminal Court in The Hague in 2019. Siobhain's research for and contribution to the writing of this chapter was undertaken while she was a student at the University of Tasmania Law School.

ROSEMARY GREY is Senior Lecturer at Sydney Law School and Co-Director of the Sydney Centre for International Law. She is also an active member of the Sydney Southeast Asia Centre at the University of Sydney. Her research focuses on gender and international criminal law, particularly in the International Criminal Court (ICC) and Extraordinary Chambers in the Courts of Cambodia (ECCC). Her book *Prosecuting Sexual and Gender-Based Crimes in the International Criminal Court* was published by Cambridge University Press in 2019. She has been invited to present her research at international forums, including the ICC Assembly of States Parties and the ICC Office of the Prosecutor.

MARK KERSTEN is Assistant Professor in the Criminology and Criminal Justice Department at the University of the Fraser Valley and Senior Consultant at the Wayamo Foundation. Mark is the founder of the blog Justice in Conflict and author of the book, published by Oxford University Press, of the same name. He holds an MSc and a PhD in International Relations from the London School of Economics and a BA (Hons) from the University of Guelph. Mark has previously been a research associate at the Refugee Law Project in Uganda and a researcher at Justice Africa and Lawyers for Justice in Libya in London.

MATT KILLINGSWORTH is Senior Lecturer in International Relations at the University of Tasmania. His research focuses on the history of the laws of war, international criminal justice, and international order. He has held visiting fellowships at the University of Oxford's Institute for Ethics and Armed Conflict and the European University Institute, is the co-editor of *Violence and the State* (Manchester University Press, 2016), with Matthew Sussex and Jan Pakulski, and is the author of several chapters and journal articles on the relationship between international criminal justice and international order.

RAIN LIIVOJA is Professor and Deputy Dean (Research) at the University of Queensland Law School, where he leads the Law and the Future of War research group. Rain is also Visiting Legal Fellow at the Australian Department of Foreign Affairs and Trade and Senior Fellow with the Lieber Institute for Law and Land Warfare at the US Military

Academy at West Point. Rain's current research focuses on the legal challenges associated with military applications of science and technology. His broader research and teaching interests include general international law, the law of armed conflict, and human rights law. He is the author of *Criminal Jurisdiction over Armed Forces Abroad* (Cambridge University Press, 2017) and a co-editor of *Autonomous Cyber Capabilities under International Law* (NATO CCDCOE, 2021) and the *Routledge Handbook of the Law of Armed Conflict* (Routledge, 2016). Rain is Co-Editor-in-Chief of the *Journal of International Humanitarian Legal Studies* (published by Brill | Nijhoff).

TIM MCCORMACK is Professor of International Law at the University of Tasmania and the Special Adviser on War Crimes to the Prosecutor of the International Criminal Court in The Hague (since 2010). He was the Foundation Australian Red Cross Professor of International Humanitarian Law at the University of Melbourne (1996–2010), Charles H. Stockton Distinguished Scholar-in-Residence at the US Naval War College (2015–16), and James Barr Ames Visiting Professor at Harvard Law School (January 2016 and January 2020). He is deeply interested in the historical development of international humanitarian law and particularly in the 'othering' of 'uncivilised peoples'.

REBECCA SHAW is Research Associate at the Omega Research Foundation, a UK-based human rights charity. She has an interest in the intersections between corporate actors and questions of security and human rights. At Omega, Rebecca researches the manufacture and trade of military, security, and policing weapons and equipment, and their use in human rights violations, including torture. She is currently working on the campaign for an international Torture-Free Trade Treaty. Her prior academic research – and PhD – examined the regulatory and normative environment around private military and security companies.

REBECCA SUTTON is Senior Lecturer in International Law at the University of Glasgow. Previously, Rebecca was a Leverhulme Trust Early Career Fellow at Edinburgh Law School, a post-doctoral researcher on the European Research Council-funded 'Individualisation of War' project at the University of Oxford, and a postdoctoral fellow at McGill University. Rebecca received her PhD in Law in 2018 from the London School of Economics, where she was a Pierre Elliot Trudeau Foundation scholar and a Social Sciences and Humanities Research Council doctoral scholar. Rebecca's current research agenda explores the role of emotions in IHL, frontline humanitarian negotiations, innovations in IHL pedagogy, and 'participatory action research' methodologies for working with displaced youth. Her first monograph, *The Humanitarian Civilian: How the Idea of Distinction Circulates Within and Beyond IHL*, was published by Oxford University Press in 2021.

MILOŠ VEC is Professor of European Legal and Constitutional History at Vienna University and was Permanent Fellow at the Institute for Human Sciences (Vienna) from 2016 to 2020. He received his Habilitation in Legal History, Philosophy of Law, Theory of Law, and Civil Law from Goethe University Frankfurt am Main. Until 2012 he worked and taught at the Max Planck Institute for European Legal History. He has also taught at the Universities of Bonn, Hamburg, Konstanz, Lyon, Tübingen, and Vilnius. He was Fellow to the Wissenschaftskolleg (Institute of Advanced Study), Berlin, 2011/2012; Senior Global Hauser Fellow at New York University in 2017; and an associate member of the Research Centre 'Normative Orders' at Frankfurt University. Recently, he spent his sabbatical leave from Vienna University as an honorary fellow at the Historisches Kolleg (Institute of Advanced Study), Munich, in the winter semester of 2022/23. He works as a freelance journalist, particularly for *Frankfurter Allgemeine Zeitung*.

DANIEL WESTBURY is a Policy Officer with the Department of Foreign Affairs and Trade in Canberra. He graduated from the University of Tasmania with BA/LLB and 1st class honours in Law in 2018 and Daniel's research for and contribution to the writing of this chapter was undertaken while he was a student at the University of Tasmania Law School.

PREFACE AND ACKNOWLEDGEMENTS

The genesis for this book was a question asked of Matt in a Politics and International Relations school seminar at the University of Queensland. Matt's presentation included Emer de Vattel's (1758) famous quote qualifying who the newly emerging international laws of war should protect: 'when we are at war with a savage nation, who observe no rules, and never give any quarter, we may punish them in the persons of any of their people whom we take'. The question asked was whether Vattel's dictum might still ring true; were protections in warfare still informed by notions of 'civilised' and 'uncivilised' (or 'barbarian')?

Efforts to moderate conflict are as old as conflict itself. Throughout the ages, restraint in warfare has been informed by religious and ethical considerations, chivalry, and class, and, increasingly since the mid-nineteenth century, a body of customary and treaty law variously referred to as the laws of war, the law of armed conflict, or international humanitarian law. As they evolved from the mid-nineteenth century, these laws were increasingly underpinned by humanitarianism, then, in the mid-twentieth century, were assumed to be universal, since, in the words of Jean Pictet, famous for his International Committee of the Red Cross Commentaries on the Geneva Conventions of 1949, they applied 'to all men and countries'.

But violations of these restraints are also as old as conflict itself. The history of conflict is replete with examples of exclusions from protections designed to moderate warfare. This edited volume explores the degree to which protections in modern warfare might be informed by notions of 'civility' and 'barbarism', or, to put it another way, asks if only those deemed to be civilised are afforded protections prescribed by the laws of war.

This question formed the basis of a workshop hosted by the University of Tasmania in November 2016, funded by a grant from the University's College of Arts, Law and Education. The papers presented by local and international colleagues from international relations, history, and law suggested to us that not only was there academic merit in these questions but that an interdisciplinary approach was necessary to interrogate these questions more fully. We were delighted to be able to bring together colleagues from various disciplines including history, law, politics, and international relations. The ensuing conversations were rich, and we are confident that the various contributions to this volume have each benefitted from interdisciplinary collegiality so evident throughout the workshop.

The success of this workshop was in no small part due to the amazing organisational support provided by Bronwyn Peters and Hannah Salisbury, and we acknowledge their important contribution to this volume. We also wish to express our heartfelt thanks to Julia Flint for her fantastic editing skills. We are indebted to Julia's keen eye for detail, her patience, and her skill in harmonising ten authors into a uniform and coherent volume.

Matt and Tim are each grateful to the other for shared friendship and mutual encouragement to continue exploring the important nexuses between international law and international relations. The fact that we support rival football teams (of equal ill-repute) only adds to the mirth and jocularity in our collaboration!

ABBREVIATIONS

CIJA	Commission for International Justice and Accountability
CPA	Comprehensive Peace Agreement
DCAF	Democratic Control of Armed Forces
DRC	Democratic Republic of Congo
EAC	Extraordinary African Chambers
FPLC	*Forces patriotiques pour la libération du Congo*
IASC	Inter-agency Standing Committee
ICC	International Criminal Court
ICJ	International Court of Justice
ICRC	International Committee of the Red Cross
ICTR	International Criminal Tribunal for Rwanda
ICTY	International Criminal Tribunal for the former Yugoslavia
IDP	Internally Displaced Person(s)
IHL	International Humanitarian Law
LOAC	Law of Armed Conflict
LRA	Lord's Resistance Army
MCDA	Military and Civil Defence Assets
MDF	Montreux Document Forum
NATO	North Atlantic Treaty Organisation
NGO	Non-governmental Organisation
OTP	Office of the Prosecutor
PMSC	Private Military and Security Company(ies)
PoC	Protection of Civilians
SPLM/A	Sudan People's Liberation Movement/Army
UN	United Nations
UNHAS	United Nations Humanitarian Air Services
UNHCR	United Nations High Commissioner for Refugees
UNMIS	United Nations Mission in Sudan
UNMISS	United Nations Mission in South Sudan
UNSC	United Nations Security Council
UPC	*Union des patriotes congolais*

1

Introduction

Civility, Barbarism, and the Evolution of International Humanitarian Law

MATT KILLINGSWORTH AND TIM MCCORMACK

For as long as wars have been fought, there have been rules that attempted to limit their occurrence and moderate their conduct. Beginning in the mid-nineteenth century, these rules have since developed into an almost universal system of customary and treaty laws determining under what circumstances states can go to war (*jus ad bellum*) and what constitutes acceptable conduct during war (*jus in bello*).

Modern *jus in bello* has two principal components: so-called Geneva law, which is mainly concerned with the protection of victims of armed conflict, and rests primarily on the four 1949 *Geneva Conventions* and the two 1977 *Additional Protocols*; and so-called Hague law, named in reference to the 1899 and 1907 *Hague Conventions*, which is concerned with controlling types of weapons and means and method of warfare. Historically, international humanitarian law (IHL) was used in reference primarily to 'Geneva' law; however, it has become the norm for IHL to incorporate both the 'Geneva' and 'Hague' dimensions of *jus in bello* law, and this is how the term is used and understood in this volume (McCoubrey, 1998, p. 2).

Attempts to moderate behaviour in war, as observed by John Keegan (2001, p. 26), are as old as war itself: while 'war may have got worse with the passage of time, . . . the ethic of restraint has barely been absent from its practise . . . Even in the age of total warfare . . . there remained taboos, enshrined in law and thankfully widely observed'. Up until the middle of the nineteenth century, attempts to restrain the use of force during conflict existed mainly as customary rules, often agreed to among warring (European) parties and, most importantly, generally existing without consistent punishments for violations of said rules and customs.

The pre-World War I enthusiasm for laws designed to limit warfare was understandably quashed by the events of the Great War. The mood following the end of World War II, however, was discernibly different. Policy makers, scarred by two world wars and the Great Depression, set about the construction of a new, liberal world order, underpinned by the idea of 'never again', to be realised through the establishment of multilateral institutions. Of greatest significance with respect to IHL are the four 1949 *Geneva Conventions* (and the subsequent 1977 *Additional Protocols*). Indeed, the *Geneva Conventions* signal the beginning of a shift away from laws focused on belligerents towards 'humanitarian law', primarily concerned with the well-being and protection of individual war victims (Neff, 2005).[1] In the post-war era, so-called Geneva law has been complemented by humanitarian-focused progress in so-called Hague laws, with international conventions banning chemical and biological weapons, land mines, cluster munitions, and, most recently, a treaty that bans nuclear weapons (see United Nations General Assembly, 2017).

While *jus ad bellum* is not the focus of this book, the *jus in bello* 'cannot be properly understood without some examination of the separate body of rules which determines when resort to force is permissible' (Greenwood, 2008, p. 1). For much of the modern period, the *jus ad bellum* was recognised as the sovereign right of the state to go to war (Kreβ and Barriga, 2017, p. 1). Indeed, up until the end of World War I, attempts to bound warfare in a legal framework had focused primarily on the *jus in bello*. The horrors of the Great War, however, served to focus policy makers' attentions on efforts to place legal restrictions on future resorts to war; 'to replace the anarchic Hobbesian world with a more regulated order' (Neff, 2005, p. 285). In the interwar years, these efforts were realised first through the League of Nations Covenant, which focused on the provision of mechanisms to prevent war, and second through the 1928 *Pact of Paris* (also known as the Kellogg–Briand Pact), which explicitly condemned 'recourse to war' for the solution of international disputes, combined with a renunciation of war 'as an instrument of foreign policy' (cited in Neff, 2005, p. 294; see also Hathaway and Shapiro, 2017). In the contemporary era, the use of force is prohibited under Article 2 (4) of the United Nations (UN) Charter. Overcoming the

[1] For Robert Kolb (2013, p. 45), the importance of the Geneva Conventions was far-reaching: 'The Law was now clearly influenced by the idea of a thorough international codification of mandatory norms of behaviour imposed on belligerents.'

limitations of both the Covenant and Kellogg–Briand Pact (see Neff, 2005, pp. 285–313), the Charter bans all resorts to armed force, except in the case of individual or collective self-defence (Article 51 of the UN Charter) or when authorised by the UN Security Council (arts. 43–48 of the UN Charter).

International legal positivists tend to stress that the two bodies of law are distinct from each other and that irrespective of the merits of resort to force consistently with, or in violation of the *jus ad bellum*, all parties to an armed conflict are bound equally by the *jus in bello* in the conduct of military operations. This distinction may be fine in theory, but it constitutes a superficial analysis of some contemporary realities that reveal significant overlap between the *jus ad bellum* and *jus in bello*. Frédéric Mégret's 'original sin' concept not only exposes such an over-simplification but also serves as an informant for the ideas and themes explored in this volume; in the rush to embrace the humanitarian imperative underlying the late nineteenth-century emergence of the *jus in bello*, contemporary scholars often conveniently overlook that the colonial powers that developed multilateral legal constraints on the waging of war in the name of humanity and civilisation only did so on the basis that it applied to war between civilised peoples, and certainly not to war involving 'uncivilised savages' (Mégret, 2006, pp. 265, 268). Indeed, the historical exclusion of 'uncivilised savages' from the protection of the newly emergent multilateral humanitarian constraints on the waging of war again rears its unprincipled head in the justification of the endless global war on terror. Western liberal democracies, and the United States in particular, justify their resort to lethal military force on the basis of the *jus ad bellum* ('the terrorists dared to attack us') but then justify the non-extension of the protections of the *jus in bello* on the basis of the 'lawlessness' of terrorists, who disregard all notions of human dignity (these are 'unlawful combatants' who have forfeited their rights of protection under the law). This rationale, used for the denial of prisoner of war status and to justify torture of detainees, is the twenty-first-century manifestation of the nineteenth-century 'uncivilised savages' concept. And, just as the supposedly 'civilised and humane' descended into savagery in their wars against indigenous peoples, so too the self-declared defenders of the dignity of humanity have descended into their own terrorising savagery in dealing with the 'terrorists'.

There are a couple of points worth making with regard to this short chronology of attempts to moderate and restrain war via international legal frameworks. The first concerns the extraordinary speed of change:

when one considers the historically central (and generally accepted) role that war played in maintaining international order, and the degree to which war was a legitimate way of righting wrongs, the relative alacrity with which war was delegitimised as a tool of statecraft through a period of no more than fifty years is extraordinary. Similarly, where once only the state exercised jurisdiction over the definition and prosecution of war crimes committed by its citizens or on its territory, the establishment of new judicial mechanisms, such as the International Criminal Tribunal for the Former Yugoslavia (ICTY), International Criminal Tribunal for Rwanda (ICTR), and more recently the International Criminal Court (ICC), provides evidence of a progressive 'movement away from a legal system in which states are the sole legal subjects' (Reus-Smit, 2004, p. 7).

The second point is also historical. In the period between the late nineteenth century and the end of World War II, there was general parity in the development of humanitarian efforts to progress the *jus in bello* and *jus ad bellum*. Since 1945, however, there has been uneven progress of the law. Nowhere is this more evident than in the case of punishing violations of these laws. High-profile *jus in bello* prosecutions at the ICTR, ICTY, ICC, and various special tribunals are contrasted with an absence of prosecutions for violations of *jus ad bellum* law.[2] Given the profound significance of the Nuremberg and Tokyo War Crimes Trials on the subsequent development of international criminal law, and the overwhelming focus of both trials on the crime of aggression as the pre-eminent crime on trial, the more recent atrophying of a multilateral commitment to accountability for the crime of aggression in the face of spectacular advances in the prosecution of war crimes is staggering. The current proposal for an ad hoc international tribunal to try Russian leaders for the crime of aggression undoubtedly represents an opportunity to reinforce the normative prohibition on violations of the *jus ad bellum*. But that same proposal is also fraught with the unsettling reality that Western nations would relish the prosecution of Russian leaders but perhaps not at the risk of subjecting themselves to similar processes in the future wars that they initiate unlawfully. While the state has acquiesced (to a degree) to being held to account for the worst violations of IHL at a level beyond the state, it continues to resist efforts to be held responsible by supra-state legal mechanisms for going to war.

[2] There is the potential for this situation to change now that the defined crime of aggression falls within the jurisdiction of the International Criminal Court (see Kreβ and Barriga, 2017).

There is also a degree to which the historical epoch in which the modern laws of war were created compounds the tension identified above. As war fighting in continental Europe became increasingly monopolised by the emerging nation-state, so too was the consent of nation-states a key principle in the establishment of mechanisms that sought to place legal boundaries around organised violence (Killingsworth, 2016, p. 101). Thus, for much of the modern period, states regarded the right to conduct war as a legitimate tool of statecraft; commenting in 1880, German Field-Marshall-General Count von Moltke wrote that 'war is an element in the order of the world ordained by God' (cited in Phillipson, 2015, p. 139).

The nature and character of war means that there have always been limitations to the efficacy of laws of war in limiting and moderating conflict. Current events, though, reveal these limitations more starkly than even before. The illegal invasion and subsequent annexation in 2014 of Crimea by Russia and more recently the illegal invasion of Ukraine and the purported Russian annexation of the Donbas provinces in Eastern Ukraine; the horrific and repeated violations of IHL in Syria, Ukraine, and Afghanistan, including the targeting of civilians and medical facilities, the use of torture, the recruitment of child soldiers, widespread rape – particularly of women – and the use of barrel bombs and chemical weapons; all serve to create scepticism, even despair, about the existence of any effective constraints on the waging of war.

Similarly, when one considers the nature and character of war, it is understandable that the evolution of attempts to moderate and constrain warfare through recourse to international law is replete with contradictions and tensions: discord between the growing language of humanity juxtaposed with ongoing atrocity, discord between multilateral mechanisms of accountability and ongoing impunity for violations of the law, and military operations conducted in compliance with the law which nevertheless result in extensive loss of civilian life.

In appreciating the institutional perpetuity of war, while simultaneously acknowledging the historically informed, inherent limitations of attempts to bound its conduct by international law, this book aims to provide answers to the following three, interrelated questions: first, is there an historical continuity with legal protections in war being informed by notions of 'civility' and 'barbarity'?; second, what is the relationship between the ideals and operational realities in IHL?; and third, what are the limitations of international laws designed to restrain excess in war?

The first question that the volume addresses is underpinned by two interrelated concepts that emerge in nineteenth-century Europe: humanitarianism and civilisation.

There is a tendency for over-simplification on the origins of the laws and customs of war – often by claiming that the starting point for the international legal regulation of the *jus in bello* is the 1864 *Geneva Convention*, the first multilateral treaty regulating the conduct of war. Occasionally, there is a concession to the existence of antecedent cultural values favouring constraints on the conduct of war in all human cultural, legal, and religious traditions – a convenient way of demonstrating the universality of humanitarianism in the conduct of war and, therefore, of substantiating the inevitability of the advent of the *jus in bello* in the late nineteenth century. One significant benefit of the cross-disciplinary nature of the current volume is a more wholistic and nuanced approach to the historical origins of the *jus in bello*. When the terms of the 1868 *St Petersburg Declaration* were negotiated, for example, repeated references to the 'laws of humanity' as a counterbalance to the necessities of war was not simply some amorphous humanitarian aspiration. In this volume's second chapter, Daly's exploration of the history of the law of siege warfare – particularly in eighteenth-century Europe – provides an excellent example of what the drafters of the *St Petersburg Declaration* meant by 'the laws of humanity': a town under siege that surrendered would be spared but a failure to capitulate, and the mounting of an 'obstinate defence', invited a violent three-day sack.

Of course, to use Rain Liivoja's inciteful phrase, there are 'challenges inherent in funnelling broad ideas of military necessity and sentiments of humanity into technical legal language'. Liivoja refers specifically to the rule prohibiting superfluous injury or unnecessary suffering as a 'vivid' example of what he is referring to, but his observation also has general application. It is challenging to formulate rules to strike a balance between military necessity and humanity, but that technical legal drafting challenge is symptomatic of the much broader paradox that attempts to moderate and constrain war through international legal means represents. This paradox is primarily due to the inherent tension between war and law: 'law implies order and restraint, war epitomises the absence of both' (af Jochnick and Normand, 1994, p. 54). Vec, in the volume's third chapter, claims that 'the progress narrative often attached to [international humanitarian law] is misleading, primarily due to the failure to acknowledge the inherent complexity of this narrative. The juridification was said to humanise warfare but … it also served to legitimate aggression, violence and warfare'.

The turn to humanitarianism that purportedly underpins the development of contemporary, codified international laws of war is also underpinned by a liberal-informed notion of universalism; all parties to an armed conflict – both states and non-state armed groups – are responsible for complying with the requirements of IHL. But, as Devetak identifies in Chapter 4, humanitarianism, as part of a broader 'civilising process', underpinned by a 'growing moral sentiment to alleviate human suffering on the battlefield', has limitations; moral sentiments are inherently ambiguous in their transference to the political domain and in their contribution to 'civilising processes', the result being a somewhat empty Western claim to civilisation.

The second informant, civilisation, came to be associated in its nineteenth-century usage with the idea of progress 'and the theory that nations advance through different stages of development' (Obregon, 2012, p. 917). Europeans increasingly came to use the term as a comparative 'other', believing they were 'endowed with an advanced level of social complexity, in opposition to "barbarous" nations, who could possible acquire civilisation if they conformed to certain values, or "savages", who were condemned to never access it' (Obregon, 2012, p. 917). Writing in 1758, and articulating the principles of non-combatant immunity, eminent Swiss jurist Emer de Vattel (2008, pp. 549, 562) argued that the existence of the rules of war 'is so plain a maxim of justice and humanity, that at present every nation, in the least degree civilised, acquiesces in it', and violators of them should be regarded as 'the enemy of the human race'. Intriguingly, Vattel is explicit in his qualifier that only citizens of civilised states are extended the protections of the law. This is further reinforced when Vattel writes that 'when we are at war with a savage nation, who observe no rules, and never give any quarter, we may punish them in the persons of any of their people whom we take' (de Vattel, 2008, p. 544).

Writing seventy years later, the Prussian military theorist, Carl von Clausewitz (1976, p. 14), argued that it was not the laws of war that moderated behaviour but rather the social 'status' of the belligerents:

> If wars between civilised nations are far less cruel and destructive than wars between savages, the reason lies in the social conditions of the states themselves and in their relationship to one another. These are the forces that give rise to war, the same forces circumscribe and moderate it. They themselves, however, are not part of war; they already exist before fighting starts.

For Vattel, being civilised was the criteria upon which protections under the laws of war were extended. Similarly, Clausewitz assumed that civilised nations are more likely to display restraint in their warfighting conduct. But this assumption is neither entirely modern nor in any sense accurate. As Mégret (2006, p. 294) observes regarding colonial wars against indigenous peoples:

> Ironically, what came to haunt European nations was not the warfare of the 'savages', as had been feared. Rather, it was the West's own savageness, revealed to itself in the process of repressing the colonial 'other'. Wars of colonization kept alive the savagery within that the laws of war were supposed to have expunged. . . . In the end, it was less the 'savages' who were 'civilized', than the 'civilized' who 'savaged' themselves, through no responsibility other than their own.

Again, we are reminded of Mégret's concept of an 'original sin': that the colonial powers that developed multilateral legal constraints on the waging of war in the name of humanity and civilisation only did so on the basis that it applied to war between civilised peoples and certainly not to war involving 'uncivilised savages' (Mégret, 2006, pp. 265, 268). In Chapter 5, McCormack, Galea, and Westbury discuss this major limitation on the scope of 'humanity' as a constraint on the waging of war in this volume and identify some of the profoundly devastating consequences for indigenous opponents in nineteenth-century wars.

Engaging further with the artificial distinction between 'civilised' and 'barbarian' in Chapter 6, Killingsworth explores the 'standard of civilisation' concept and argues that its application reveals a degree of continuity with regard to protections afforded to belligerents and non-belligerents determined by subjective notions of 'civilised' and 'barbarian'.

The second and third questions that the volume seeks to answer are informed by a number of different critiques of the laws of war. The first, and perhaps most hackneyed, is that the laws of war do not work. Such criticisms are part of broader dismissals of the efficacy of international law, underpinned by John Austin's assumption that law is – and can only be – an expression of state power (Austin, 1832, p. 47, 207). Even when reluctantly admitting that international law might have some efficacy, its critics argue that it is only as a reflection of pre-existing interests of, and power between, states (see Goldsmith and Posner, 2005). Yet the laws of war clearly do work. As Best notes, 'almost all international wars, and some major civil wars, since the eighteenth century have been softened by the operation of the law of war' (Best, 1980, p. 12; see also Solis, 2010, pp. 9–10). Nonetheless, as Sutton identifies in Chapter 7, engaging with questions as they relate to universality and efficacy, there remain tensions as to the degree to which IHL is interpreted as 'Western' law.

The second critique concerns what could be regarded as an update of Immanuel Kant's 'sorry comforters' criticism of Vattel, Hugo Grotius, and Samuel Puffendorf; the laws of war legitimate activities that should otherwise be prohibited (Kant, 1971, p. 171). As identified above, the modern laws of war are informed by the nineteenth-century turn to humanitarianism; thus, it remains difficult to reconcile that conflicts conducted in accordance with the laws of war can still bear witness to civilian loss of life. Borrowing from Best (1980, p. 15), the contributors to this volume accept war as a regrettable occurrence that should ideally be reduced in time to non-existence, and in the meantime, acknowledge that 'restricting the extent of its horrors by observing the laws and rules of war 'will continue to do more good than harm'.

Another element, identified by Christine Chinkin and Mary Kaldor (2017, p. 3), is that the laws of war, constructed in the nineteenth and twentieth centuries, rest on an outmoded conception of war drawn from the experience of European wars: 'interstate clashes involving battles between regular armed forces'. Chinkin and Kaldor offer ahistorical assessments of the laws of war. For as long as the laws have existed, they have been violated. Furthermore, as Shaw identifies in Chapter 8, criticisms of the laws of war that rest on the changed nature of belligerents are a proverbial strawman; using private military companies and contractors as an example, she argues that 'firms within the industry do not operate beyond the bounds of legal recourse'. Rather than rendering them useless, the laws of war continue to provide a framework by which unacceptable behaviour and illegal acts can be determined.

The critique informing the third question concerns the degree to which changes in the way that wars are fought render modern laws of war unfit for purpose. This assessment has a number of elements to it, some of which are addressed in this volume. One element concerns new technologies in warfare. As Rain Liivoja, Kobi Lens, and Tim McCormack point out: 'advances in science and technology have had a major impact on the conduct of war throughout history . . . the question arises as to whether it should be accompanied by a "revolution in military legal affairs"' (Liivoja, Lens and McCormack, 2016, p. 603). In Chapter 9, Liivoja, engaging with the concept of superfluous injury or unnecessary suffering, considers the origins of the rule in question, and how key aspects of the rule are interpreted. The chapter then examines one of the more contentious issues about the rule, namely whether it is only concerned with the inherent properties of particular weapons or whether it also deals with the use of weapons generally.

A final element as it relates to the third question addressed in this volume concerns prosecuting violations of IHL. As noted above, the evolution of supranational legal mechanisms to prosecute so-called atrocity crimes (including gross violation of the laws of war) when states were either unwilling or unable to prosecute was a critical moment in the longer evolution of the laws of war. But as the final two chapters identify, prosecutions of gross violations of IHL become problematic when reality conflicts with the neat boundaries prescribed by the Geneva Conventions. In Chapter 10, Grey poses the question of what legal protections young women and girls who, over the course of a single conflict, may occupy the roles of a child, a civilian, a combatant, a killer, a victim of sexual violence, and/or a mother, enjoy in theory, what these protections offer in practice, and what this means when prosecuting gross violations of the laws of war? Focusing on the activities of the ICC, Kersten, in Chapter 11, identifies a number of limitations, and subsequent solutions, for the Court to bring the 'civility' of international criminal justice to the 'barbarity' of modern violent political conflicts.

The contributions to this volume are united in acknowledging the indispensability of laws of war, while also being acutely aware of their imperfections. Appreciating the contested and pejorative nature of the terms 'civility' and 'barbarism', we have not sought to define either of these terms. Rather, through historical, political, and legal lenses, each of the contributions draws a range of conclusions about the degree to which 'civility' and 'barbarism' are valuable concepts when seeking to understand the distinction between who should be, and who actually is, afforded protections under IHL.

References

Austin, J. (1832). *The Province of Jurisprudence Determined*, London: J. Murray.

Best, G. (1980). *Humanity in Warfare: The Modern History of the International Law of Armed Conflicts*, London: Weidenfield & Nicolson.

Chinkin, C. and Kaldor, M. (2017). *International Law and New Wars*, Cambridge: Cambridge University Press.

Clausewitz, Carl Von. (1976). *On War*, trans. Michael Howard and Peter Paret, Oxford: Oxford University Press.

Greenwood, C. (2008). Historical development and legal basis. In D. Fleck, ed., *The Handbook of International Humanitarian Law*, 2nd ed., Oxford: Oxford University Press.

Goldsmith, J. and Posner, E. (2005). *The Limits of International Law*, New York: Oxford University Press.

Hathaway, O. and Shapiro, S. (2017). *The Internationalist: How a Radical Plan to Outlaw War Remade the World*, London: Simon & Schuster.

af Jochnick, C. and Normand, R. (1994). The legitimation of violence: A critical history of the laws of war. *Harvard International Law Journal* 35(1).

Kant, I. (1971). The metaphysics of morals. In H. Reiss, ed., *Kant's Political Writings*, Cambridge: Cambridge University Press.

Keegan, J. (2001). *War and Our World*, New York: Vintage Books.

Killingsworth, M. (2016). From St Petersburg to Rome: Understanding the evolution of the modern laws of war. *Australian Journal of Politics and History* 62(1).

Kolb, R. (2013). The main epochs of modern international humanitarian law since 1864 and their related dominant legal constructions. In K. Mujezinović Larsen, C. Guldahl Cooper and G. Nystuen, eds., *Searching for a 'Principle of Humanity' in International Humanitarian Law*, Cambridge: Cambridge University Press.

Kreβ, C. and Barriga, S. (2017). *The Crime of Aggression: A Commentary*, vol. 1, Cambridge: Cambridge University Press.

Liivoja, R., Lens, K. and McCormack, T. (2016). Emerging technologies of warfare. In R. Liivoja and T. McCormack, eds., *Routledge Handbook of the Law of Armed Conflict*, Abingdon: Routledge.

McCoubrey, H. (1998). *International Humanitarian War: Modern Developments in the Limitation of Warfare*, Aldershot: Ashgate.

Mégret, F. (2006). From 'savages' to 'unlawful combatants': A postcolonial look at international law's 'other'. In A. Orford, ed., *International Law and Its Others*, Cambridge: Cambridge University Press.

Neff, S. (2005). *War and the Law of Nations: A General History*, Cambridge: Cambridge University Press.

Obregon, L. (2012). The civilised and uncivilised. In B. Fassbender and A. Peters, eds., *The Oxford Handbook of the History of International Law*; Oxford: Oxford University Press.

Phillipson, C. (2015). *International Law and the Great War*, Clark, NJ: The Law Book Exchange.

Reus-Smit, C. (2004). Introduction. In C. Reus-Smit, ed., *The Politics of International Law*, Cambridge: Cambridge University Press.

Solis, G. (2010). *The Law of Armed Conflict: International Humanitarian Law in War*, Oxford: Oxford University Press.

United Nations General Assembly (2017). *Treaty on the Prohibition of Nuclear Weapons*, available at http://undocs.org/A/CONF.229/2017/8.

de Vattel, E. (2008). *The Law of Nations, or, The Principles of the Law of Nature, Applied to the Conduct and Affairs of Nations and Sovereigns, with Three Early Essays on the Origin and Nature of Natural Law and on Luxury*, eds. Bela Kapossy and Richard Whatmore, Indianapolis, IN: Liberty Fund.

2

Sieges and the Laws of War in Europe's Long Eighteenth Century

GAVIN DALY

Introduction

Throughout most of the long history of European warfare, certainly until the late eighteenth century, sieges were more common than battles (Wright, 1934, p. 629). Indeed, one estimate is that in Western Europe between 1550 and 1714, sieges outnumbered battles by a ratio of 10:1 (Childs, 2012, p. 158). They were a more complex phenomenon too, operating within fortified town spaces and their immediate hinterlands over a lengthy period of time, and concerning both military and civilian populations. Sieges have been described as the 'oldest form of total war' (Walzer, 1977, p. 160). They were the most common form of warfare, where civilians could be exposed to direct and indirect violence, and where they might become actively involved in defence and armed resistance.[1]

Given this, it is not surprising that sieges were more important than battles in the historical development of laws on the conduct of war (*jus in bello*), a point that John Lynn has highlighted (Lynn, 2012, p. 102). Under customary laws of war, if a besieged town refused to surrender and was eventually taken by a general storm, then the besieging forces had the right to deny quarter to the garrison and to sack the town, which invariably involved not only plunder and damage to property but the murder and rape of civilians. Yet as Philip Dwyer has noted of the tradition of sacking towns, 'there is surprisingly little literature on the phenomenon' (Dwyer, 2009, p. 385). This has begun to change only in very recent years, including for the Revolutionary-Napoleonic Wars, an era whose siege warfare, especially regarding the laws of war, has been traditionally neglected by historians.

[1] For the impact of sieges on civilians over history, see Dowdall and Horne (2017).

This chapter explores the history of sieges and the laws of war in Western Europe over the course of the 'long eighteenth century' (c.1660–1815), with a specific focus on the sack of besieged towns and direct violence to garrisons and civilians within this context. Josh Levithan has noted the traditional treatment of sack within military history generally: 'the latter stages of the narrative are likely to feature a statement (mostly generalized and unsourced) that the sack was well known and understood to be the inalienable right of assaulting troops, and that this has always been the case' (Levithan, 2013, pp. 205–6). Yet rather than being a historic constant, both attitudes and practices towards the sack of besieged towns evolved and shifted over time. This is especially so for the period of the long eighteenth century: a crucial era between the sixteenth- and seventeenth-century wars of religion and the later mass industrial warfare of modern nations, and between older customary laws of war and the emergence of international treaty law in the late nineteenth century, including the eventual outlawing of sack itself under Article 28 of the 1899 Hague Convention. Anchored as it was in classical and medieval traditions, and occurring on many occasions in the sixteenth and seventeenth centuries, sack largely disappeared from eighteenth-century Western European siege warfare, only to experience a revival, to a degree, in the era of the Revolutionary-Napoleonic Wars. This chapter highlights sieges as an important site for examining changes and continuities in customary laws of war; practices and cultures of war; ideas of civility and barbarism; and the strengths, limitations, and paradoxes of humanitarian discourses over the long eighteenth century.[2]

2.1 The Laws of War and Siege Violence

Throughout the early modern period, the siege remained the classic positional form of European warfare. A formal siege during the eighteenth century conventionally adhered to the same broad processes: after surrounding (investing) the fortress or fortified town, and establishing a defensive parameter, the attacking forces dug parallel systems of trenches that slowly advanced closer to the defensive walls. The aim was to edge closer with breaching batteries so that concentrated fire could produce a practicable breach in the outer walls, which triggered either surrender or, failing that, a general storm.[3] This was known as the 'siege in form'.

[2] The themes of this chapter are explored at length in Daly (2022).

[3] For an overview, see Falkner (2007, pp. 9–11).

Sieges in early modern Europe were conducted according to rules and norms that had evolved over the centuries. These unwritten rules drew upon traditions of natural, divine, and military law, and a pan-European military honours system, grounded in chivalric traditions and aristocratic martial culture. In an age before binding international treaty law, these customary laws of war were mutually recognisable, and culturally self-regulated, underpinned by the principle of reciprocity.[4] Sieges played out according to time-honoured rituals, with etiquette demanding that at the start of the siege the attacking commander would send in a summons to the governor of the fortress town, seeking capitulation terms. This was nearly always declined, with the siege then progressing. The critical juncture, and most dangerous phase, especially for soldiers and civilians within the fortified space, was when a practicable breach was made in the outer walls. The defenders then had a stark choice: capitulate or fight on, with the latter decision running the very high risk, if the defences were overwhelmed, of the garrison being put to the sword and the town sacked. A capitulation document, signed by both parties, set out in a series of articles the terms and protections accorded to the garrison and civilian inhabitants. For the governor and garrison, the matter of capitulating with martial 'honour' was paramount: the best outcome here was leaving the fortress with full military honours, bearing arms amidst much fanfare and ceremony, and with all private possessions in tow. Civilians would be guaranteed that no harm would befall their persons or private property when the enemy took possession of the town.

Yet under the laws of war, if the defenders failed to capitulate in the face of a practicable breach and mounted an 'obstinate defence', then another likely fate awaited the garrison and town if the assault was successful. If the attacking troops stormed the breaches, the town could be sacked, for up to three days, with the garrison put to the sword, the town plundered, and violence to civilians. A garrison might manage to withdraw into an inner citadel (if one existed) to continue the defence, but the civilian inhabitants were completely exposed to the storming troops. This customary law of war was unique, the one conventional wartime context in which it was 'lawful' to deny quarter or to murder and rape civilians. This law legitimised the very violence that was specifically outlawed on a field of battle: killing soldiers who were in the act of

4 On the laws of war and early modern European sieges, see Parker (1994); Childs (2012); Wright (1934); Lesaffer (2007).

surrendering or who had thrown down their arms, killing wounded soldiers who were incapable of resistance, and killing prisoners of war. The act of storm theoretically removed all protections for both enemy combatants and civilians within the fortress or town walls.

This 'law of sack' was traditionally justified on a number of grounds.[5] First, it was seen as a form of retribution and natural justice for the lives that attackers lost in the act of storming a practicable breach; the garrison and town as a whole were considered to bear a collective responsibility. Second, it was considered exemplary punishment, a warning to all future garrisons and civilian authorities that they should capitulate rather than mount an 'obstinate defence'. And finally, the plunder of a town acted as an incentive for attacking troops to risk their lives in the most dangerous of all military operations – storming a well-defended breach.

These customary laws of war were acknowledged by all the leading early modern European law of nations jurists, from Francisco de Vitoria (1485–1546) and Alberico Gentili (1552–1608) to Hugo Grotius (1583–1645) (Lesaffer, 2007, pp. 180–83). As Grotius noted on the granting of quarter, its deep lineage stretched back to classical times: 'In besieged Towns, the Romans observed this Custom before the battering Ram struck the walls.' This principle, 'is still observed, viz. in weak Towns, before the playing of the Batteries; and in fortified Cities, before *the giving of a Storm*' (Grotius, 2005, pp. 1449–50, emphasis in the original). Sack was taken almost as a given when besieged towns were captured by storm. As Gentili put it: 'Cities are sacked when taken; they are not sacked when surrendered' (Gentili, 1933, p. 315). In establishing the long historical tradition and right of sack, jurists conjured up nightmarish horrors of sieges long past, from biblical and classical authorities, Gentili evoking the Roman destructions of Corinth, Carthage, and Jerusalem (Gentili, 1933, pp. 316–19). While jurists stressed restraint, morality, and proportionality in siege warfare, they nevertheless upheld the principle of strategic necessity. In such circumstances, conceded Vitoria, sacking a besieged town was 'not unlawful', even if it gave licence for soldiers to 'commit every kind of inhuman savagery and cruelty, murdering and torturing the innocent, deflowering young girls, raping women, and pillaging churches' (Vitoria, 1991, p. 317).

[5] I have taken the term 'law of sack' from Showalter (2007).

This law of war informed behaviour in numerous sieges in the sixteenth and seventeenth centuries (Lesaffer, 2007, pp. 177–90; Lynn, 2012, pp. 102–7). A number of wars, in particular, attracted notoriety for sack violence visited upon both garrisons and town inhabitants.[6] Sack was not uncommon in the sieges of the Italian Wars in the first half of the sixteenth century.[7] The Eighty Years War between the Spanish and the Dutch witnessed a number of sieges that ended in garrisons being put to the sword or towns sacked or both – most notoriously at the hands of the Duke of Alba (Kamen, 2004, pp. 110–16, 122–23). But the most infamous sack of all, one that came to rival in legend even those of classical and biblical times, was that of Magdeburg in 1631 during the Thirty Years War, where Imperial troops slaughtered an estimated 20,000 Protestants and left the city a smouldering ruin (Wilson, 2009, pp. 467–70).

2.2 Siege and Sack in the Eighteenth Century

Nonetheless, the practice of sack increasingly disappeared from eighteenth-century siege warfare – at least in Western Europe. Eighteenth-century European warfare has traditionally been characterised by historians as one of restraint and moderation, relative to the earlier excesses of the wars of religion. Deconfessionalisation; the Enlightenment; the Westphalian state system; the rise of professional, uniformed, and regularly paid state armies; the regularisation of requisitioning; and more comprehensive and enforceable military justice systems have all been seen as contributing to more 'limited' forms of warfare (Parker, 1994, pp. 51–55; Lesaffer, 2007, pp. 183–84; Childs, 2012, p. 158). Scholarship over the past twenty-five years has strongly challenged how restrained European warfare was in practice after 1648: the French 'devastation of the Palatinate' in 1688–89 and the destruction of the Seven Years War in Eastern Europe, including to towns and villages, are stark reminders of the traumas of war visited upon civilian populations during this period.[8]

With respect to sieges, the first half of the eighteenth century was the high age of European siege warfare, from roughly 1680 to 1748, with the epicentre the long wars of Louis XIV. Sieges became more ritualised and scientific than ever before. No name was more associated with this

[6] For an overview of the sacking of cities in these centuries, see Martines (2013).
[7] See esp. Bowd (2018); Sherer (2017).
[8] See, for example, contributions to Frey and Frey (2007).

perceived perfection of siege warfare than Louis XIV's master military engineer, Vauban.[9] Part of Vauban's legend was that he famously set out a timetable for the number of days for an ideal typical siege – forty-one (Ostwald, 2009, p. 201). Moreover, there was also an important humanitarian dimension to Vauban's conception of siege warfare, wanting to minimise not only time and costs but human lives too, famously pleading to 'burn more powder and spill less blood' (quoted in Ostwald, 2009, p. 228).[10] The 'Vaubanian siege', with its sense of economy, precision, reason, mathematics, and predictability became the aspirational enlightened model for sieges.

Yet as Jamel Ostwald has argued, eighteenth-century sieges in practice did not always match Vaubanian scientific and humane ideals and could be costly operations in terms of human lives (Ostwald, 2009, chs. 6–8). Civilians continued to suffer in post-1650 sieges (Duffy, 1979, pp. 249–53). They could suffer from disease and famine in long sieges. They suffered when homes and livelihoods were destroyed in the suburbs outside the town walls. They could be pressured and targeted by the attacking forces to turn on garrisons. Civilians were especially vulnerable to bombardment, one that desperate siege commanders could draw upon to press for a resolution (Ostwald, 2009, pp. 290–95). Artillery, mortars, and incendiaries could be fired indiscriminately into the town, sometimes deliberately terrorising civilians. The French bombardments of Brussels in 1695 and Frederick the Great's 1760 destruction of Dresden were among the most notorious examples (Duffy, 1979, p. 251; Szabo, 2008, pp. 281–83). The morality of bombardment became part of the Enlightenment debate about limiting the impact of war on civilians, one that historians have pointed out was a forerunner to debates over twentieth-century aerial bombardment of cities (Best, 1980, p. 67). Finally, civilians continued to play active roles in siege defences, with the sieges of Turin (1706) and Barcelona (1714) among the more famous examples (Duffy, 1979, pp. 50–56; Hugill, 1991, ch. 10).

Nevertheless, there was one fundamental change when it came to siege violence: over the course of the eighteenth century, besieged garrisons and civilians were less likely to experience the trauma of sack than previous generations. John Lynn has pointed to a shift in siege surrender rituals that took hold in the early eighteenth century, with capitulation becoming more managed and predictable, increasingly ending on

[9] See esp. Ostwald (2009).

[10] On Vauban's humanitarian side, see Ostwald (2009, pp. 49–52).

honourable and humane terms (Lynn, 2012, pp. 106–7). Technological advances in the destructive firepower of siege trains reduced the likelihood of successfully defending a breach, and there was an understanding that a respectable or honourable defence was reached when the walls were breached, if not earlier, when the covered way was taken by the attacking forces (Ostwald, 2009, pp. 271–77; Childs, 2012, p. 159). The emergence of this trend was most marked in the many sieges conducted in the Low Countries during the War of the Spanish Succession (1701–14). In 1705, Louis XIV issued a regulation to his garrison commanders that they should withstand at least one assault on the breach (Louis XIII's regulation in the first half of the seventeenth century had stipulated 'several assaults') – but this was rarely observed in practice (Wright, 1934, p. 630; Ostwald, 2009, p. 274). Surrendering a town before or at the moment of a practicable breach became the normative framework. This was not lost on contemporaries. John Millner, a sergeant in the Irish Foot, recorded in his journal of the Duke of Marlborough's campaigns in Flanders: 'of all the cities and towns taken throughout the whole of the war on our side thereof, none stood a storm, but at the last extream surrender'd on reasonable conditions' (quoted in Ostwald, 2009, p. 271). Indeed, Marlborough conducted twenty-six sieges during the war, without a single town falling to storm and sack.[11] In the many sieges of the Spanish theatre of the same war, obstinate defences persisted, with a number of celebrated defences of practicable breaches, but the majority of sieges nevertheless ended in negotiated surrender beforehand, with few instances of wholesale sack.[12] As the eighteenth century progressed, sack became a very rare occurrence in Western European siege warfare, the most notorious case being the French sack of Bergen-op-Zoom in 1747 during the War of the Austrian Succession, when an estimated 2,000 civilians were killed (Browning, 1993, pp. 318–21). But this was an exception to the norm. In 1769, the British officer and deputy judge advocate, Stephen Payne Adye, wrote in his *A Treatise on Courts Martial* thus: 'Towns taken are never now given up to plunder, as was formerly the practice among the Ancients' (Adye, 1769, p. 138).

Tellingly, unlike his earlier sixteenth- and seventeenth-century counterparts such as Grotius, the eighteenth century's leading jurist on the laws of nations, Emer de Vattel in *The Law of Nations* (1758), did not

[11] On Marlborough's sieges, see Falkner (2007).

[12] The most infamous case was the sack and razing of the Valencian town of Xativa in 1707 (Kamen, 2001, pp. 66–67). On the sieges of the war, see Hugill (1991).

specifically address the question of violence to civilians in the context of the sack of cities. Gone are references to horrific sacks from the scriptures or the classical world. Vattel singled out for criticism the traditional custom of putting governors and garrisons to the sword for mounting obstinate defences, a practice he condemned as being at complete odds with the age's spirit:

> How could it be conceived in a knowing age, that it is lawful to punish with death a governor who has defended his place to the last extremity . . . Yet even in the last century this was so common as to make an article in the law of war, and even at present it is not totally exploded. What a thought! To punish a brave man for having performed his duty.
>
> (Vattel, 1796, p. 417)

To exact punishment in these circumstances, Vattel went on, would simply be 'unjust', 'barbarous', and 'horrible'. Only in rare cases, when defending to the last extremity was 'manifestly useless', declared Vattel, was the punishment of death justified. Vattel's example was if an entire state had fallen to the enemy with the exception of a sole remaining fortress – to defend to the last extremity here was 'absolutely fruitless', leading only to the unnecessary 'effusion of human blood' (Vattel, 1796, pp. 418–19). Vattel's approach to moderation in war, however, applied first and foremost to civilised enemies who abided by accepted laws of war, not to an 'inhuman enemy' who violated them (Vattel, 1796, p. 417).

2.3 Siege and Sack in the French Revolutionary-Napoleonic Wars

Yet the practice of sack witnessed a revival, to some degree, at the end of the century in the era of the Revolutionary-Napoleonic Wars (1792–1815). Over the past few decades, there has been considerable historical debate over the nature of the Revolutionary-Napoleonic Wars, and their place within the long-term history of warfare more generally.[13] Much of this has centred on the degree to which the French Revolution gave rise to a new era in warfare relative to the eighteenth century: one characterised by ideology, nationalism, nations-in-arms, people's wars, and the erosion of conventional distinctions between combatants and non-combatants. David Bell, in particular, has argued that this era was the crucible of modern 'total war', where a new culture of war 'drove the participants relentlessly toward a condition of total engagement and the

[13] For an overview, see Chickering and Förster (2010).

abandonment of restraints' (Bell, 2007, p. 8). For Bell, there was a transformative qualitative shift in the nature of wartime violence, with eighteenth-century constraints abandoned in the face of a new-found absolute enmity towards the enemy, whether military or civilian.

Sieges have always been the poor cousin to battles in historical coverage of the Revolutionary-Napoleonic Wars – their traditional neglect by historians based largely on the assumption that they were an increasingly obsolete and archaic form of warfare in an age of mass armies, mobility, and major battles (Collins, 2017, pp. 2–7). Yet there were scores of formal sieges across the many theatres of the Revolutionary-Napoleonic Wars, none more so than in the Peninsular War in Spain, which saw about thirty formal sieges between 1808 and 1814 (Haythornthwaite, 1999, pp. 419–23). The era saw a number of notorious siege-related sacks. Before the Revolutionary Wars, Russian forces sacked Ochakov (1788) and Ishmail (1790) in the Russo-Turkish Wars (Aksan, 2012, pp. 343–45), and there were sacks and massacres in European colonial siege contexts: Bonaparte's systematic execution of between 2,400 and 3,000 Turkish prisoners at Jaffa in 1799 (Dwyer, 2009, pp. 381–83) and a number of British sacks in India, most notably the 1799 storm and sack of Seringapatam (Collins, 2017, pp. 227–29). In all these instances, there was an erosion of European restraint in the face of enemies deemed barbaric. Yet the sack of besieged towns did not occur only within Christian–Turkish and colonial siege contexts. Within Europe, there was a series of notorious French and British sacks in the Peninsular War, which was both the most siege-intensive theatre of the Napoleonic Wars and its most barbarous. The most infamous of the French sacks occurred at the siege of Tarragona in 1811, when storming French troops under the command of Suchet fell upon the garrison and civilians.[14] But sack was not the work of the French alone. In the later years of the war, Wellington's Anglo-Portuguese army stormed and sacked the French-held Spanish cities of Ciudad Rodrigo (January 1812) and Badajoz (April 1812), and then in the final months of the war stormed and sacked San Sebastian (August 1813) – the latter

[14] Highlighting the large variations that sometimes arise in sack death tolls, as cited in the secondary literature, Gunther Rothenburg (1994, p. 93) claims that 15,000 Spaniards died at Tarragona, the majority being civilians, whereas historians of the Peninsular War mention a much lower estimate of 2,000 (Oman, 1902–30, vol. IV, p. 525; Esdaile, 2003, p. 362).

two sacks lasted three days and involved atrocities against Spanish civilians.[15]

Despite this, only in recent years have historians begun to turn their attention to the sack of besieged towns in this era – either as a subject in its own right or within the context of wartime massacres more generally.[16] Bruce Collins, taking issue with Bell's general thesis on the violence of the Revolutionary-Napoleonic Wars, claims there was nothing new with regard to the sack of besieged towns: 'The sacking of defended cities did not essentially differ in the 1810s from such actions before the 1790s' (Collins, 2017, p. 238). Philip Dwyer, on the other hand, on the subject of French wartime massacres of civilians, argues that while such massacres were no less violent in the revolutionary era than before, they nevertheless took on new dimensions: for French armies, massacre became a political and imperial tool of liberation, conquest, and pacification; the ideology of 'enlightened civilization' helping to frame the justness of the wars, and the dehumanisation of enemies and peoples deemed less than civilised (Dwyer, 2009). For Fergus Robson, operating within a very broad definition of siege, including the military pacification of rural regions where insurrection and insurgency were rife, the French siege violence of this era witnessed new historical heights of intensification, where 'we can see the brutality of the wars of religion, and the routine sacking of enemy towns merge with more 'modern' national and ideological enmities to make sieges more dangerous than ever for both soldiers and civilians' (Robson, 2017, p. 101).

It is important here to distinguish between the sack of formally besieged towns from other sacks and massacres, whether in urban or rural contexts. While there were scores of towns and villages sacked by French troops during the Napoleonic Wars, especially in southern Italy and Spain, these were typically not in the context of regular siege warfare. The sack of 'open' or poorly protected towns generally occurred soon after the arrival of the attacking forces, without any regular siege having taken place. Such was the case when the French sacked Pavia in 1796 (Dwyer, 2007, pp. 230–32). Moreover, when it came to dealing with rural insurrection and guerrilla warfare, regular forces operated outside conventional laws of war as a matter of course, with villages sacked and

15 On Badajoz, see Daly (2019); on San Sebastian, Collins (2017).

16 On the British sacks of the Peninsular War, see Daly (2019, 2020); Collins (2017); Parker (2015); Coss (2010, ch. 7). On French massacres and sacks, see Dwyer (2013, pp. 117–31); Robson (2017, pp. 83–105).

razed, collective reprisals, and the systematic killing of those bearing arms, who were categorised as criminals and 'brigands'.[17]

Were formal sieges more dangerous than ever during the Revolutionary-Napoleonic Wars in terms of sack? A whole mix of variables – military, circumstantial, cultural – could shape the particular fates of garrisons and civilians in any given siege, as was the case in any era. Certainly, in comparison to eighteenth-century sieges, there was a greater emphasis placed on obstinate defence in this era. In the French context, this was formalised through a general order that Napoleon issued in 1810 to all his garrison commanders – they were to withstand at least one general assault of a practicable breach, lest they risk court martial or even execution.[18] Napoleon's garrison commanders in Spain duly adhered, meaning that Wellington was forced to storm the breaches at Ciudad Rodrigo, Badajoz, and San Sebastian. Wellington later condemned this practice as a violation of eighteenth-century siege capitulation norms, the French having 'availed themselves of the humanity of modern warfare' (quoted in Oman, 1902–30, vol. V, p. 260). Yet the matter was more complex than Wellington made out, not least being that obstinate defences were also mounted by Spanish and British defenders in the same war.[19] Moreover, Napoleon's order was part of a broader long-term shift in cultures of war: over the eighteenth century, there was a growing sense that military honour needed to be reinvigorated, with leading theorists of the 'Military Enlightenment' looking to classical role models of martial virtue and heroic self-sacrifice.[20] Further, while civilians had historically played active roles in numerous siege defences, this reached a new intensity in the Peninsular War, exemplified in the joint military-civil-religious defences at the sieges of Zaragoza (1808–9) and Gerona (1809).[21] In the end, a greater store on obstinate defence meant that more fortresses were stormed out of strategic necessity, which in turn increased the likelihood of massacre and sack. At Tarragona, the French commander, Suchet, levelled the blame for the sack firmly on the Spanish governor and garrison 'by defying the last assault, which the laws

[17] On such French tactics in Spain and Calabria, see Bell (2007, pp. 270–74, 284–91).

[18] Napoleon had Lazare Carnot draw up a treatise (Carnot, 1810).

[19] Seven Spanish towns mounted obstinate defences; Haythornthwaite (1999, pp. 419–23). At Tarifa (1811) an Anglo-Spanish garrison repulsed a French storm (Oman, 1902–30, vol. v, pp. 114–29).

[20] On eighteenth-century military honour, see Starkey (2003).

[21] On the sieges, see Oman (1902–30, vol. I, pp. 145–62; vol. II, pp. 90–136; vol. III, pp. 19–60).

of honour excused them from awaiting, and with which the conqueror would rather have dispensed' (Suchet, 1829, vol. II, p. 102).

Furthermore, Enlightenment conceptions of civilisation on the one hand, and the interrelated framing of laws of war around civility on the other, added an extra dimension to the 'othering' of certain enemies in this era.[22] Over the course of the eighteenth century, 'Enlightened' Europe increasingly read the conduct of warfare as a sign of civilisation and historic development. This was apparent not only with the colonial sphere but within Europe itself and is especially evident in the Peninsular War in Spain, where deep cultural fault lines cut across the formal military relationships of the war. Enemies on the field of battle, French and British combatants nevertheless saw themselves as sharing a civilised martial culture and honour code, with a high degree of mutual respect, fraternisation, reciprocity, and humane treatment of prisoners. In contrast, both the French and British saw the Spanish peoples as relatively backward, superstitious, and unenlightened, with many British soldiers seeing French reform in Spain as progressive and necessary. The atrocities committed by Spanish regulars and guerrillas against French soldiers only confirmed in their eyes that they were in a relatively barbaric region. In one such instance, a British officer condemned Spanish soldiers for having 'displayed ignorance and barbarity more suited to savages than a Christian people claiming to rank in the order of civilization' (Swabey, 1984, p. 155). This shared Anglo-French sense of Iberian backwardness formed part of a broader construction of a 'civilized' northern Europe and a backward southern Europe.[23]

Given the general level of enmity between French and Spanish troops, it is not altogether surprising that the French stormers initially gave no quarter to the Spanish garrison at Tarragona, although French officers tried to restrain their men (Suchet, 1829, vol. II, p. 100). In stark contrast, British stormers spared the French garrisons at Ciudad Rodrigo, Badajoz, and San Sebastian, despite suffering horrendous and traumatic losses in the breaches (Daly, 2020). As one British officer wrote from Badajoz: 'It is most extraordinary that, notwithstanding the obstinate defence, and causes of animosity which our men had, and all their previous

[22] On laws of war and enlightenment stadial theories of civilization, politeness, and progress, see Buchan (2011, pp. 64–71); Smith (2014, pp. 1–15). On Vatellian conceptions of laws of war not applying to inhuman enemies, see Edelstein (2008, pp. 240–48).

[23] On martial constructions of civility and barbarism in the war, see Daly (2016). On British soldiers' perceptions of Iberian backwardness, see Daly (2013), esp. ch. 5.

determinations, they gave quarter to almost every Frenchman' (Warre, 1999, p. 159). Instead, British soldiers turned on the Spanish civilians, allies they were meant to be liberating. Yet this was not simply a case of discriminating against civilians, as the British also drew distinctions among combatants. During the storming of Ciudad Rodrigo, British soldiers reportedly deliberately gave no quarter to a contingent of Italian soldiers who formed part of the Imperial garrison, claiming they harboured a 'horrible antipathy' towards them (Kincaid, 1830, pp. 112–13).

British mercy towards French soldiers is even more striking when compared to the fate of obstinate garrisons in colonial sieges, where greater cultural divides and a weaker sense of reciprocated laws of war lowered restraints. In India, British stormers at the sieges of Seringapatam in 1799 and at Gawilghur in 1803 showed no mercy to the Mysorean and Marathan garrisons (Vibart, 1881, vol. I, pp. 318–19; Cooper, 2003, p. 136). Moreover, at the siege of Montevideo in 1807, British stormers initially put to the sword Spanish and Creole troops, whom they held in little regard, like Spanish America more generally.[24] One British officer later wrote: 'If the European Spaniards are supposed to be two centuries behind the rest of Europe, half a century more may be added to the distant colonies' (Wilkie, 1836, p. 507).

Yet for all this, there were also counter-prevailing moderating influences on the sieges of this era. Despite a renewed commitment to obstinate defence, and a number of notorious sacks in the Peninsular War, the majority of formal sieges ended exactly as they had in the eighteenth century: negotiated capitulation. This was true, for example, of the Prussian fortresses that fell to the French in the wake of the Battle of Jena in 1806 (Gallaher, 2008, pp. 155–80).[25] The ten-week French siege of Danzig in 1807 was in the vein of a classic eighteenth-century siege, ending with a formal capitulation, and the Prussian garrison departing with the full honours of war (Petre, 1976, pp. 245–61). And this also holds up even for the Peninsular War itself. French commanders in Spain often invoked (with expressed regret and lament) the threat of

[24] On the storming of Montevideo and its aftermath, see Daly (2021, pp. 103–19). On the 1806–7 British campaign in South America, see Hughes (2015).

[25] Kolberg was the noted exception, holding out until the peace of Tilsit in July 1807 (Esdaile, 2008, p. 291).

storm and sack in the face of determined resistance.[26] But the majority of besieged towns did not fall to storm or experience sack but rather capitulated beforehand.[27]

Moreover, it is also clear that we need to rethink the notorious reputations of some of these sacks and their place within the long-term history of siege violence (Daly, 2019). This is most apparent with the sack of Badajoz, which has sometimes been likened to 'some of the worst atrocities of the Thirty Years War' (Myatt, 2008, p. 104). The city was sacked for three days, with the murder and rape of civilian inhabitants. Yet the violence that British troops perpetrated against civilians there was not remotely comparable in ferocity or scale to that of the sacks of the sixteenth- or seventeenth-century wars of religion. British soldiers' accounts vary widely in their own estimations of the severity and scale of the sack, but it seems very likely that about a hundred Spanish civilians died at the hands of British redcoats – a tragic figure but one much lower than the sack's infamy would suggest (Coss, 2010, pp. 226–34; Muir, 2013, pp. 456, 548; Daly, 2019, pp. 167–68).[28]

Further, British officers especially, but also men from within the ranks, expressed moral and humanitarian concerns about the practice of sack. Certainly, among eyewitness accounts within the British army, we find officers and rankers trying to make sense of the sackings in the context of 'laws of war' and 'right of conquest'. Some argued the sacks were unavoidable given the circumstances in which the towns fell, that plunder was the traditional incentive for storming the breaches, and that retributive vengeance arose from the number of British soldiers killed in the breaches. Some accounts also levelled a degree of blame on the Spanish civilians themselves – accused of firing on British soldiers or of collaborating with the French by virtue of remaining in the city or of having been uncivil to the British on earlier occasions (Daly, 2019, pp. 170–71).

Yet the far greater weight of sentiment was one of horror, moral outrage, and shame (Daly, 2019, pp. 171–78). What comes across in soldiers' writings is that the violence of sack, permissible under customary laws of war, was abhorrent to prevailing standards of military honour

[26] See, for example, Ney before Ciudad Rodrigo in 1810, and Augereau before Gerona in 1809 (Oman, 1902–30, vol. III, p. 54; Howard, 1980, p. 141).

[27] Based on the siege outcomes in Haythornthwaite (1999).

[28] Spanish figures collected at the time from Badajoz list 125 dead and gravely injured (Venegas, 1983, pp. 164–69). For a summary of Venegas' study of the Spanish parish figures, see Ortiz (2001). I'm grateful to Richard Tennant for bringing this to my attention.

and professional conduct on the one hand, and moral and humane sensibilities on the other. William Napier, a senior veteran officer and author of the most famous early history of the Peninsular War, described sack as a 'remnant of barbarism' (quoted in Oman, 1902–30, vol. III, p. 308). Among some British officers, there was a degree of tolerance for plunder – up to a point – but violence against Spanish civilians was generally condemned by officers and rankers alike. Studies of British military writing of the era have demonstrated how officers, first and foremost, but also common soldiers to a degree, were influenced by the language of empathy and feeling that characterised the late eighteenth-century culture of sentimentalism.[29] We find this language evident in how soldiers responded to sack. On Badajoz, one officer wrote: 'my blood has frozen with the outrages I have witnessed' (Oman, 1913, p. 303); another found it 'revolting to any man of feeling'(Harley, 1838, p. 90). For the officer, George Bingham, sack itself was utterly inexcusable: 'the disgraceful scenes . . . could not be justified, even if the town had been an enemy's town, and the inhabitants had entered warmly into the defence of it; but the population were our allies' (Glover, 2004, p. 114).

The Duke of Wellington himself, as siege commander, shared to a degree these concerns. Throughout his career in India and Spain, Wellington perhaps witnessed more sacks in the context of siege warfare than any other commander of this era.[30] Wellington was caught between the military necessity of taking obstinate towns by storm, on the one hand, and knowing that those actions would invariably trigger sack, on the other; between an understanding that plunder was the traditional motivation for common soldiers to storm and a moral sensitivity to the suffering of the inhabitants. In response to the controversy over the sack and destruction of San Sebastian, he acknowledged that sack was a multifaceted 'evil' that 'every officer laments', on account of both the breakdown in troop discipline and of the suffering 'inflicted on the inhabitants'. He also believed that 'it is impossible to prevent a town in such a situation from being plundered' (Wellington to his brother, Henry, 1813, in Gurwood, 1844–47, vol. VII, pp. 47–48). A fundamental challenge here was that there was nothing specifically under British military law – as set out in the Articles of War and Mutiny Act – that criminalised the sack of besieged towns, in accordance with existing customary laws of war. As Lieutenant General Sir Thomas Graham wrote to Wellington

[29] See esp. Ramsey (2011).
[30] On Wellington and sacks in India, see Collins (2017, pp. 227–29).

after San Sebastian: 'It would require a different military code from ours to stop men from being disorderly on such an occasion' (Second Duke of Wellington, 1861, p. 301).

Still, over the course of the Peninsular War, the British military justice system increasingly encroached into the space of sack itself. At Badajoz, rather belatedly, Wellington issued general orders to try and end the sack, which included dispatching a Provost Marshal into the town with the power to 'execute any men [British or Portuguese] he may find in the act of plunder' (Gurwood, 1844–47, vol. V, p. 577). The following year, the preventive and containment measures at San Sebastian went much further, Wellington declaring 'upon this occasion particular pains were taken to prevent it' (Gurwood, 1844–47, vol. VII, p. 48). Major-General Hay, in charge of San Sebastian after its fall, stressed that all commanding officers before the storm had 'endeavoured to impress in the strongest manner on the minds of the men the absolute necessity that was for strict discipline and to abstain from plunder, more perhaps than at any former assault' (Second Duke of Wellington, 1861, p. 311). Hay ordered provost marshals into San Sebastian the morning after its fall, with powers to punish offenders and to confiscate plunder. Similarly, when French troops sacked the neutral Hanseatic city of Lübeck in 1806, Marshal Bernadotte set up a military commission with the power to execute soldiers guilty of pillage, reminding his men that this was not an enemy city, and imploring them to be 'sensitive and humane' to the civilian inhabitants (Foucart, 1890, pp. 783–84). Moreover, British and French officers, at some personal risk, often took matters into their own hands to try and restrain the violence and plunder of their men in the aftermath of a storm: this was the case, for example, with British officers in Spain (Daly, 2019, pp. 178–80), and with French officers at Lübeck (Petre, 1914, pp. 284–85).

Conclusion

Lynn Hunt has highlighted the 'paradox of human rights' in the late eighteenth and early nineteenth-century Age of Revolution: the period witnessed an unprecedented outpouring of empathy towards the suffering of fellow human beings, and yet at the same time the self-proclaimed 'universalism' of that sentiment was often circumscribed and violated in practice, with the language of rights and moral sentiment coexisting with extraordinary revolutionary violence (Hunt, 2007, pp. 3–17). The siege warfare at the end of the long eighteenth century in many ways embodies a similar paradox: tensions between military necessity and moderation, between a centuries-old law of war that sanctioned violence against combatants and civilians in the aftermath of a storm and counter-prevailing martial honour codes and moral and humanitarian sentiments that sought to minimise or prevent such violence, and between both the preservation and the erosion of constraint inherent within enlightened laws of war framed around the self-limiting boundaries of civility.

Notorious massacres and sack atrocities were part of the regular siege warfare of the era, yet within the Napoleonic Wars this was confined to the Peninsular War, and it operated alongside and within continuing restraints and moderating influences that led to most sieges in Europe ending in negotiated capitulation. Notwithstanding the attendant civilian suffering that came with bombardment or a long siege, the overwhelming number of besieged civilians were at least spared the direct violence of sack at the hands of soldiers. In those instances where besieged towns were sacked after a storm, there were variations in the scale, duration, and forms of violence, shaped by campaign and operational circumstances, as well as the level of cultural enmity between the besieger and besieged. Enlightenment ideals of 'civility' and 'barbarity' influenced to a degree post-storm behaviour towards garrisons and civilian inhabitants, both within Europe and especially within the colonial sphere. In the end, the law of sack provoked not only plunder and atrocity but restraint, protective intervention, and moral outrage. We should not lose sight of the fact that only eight decades after the end of the Napoleonic Wars, the practice of sack was finally criminalised in Article 28 of the 1899 *Hague Convention*: 'The pillage of a town or place even when taken by assault, is prohibited' (Schindler and Toman, 1988, p. 84). The long eighteenth century laid much of the early groundwork for that change.

References

Adye, S. P. (1769). *A Treatise on Courts Martial: To Which Is Added, An Essay on Military Punishments and Rewards*, New York: Gale ECCO.

Aksan, V. H. (2012). Ottoman Military Power in the Eighteenth Century. In B. L. Davies, ed., *Warfare in Eastern Europe, 1500–1800*, Leiden: Brill.

Bell, D. A. (2007). *The First Total War: Napoleon's Europe and the Birth of Warfare as We Know It*, New York: Bloomsbury.

Best, G. (1980). *Humanity in Warfare: The Modern History of the International Laws of Armed Conflicts*, London: Weidenfeld & Nicolson.

Bowd, S. D. (2018). *Renaissance Mass Murder: Civilians and Soldiers during the Italian Wars*, Oxford: Oxford University Press.

Browning, R. (1993). *The War of the Austrian Succession*, New York: St Martin's Press.

Buchan, B. (2011). Civilized Fictions: Warfare and Civilization in Enlightenment Thought, *Alternatives: Global, Local, Political*, 36: 1.

Carnot, L. (1810). *Traité de la défense des places fortes*, Paris.

Chickering, R., and Förster, S., eds. (2010). *War in an Age of Revolution, 1775–1815*, New York: Cambridge University Press.

Childs, J. (2012). Surrender and the Laws of War in Western Europe, c. 1660–1783. In H. Afflerbach and H. Strachan, eds., *How Fighting Ends: A History of Surrender*, Oxford: Oxford University Press.

Collins, B. (2017). *Wellington and the Siege of San Sebastian 1813*, Barnsley: Pen & Sword Military.

Cooper, R. G. S. (2003). *The Anglo-Maratha Campaign and the Contest for India: The Struggle for Control of the South East Asian Military Economy*, Cambridge: Cambridge University Press.

Coss, E. J. (2010). *All for the King's Shilling: The British Soldier under Wellington, 1808–1814*, Norman: University of Oklahoma Press.

Daly, G. (2013). *The British Soldier in the Peninsular War: Encounters with Spain and Portugal*, Basingstoke: Palgrave Macmillan.

(2016). 'Barbarity More Suited to Savages': British soldiers' Views of Spanish and Portuguese Violence during the Peninsular War, 1808–1814, *War and Society*, 35: 4.

(2019). 'The Sacking of a Town Is an Abomination': Siege, Sack and Violence to Civilians in British Officers' Writings on the Peninsular War – The Case of Badajoz, *Historical Research*, 92: 255.

(2020). Anglo-French Sieges, the Laws of War, and the Limits of Enmity in the Peninsular War, *English Historical Review*, 125: 574.

(2021). British Soldiers, Sieges, and the Laws of War: The 1807 Siege of Montevideo. In Kevin Linch and Matthew Lord, eds., *Redcoats to Tommies: The Experience of the British Soldier from the Eighteenth Century*, Woodbridge: Boydell Press.

(2022). *Storm and Sack: British Sieges, Violence and the Laws of War in the Napoleonic Era, 1799–1815*, Cambridge: Cambridge University Press.

Dowdall, A., and Horne, J., eds. (2017). *Civilians under Siege from Sarajevo to Troy*, Basingstoke: Palgrave Macmillan.

Duffy, C. (1979). *Siege Warfare: The Fortress in the Early Modern World, 1494–1660*, London: Routledge.

Dwyer, P. G. (2007). *Napoleon: The Path to Power, 1769–1799*, London: Bloomsbury.

(2009). 'It Still Makes Me Shudder': Memories of Massacres and Atrocities during the Revolutionary and Napoleonic Wars, *War in History*, 16: 4.

(2013). 'Violence and the Revolutionary and Napoleonic Wars: Massacre, Conquest and the Imperial Enterprise', *Journal of Genocide Research*, 15: 2.

Edelstein, D. (2008). War and Terror: The Law of Nations from Grotius to the French Revolution, *French Historical Studies*, 31.

Esdaile, C. (2003). *The Peninsular War*, London: Penguin.

(2008). *Napoleon's Wars: An International History, 1803–1815*, London: Penguin.

Falkner, J. (2007). *Marlborough's Sieges*, Stroud: Spellmount.

Foucart, P.-J. (1890). Vol. II of *Campagne de Prusse (1806): D'après les archives de la guerre*, 2 vols. Paris.

Frey, L., and Frey, M., eds. (2007). *Daily Lives of Civilians in Wartime Europe*. Westport, CT: Bloomsbury.

Gallaher, J. G. (2008). *Napoleon's Enfant Terrible: General Dominique Vandamme*, Norman: University of Oklahoma Press.

Gentili, A. (1933). Vol. II (trans. of the 1612 ed. by J. C. Rolfe) of *De Jure Belli Libri Tres*, 3 vols. Oxford: Clarendon Press.

Glover, G., ed. (2004). *Wellington's Lieutenant, Napoleon's Gaoler: The Peninsula and St Helena Diaries and Letters of Sir George Ridout Bingham 1809–21*, Barnsley: Pen & Sword Military.

Grotius, H. (2005). Book 3 of *The Rights of War and Peace*, ed. R. Tuck, Indianapolis, IN: Liberty Fund.

Gurwood, J., ed. (1844–47). *The Dispatches of Field Marshal the Duke of Wellington*, 2nd ed., 8 vols. London.

Harley, J. (1838). Vol. II of *The Veteran, or Forty Years in the British Service*, London.

Haythornthwaite, P. (1999). Appendix 5: A List of Peninsular War Sieges. In P. Griffith, ed., *A History of the Peninsular War: Vol IX: Modern Studies in Spain and Portugal, 1808–1814*, London: Greenhill Books.

Howard, D. D. (1980). *Napoleon and Iberia: The Twin Sieges of Ciudad Rodrigo and Almeida, 1810*, Tallahassee: University Presses of Florida.

Hughes, B. (2015). *The British Invasion of the River Plate 1806–1807: How the Redcoats Were Humbled and a Nation Was Born*, Barnsley: Pen & Sword.

Hugill, J. A. C. (1991). *No Peace without Spain*, Oxford: Kensal Press.

Hunt, L. (2007). The Paradoxical Origins of Human Rights. In J. N. Wasserstrom, L. Hunt, and M. B. Young, eds., *Human Rights and Revolution*, Lanham, MD: Rowman & Littlefield.

Kamen, H. (2001). *Philip V of Spain*, London: Yale University Press.

(2004). *The Duke of Alba*, London: Yale University Press.

Kincaid, J. (1830). *Adventures in the Rifle Brigade*, London: T. & W. Boone.

Lesaffer, R. (2007). Siege Warfare in the Early Modern Age: A Study on the Customary Laws of War. In A. Perreau-Saussine and J. B. Murphy, eds., *The Nature of Customary Law*, Cambridge: Cambridge University Press.

Levithan, J. (2013). *Roman Siege Warfare*, Ann Arbor: University of Michigan Press.

Lynn, J. A. (2012). Introduction: Honourable Surrender in Early Modern European History, 1500–1789. In H. Afflerbach and H. Strachan, eds., *How Fighting Ends*, Oxford: Oxford University Press.

Martines, L. (2013). *Furies: War in Europe, 1450–1700*, New York: Bloomsbury.

Muir, R. (2013). *Wellington: The Path to Victory, 1769–1814*, New Haven, CT: Yale University Press.

Myatt, F. (2008). *British Sieges of the Peninsular War*, Stroud: Spellmount.

Oman, C. (1902–30). *A History of the Peninsular War*, 7 vols. Oxford: Clarendon Press.

(1913). A Dragoon of the Legion. *Blackwoods Magazine*, vol. CXCIII, no. MCLXIX.

Ortiz, F. (2001). Civilian Casualties during the Sack of Badajoz 1812, The Napoleon Series, Hawaii. Available at: www.napoleon-series.org/military-info/battles/1812/Peninsula/Badajoz/CivilianCasualtiesBadajoz/c_civiliancasuatiessackofBadajoz.html.

Ostwald, J. (2009). *Vauban under Siege: Engineering Efficiency and Martial Vigor in the War of the Spanish Succession*, Leiden: Brill.

Parker, A. (2015). 'Incorrigible Rogues': The Brutalisation of British Soldiers in the Peninsular War, 1808–1814, *The British Journal of Military History*, 1:3, 42–59.

Parker, G. (1994). Early Modern Europe. In M. Howard, G. J. Andreopoulos, and M. R. Schulman, eds., *The Laws of War: Constraints on Warfare in the Western World*, New Haven, CT: Yale University Press.

Petre, F. L. (1914). *Napoleon's Conquest of Prussia – 1806*, London: John Lane.

(1976). *Napoleon's Campaign in Poland*, 3rd ed., London: John Lane.

Ramsey, N. (2011). *The Military Memoir and Romantic Literary Culture, 1780–1815*, Farnham: Ashgate.

Robson, F. (2017). Siege Warfare in Comparative Early Modern Contexts: Norms, Nuances, Myth and Massacre during the Revolutionary Wars. In A. Dowdall and J. Horne, eds., *Civilians under Siege from Sarajevo to Troy*, New York: Springer.

Rothenberg, G. (1994). The Age of Napoleon. In M. Howard, G. J. Andreopoulos, and M. R. Schulman, eds., *The Laws of War: Constraints on Warfare in the Western World*, New Haven, CT: Yale University Press.

Schindler, D., and J. Toman, eds. (1988). *The Laws of Armed Conflicts: A Collection of Conventions, Resolutions, and Other Documents*, 3rd revised ed., Leiden: Brill-Nijhoff.

Second Duke of Wellington, ed. (1861). Vol. VIII of *Supplementary Despatches and Memoranda of Field Marshall Arthur Duke of Wellington*, London.

Sherer, I. (2017). *Warriors for a Living: The Experience of the Spanish Infantry in the Italian Wars, 1494–1559*, Leiden: Brill.

Showalter, D. (2007). Matrices: Soldiers and Civilians in Early Modern Europe, 1648–1789. In L. S. Frey and M. A. Frey, eds., *Daily Lives of Civilians in Wartime Europe, 1618–1900*, Westport, CT: Bloomsbury.

Smith, C. (2014).'We Have Mingled Politeness with the Use of the Sword': Nature and Civilization in Adam Ferguson's Philosophy of War, *The European Legacy: Towards New Paradigms*, 19: 1.

Starkey, A. (2003). *War in the Age of the Enlightenment*, Westport, CT: Praeger.

Suchet, L. (1829). *Memoirs of the War in Spain, from 1808 to 1814*, 2 vols. London: H. Colburn.

Swabey, W. (1984). *Diary of Campaigns in the Peninsula*, ed. F. A. Whinyates, London: Ken Trotman.

Szabo, F. A. J. (2008). *The Seven Years War in Europe, 1756–1753*, Harlow: Pearson/Longman.

Vattel, E. de (1796). *Book III of The Law of Nations*, New York: Longmans, Green & Co.

Venegas, E. M. (1983). Datos para un estudio de la Guerra de la Independencia en Badajoz, *Revista de Estudios Extremeños*, 39: 1.

Vibart, H. M. (1881). *The Military History of the Madras Engineers and Pioneers*, 2 vols. London.

Vitoria, F. de (1991). On the Law of War. In A. Pagden and J. Lawrence, eds., *Vitoria: Political Writings*, Cambridge: Cambridge University Press.

Walzer, M. (1977). *Just and Unjust Wars: A Moral Argument with Historical Illustrations*, New York: Basic Books.

Warre, W. (1999). *Letters from the Peninsula 1808–1812*, ed. E. Warre, Staplehurst: Spellmount Publishers.

Wilkie, F. (1836). Recollections of the British Army in the Early Campaigns of the Revolutionary War. *The United Service Magazine*, Part 3.

Wilson, P. (2009). *The Thirty Years' War: Europe's Tragedy*, Cambridge, MA: Belknap Press.

Wright, J. W. (1934). Sieges and Customs of War at the Opening of the Eighteenth Century, *The American Historical Review*, 39: 4.

3

All's Fair in Love and War or the Limits of the Limitations

Juridification of Warfare and Its Revocation by Military Necessity

MILOŠ VEC

Introduction: A Splendorous Age of Juridification around 1900?

The decades around 1900 are commonly regarded as a formative period in the history of modern international humanitarian law (IHL) (Kolb, 2013, p. 24). This is a dominant and largely accepted narrative. Yet a more critical inspection reveals possible flaws. Did international law limit the conduct of war around 1900? Was this time really a splendorous age of juridification, and where were the limits of the limitations? These are the main questions of this chapter, which particularly addresses the normative conflict emerging from the idea of 'military necessity', which was said to be itself a limitation of the limits drawn by law – especially so-called *jus in bello* law – and other normativities. The chapter will provide an overview on the traditional narratives attached to the historical limitations of war technologies and examine these plural limitations from a meta-normative perspective. In the nineteenth century, scholars of the rising discipline of international law discussed limits of the conduct of warfare and international treaties tried to set boundaries for state practice but also to exclude other (non-state) actors from this field. However, there were also additional normative sources like ethics, moral theology, social custom, or honour codes which led to entanglements with international law and its attempts to regulate war and weapons. The ambition of the chapter is to understand the coexistence, co-operation and conflicts among these various normative orders under the term of 'multinormativity'. The regulation of war technologies is an historic example for such entanglements between normative orders. At the same time, it is another test for the validity of the master narratives of juridification, positivism, pacification, and universalisation, which are often attached not only to the fields of history of warfare or the history of IHL but also to legal history in general.

3.1 Revisiting the Master Narrative of 'Juridification' and Its Humanitarian Mission: The Need for Limits

In the field of war technology and IHL, 'the need for limits' is and was articulated in the language of law. Before I introduce and discuss the limits of these limits, I would like to give first some evidence from historical sources and secondary literature about those limits of international humanitarian law in history and their perception.

3.1.1 Codifying the Conduct of Warfare: Scholarly Records from Past to Present

The master narrative of the limitation of war through legal sources has been articulated for a very long time. It is not a phenomenon only of the nineteenth and twentieth centuries but can also be found with premodern authors. Scottish moral philosopher Adam Ferguson, as early as 1792, states in a high tone, with future promises: 'there is no branch of practical justice, which we may recommend with more hopes of success, than that which restrains nations at war, from unnecessary severities against one another' (Ferguson, 1792, p. 295). This claim of limitations by law is addressed to various fields of the laws of war, and it is replicated by contemporary international jurists. Gerry Simpson framed a chapter in his 2007 published book with the title 'Law's Hegemony: The Juridification of War' (Simpson, 2007, pp. 132ff.; see also: Jouannet, 2012, p. 130).

These examples can be understood as precursors and variations of the master narratives of juridification which is prevailing in modern legal history. The notion of juridification is an intellectual product of the 1980s, claiming an overall spread of law and points at the same time at the downsides and losses of it. Thus, it is also a critical account of law's limitations. Problematically, the concept of juridification is sometimes used with little empirical evidence. Despite these problems, I consider the idea of juridification to be seminal to the history of international law. However, this concept also has its opposite, which I want to emphasise: the avoidance of law and de-juridification.

Although there appears to be consent about the fact of 'juridification' for the nineteenth century's law of war, what does this exactly mean? From today's perspective, it seems that an 'almost universal system of multilateral laws' emerged, more recently reconceptualised under the guise of 'international humanitarian law'.[1] It is said to be the historical result of codification, using the legal instruments of conventions, declarations, and arrangements.[2]

The imposed nineteenth-century boundaries on warfare are not only a subject of intellectual curiosity for today's international lawyers and historians of international law; jurists of the day also commented on them. Summing up their observations and analysis helps in identifying at least three different aspects of those regulations.

First, the authors agree on the fact that the rules and impositions were of limiting, not enabling, nature. British international lawyer John Westlake generalised in 1907: 'These rules are always restrictive' (Westlake, 1907, p. 52). The history of the laws of war taught, according to German jurist Sigmund Cybichowski in 1912, that the laws of war were a product of a step-by-step restraint of the original freedom of the state (Cybichowski, 1912, p. 5). International lawyers saw those limitations as mitigation which was in favour of humankind. Henry Sumner Maine wrote in 1888 about 'the softening of the usages of war' and traced it back to 'the growing humanity of military commanders' (Maine, 1888, p. 126).

Second, international lawyers had already connected this development towards war's boundaries with a shift in legal sources. They claimed the basis of legal regulation shifted from customary to treaty law during the nineteenth century (Endres, 1909, p. 3). Today's international legal historians persistently repeat the narrative of such a shift, referring to the 'triumph of codification in the nineteenth century' (af Jochnik and Normand, 1994, p. 62).

Third, one can identify the rise of multilateralism in this field. Not only were treaties with obligations concluded as an expression of the positivisation of international law (which should not be confused with positivism (Vec, 2017a)), but the development also went further: law-making treaties emerged (Vec, 2006, pp. 113–19). They were regarded and estimated as a substitute for the missing proper legislation in the field

[1] See the interesting conceptual history and theoretical remarks by Alexander (2015, pp. 109–8).

[2] The triad can be found, for example, in Porter (1914, p. 4).

of international relations and international law. The 'treaty revolution of the 19th century' (Keene, 2012) also took place in the regulation of warfare.

3.1.2 'Progress' and Its Dark Side: The Enabling Force of Throttling Violence

As one might already assume from the previous section, nineteenth-century international jurists were labelling these developments in very optimistic terms. In their self-assessments, they were highlighting the progress of international law in the regulation of warfare in the nineteenth century and celebrated it as 'a great gain for humanity' (Taylor, 1901, p. 470) or as 'le triomphe de l'Humanité et du Droit' (de Martens, 1903, p. VI). This often-read progress narrative (Bex, 1910, p. VII) was part of larger developments with similar assessments. Felix Dahn, German jurist and very successful novel writer, in 1870, praised Rousseau's acknowledgement that only states not their citizens are belligerents and enemies as 'a big progress of humanity in international law' (Dahn, 1884, pp. 2 f.). Maine claimed, in 1887, that the mitigation of war increased the 'gentleness of mankind' (Maine, 1888, p. 127) and would 'humanise the law of land' (Maine, 1888, p. 128). He proclaimed that they recently encountered 'epochs in the period of humanitarian progress and voluntary codification', starting with the Geneva Convention and ending provisionally with the Brussels conference of 1874 (Maine, 1888, p. 142). US Lieutenant Colonel John Biddle Porter, judge advocate to the US Army and senior instructor of the Department of Law, repeatedly referred to the 'progress of civilisation' that imposed duties upon the belligerents (Porter, 1914, pp. 66, 70).

At the same time, international lawyers like Westlake saw clearly that this optimism and support was not uncontested, with a particular focus on resistance and opposition to the regulation of war. Writing in 1907, he noted: 'If on the other hand, with regard to the laws of war, general opinion has less external support than in other parts of international law, it speaks with more authority when it imposes restrictions on violence in the names of humanity and conscience' (Westlake, 1907, p. 5). According to his impression, the restriction of war was itself a battlefield. International law's efforts were seen here as more problematic than in other regulatory areas.

Today's observers have also to bear in mind that the language of progress and 'internationalism in the age of nationalism', as Glenda

Sluga put it (Sluga, 2013), had its inherent problems. The high tone not only of international lawyers but also of other professional groups had its ambivalences and dark sides. To those belonged the inherent general legitimation of organised political violence by banning only specific forms of hostilities of states during armed conflicts (von Bernstorff, 2018). In consequence, the laws of war became a legitimation for war itself. 'Civilizer la guerre' (Bex, 1910, p. 149) by punctual restrictions meant legalising violence in general. The 'humanisation of warfare' through the law of war might have been a Greek gift for true peace.

3.1.3 Plural Principles, Ambivalent Methods: Aiming for Peace through Humanity, Civility, or War?

Through those regulatory efforts loomed ethical understandings of international law. Humanity and civility were discovered/established as new leading principles of international law during the last decades of the nineteenth century and replaced by that, at least rhetorically, the Christian foundation of European international law (Lovrić-Pernak, 2013). Principles are guidelines or meta-rules and not rules in themselves as legal theory states. They were driving state practice and doctrine, treaty making, as well as the academic discourse.

However, humanity and civility were not the only principles in the field of international law and international relations. A range of other principles existed next to them, often in a very delicate and unclear relation such as the balance of power principle, which was very often proclaimed as another leading principle in nineteenth-century international relations. In case those principles got into problematic tensions, how could conflicts be resolved? Unfortunately, neither political doctrine nor legal writings had a clear answer to such collisions. Humanitarian postulates/notions like 'peace' also had their complicated semantics and paradoxical sides: serving peace could have meant excessive repression or waging war.

The principles of civilisation and humanity followed similar logics, accompanied in the last quarter of the nineteenth century by a high tone in the writings of contemporary international lawyers, but this is the cause of the discomfort addressed in this chapter. The self-assessment of the mostly European intellectuals, writers, and politicians as promoters of civilisation as well as peace through the institution of international law was also a hegemonic instrument. It divided the world into different spheres in a hierarchical, repressive, and unjust way. International law was framed explicitly as the law of the 'civilised nations'. Accordingly named/formulated were also the subtitles of major late nineteenth-century textbooks such as the one of Swiss-born Johann Casper Bluntschli (Bluntschli, 1868; Lorimer 1883/1884). As a rhetorical code, 'Civilisation' (Gong, 1984) obscured and indicated its roots in European legal history and in Christianity. Reciprocity of rights and duties was assumed to exist only among the members of this exclusive club.

In other words: sovereignty (itself a very flexible concept) was not the only criterion for belonging to the 'Family of Nations' and their blessings, and it led to the exclusion or at least to the attribution of a very ambivalent legal status of countries such as Brazil, China, and the Ottoman Empire. That exclusion and discrimination had harsh consequences in the case of armed conflicts in colonial settings. These armed conflicts were not conceptualised as 'wars' in the sense of this nineteenth-century understanding of international law (Kleinschmidt, 2013). Subjects beyond the borders of the 'civilised world' did not profit from the regulations and mitigations of warfare; the enemy was excluded 'from the categories of civilised human beings' (Balfour, 2001, p. 128). 'Terrifyingly ferocious forms of violence' (Witt, 2011, p. 903) were the result of these structural discriminations of the European law of nations in its perspective on the so-called uncivilised subjects; peace was reserved only for the 'civilised'.

Another limitation to promoting civility and humanity through international law must be added, and it has also something to do with the risk of stepping into the trap of back projections of our own humanitarian and political ideals: in the perspective of the nineteenth-century politicians and writers, peace was not only promoted through the limits and the mitigation of war. On the contrary, quite a number of writers emphasised openly that war itself could support the aims of peace, progress, and humanity. The aim was peace, but war was its instrument (Pfizer, 1846, p. 562).

Similar ideas were attributed to the standards and methods of warfare, and such positions were also found among (international) lawyers. Austrian Ferdinand Lentner claimed in 1880 that the reckless conduct of warfare would serve humanity (Lentner, 1880, p. V). Military inventions, according to American international lawyer Henry Wager Halleck, quoting an unnamed colleague, would have 'a life-saving and peace-promoting influence' (Halleck, 1866 reprinted 1872, p. 178). From that perspective, not the mitigation and restriction of warfare or the limitation of arms but inventions of new weapons technologies and their consequent usage would promote peace best. Thus, it would be an elementary mistake to regulate future weapons (Dülffer, 1978, p. 15). Similar positions can be found with a number of other writers, unsurprisingly also by militaries but not limited to them.

3.1.4 *Multinormativity: Numerous Normative Fundaments for Times of War*

The regulation of war and warfare took place through a variety of normative orders. But its precondition was that the subject regulated, warfare, was epistemologically perceived as distinct phenomenon – different from peace. American international lawyer David Kennedy wrote in 2006: 'The legal distinctiveness of war reinforced the idea that war was itself a discrete and limited phenomenon – over there, the domain of combat' (Kennedy, 2006, p. 67). War and peace historically constituted a dichotomy with clear boundaries, and the difference was already displayed in the order of the subjects of international law textbooks, which often constituted even separate volumes for peace and war, highlighting the legal distinction. Now, in the twenty-first century, this precondition of opposing binaries seems to have become questionable. A number of scholars are drawing our attention on the blurring boundaries between war and peace (Brooks, 2016; Kaldor and Chinkin, 2017, p. 530). But already in the nineteenth century, some authors were pointing out the entanglements and missing juxtaposition of war and peace. French philosopher Pierre-Joseph Proudhon wrote in 1861: 'La paix est donc encore la guerre, et la guerre est la paix: il est puéril de s'imaginer qu'elles s'excluent' (Proudhon, 1861, pp. 97 f.).

3.2 'International Humanitarian Law': Established Obligations under a New Term?

The nineteenth- and twentieth-century legal norms were forming a new and separate field of international law which we call 'international humanitarian law'. Before 1970, the concept seems to have been quite unknown (see Figure 3.1). This (modern) notion is often the starting point for historical interest in the field of the regulation of war. However, we have to be aware of the dangers of anachronism: the neologism displays not only a shift in language but also a shift in perception and concepts. The new label 'international humanitarian law' indicates changes within this legal field that we should take seriously. The wording

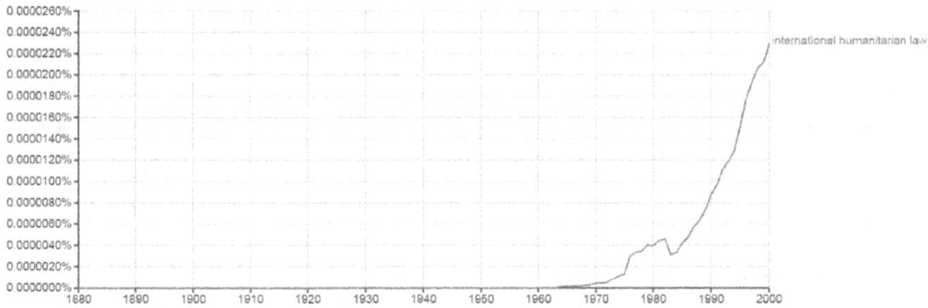

Figure 3.1 A recent and quite steep career: The rise of the term 'international humanitarian law' in printed books, according to Google n-gram viewer.

of the historical sources altered, and such differences imply elementary modifications in content (Alexander, 2015, pp. 109 f.).

The historical understanding and perception of the instruments, aims, and objectives of the regulation of war might differ from those of today's 'international humanitarian law'.

3.2.1 *Regulative Complexity: Going beyond Legal Normative Sources*

This difference between modern and historical regulation of warfare also affects the normative instruments and their constellations. Trying to identify different types of normative orders, one can see that many norms restricting nineteenth-century warfare can be found in the legal field. Thus, it would be fully adequate to speak of a 'legal pluralism' in that field and they will be named first in the following sections. But my ambition is to go beyond the limitation of the legal cosmos and to add for the sake of 'multinormativity' some other kinds of normativities which were also regulating warfare.

This pluralism of normative orders is clearly going beyond the area of the law. Thus, I would not be in favour of labelling it with the term 'legal pluralism' but prefer 'multinormativity' for it. I regard this pluralism underestimated in its practical relevance. (See the similar perspective of Liivoja, 2013, pp. 143–65.) But practically, non-legal norms very often have a clear impact on legal ideas. Just consider the problem of (missing) law enforcement. Here, very often moral convictions or social customs which are opposing the legal regulation are the driving force for the reluctance to enforce. I understand that it is, practically, very often most complicated, and sometimes probably impossible, to define the exact quality of a regulation limiting warfare. Already the distinction between customary law and social custom in the field of warfare imposes immense complications (Ziegler, 2004, p. 275). The wording from the sources needs interpretation, but frequently we are left alone with few remarks which are opaque. However, I would claim that these ideal types are a helpful tool from theory to analyse historical realities and particularly conflicts.

Careful reading of nineteenth-century sources underlines that nineteenth-century international law was not merely 'positivistic' as it was often claimed. The 'Myth of Positivism' (Vec, 2017a) was attached to this century due to the self-assessment of nineteenth-century international lawyers and the according attributions of the twentieth century. As we have seen from above, eminent nineteenth-century international law writers referred explicitly not only to positive international legal regulations. On the contrary, international lawyers saw morality, social custom, chivalry, ideas about 'just war', and finally also (uncodified) 'military necessity' as valid norms in international relations. It should have become clear that nineteenth-century IHL was not based on positivism. It might be an adequate and clever compromise to frame this époque 'A Positive Century' (Neff, 2014, pp. 217–339).

3.2.2 Multi-level Juridical Plurality: Legal Regulations of Warfare

The legal regulations addressing warfare may be principally subdivided into domestic and international law.

3.2.2.1 National Legislation Promoting Military Discipline

Domestic law, through national regulation, supplies a variety of regulations of warfare which are in principle unilateral and only bind the state's own armies. Since the Middle Ages and throughout early modern Europe, very detailed provisions were laid down in specific military orders and military manuals. Their regulations were principally driven by the ambition to uphold military discipline within the armies. As a side effect, life, liberty, and property of civilians and combatants, both foreign and domestic, were more likely to be protected by these standards of restraint (but practice was still desolate and abysmal). In other words, these territorial regulations, promoting military discipline, had a humanitarian overspill. Their ambition and ideal typical result was the emergence of the contained war ('*gehegter Krieg*': Schmitt, 1950, pp. 98, 112 f., 120–23, 139 f., 157 f., 161, 176) between states in eighteenth- and nineteenth-century Europe.

3.2.2.2 International Law Partly Originating from the Law of War

Complementary to those domestic regulations, international law supplied a number of provisions ordering war. Regulating warfare forms a separate branch of international law, and regarding the main focus of older treatises on international law, one might even have the impression that rules for warfare were of higher interest than those for international law in times of peace.

3.2.3 Ethics and Moral Philosophy and Their Interfaces with Jurisprudence

A normative order separate from law would be ethics or morals, which also impose principles and provisions about adequate behaviour in cases of armed conflicts. This type of normativity was historically elaborated in the theoretical form of moral philosophy, which again had interfaces through the field of natural law with jurisprudence. It is classically attributed to the individual. As a nineteenth-century scholarly reference to it, one might think about Maine's statement from 1888 that 'the softening of the usages of war was ... due to ... the growing humanity of military commanders' (Maine, 1888, p. 126). International law writers did not have a homogeneous position on the degree to which ethics restrained the use of force, particularly those who believed in a project called positivism, who were trying not only to separate but to exclude explicitly all issues of 'international ethics' from international law (Oppenheim, 1906, p. 69; see on the project: García-Salmones Rovira, 2013). And they wrote little about ethics justifying specific techniques and attitudes of warfare or moral philosophy promoting warfare itself.

3.2.4 Moral Theology as a Pillar of Historical Restrictions of Warfare

A very specific or even autonomous form of ethics might be seen in moral theology, which refers to religion as a normative order. Moral theology has historically been one of the pillars within the development of the restriction of warfare. Religions like Christendom, Islam, or Judaism have imposed, over time, rules of adequate warfare (while at the same time justifying warfare itself). Theologians and other spiritual leaders have henceforth developed them further. Probably the best-known example of an outcome is the 'just war' doctrine, which imposed requirements on declaration and conduct of going to war (Ziegler, 2004, pp. 273–5, 292). Even nineteenth-century international lawyers still referred to it (Halleck, 1866 reprinted 1872, pp. 145, 157; Bluntschli, 1868, p. 3; Simon, 2018, p. 124).

3.2.5 Social Custom Constituting the Military's Attitudes and Acting

A very different type of normative order is social custom. Social custom is also constituting attitudes and acting in the field of warfare, traditionally often phrased as 'chivalric practices' (af Jochnik and Normand, 1994, p. 60; Liivoja, 2012, 2013), thus referring to pre-modern language and notions. In nineteenth-century sources, it appears under the labels as 'Military honour and etiquette' (Halleck, 1866 reprinted 1872, p. 178), 'proper manner of war', and 'customs of war'. The American legal historian James Q. Whitman also used the terms 'manners', 'ritual etiquette', and 'social ceremonial' as labels for this type of norm (Whitman, 2014, pp. 203 f.). Some authors around 1900 phrase an explicit preference for this concept as they clearly distinguish it from legal restraints: the notorious German publication 'Kriegsbrauch im Landkriege' conceptualised *Kriegsgebrauch, Kriegssitte oder auch Kriegsmanier* in 1902 as a voluntary self-restraint, emerging from chivalry, Christendom, and higher education, as well as from the insight into one's own benefits (Großer Generalstab. Kriegsgeschichtliche Abteilung I, 1902, p. 2).

3.2.6 Necessity; Raison de guerre; Kriegsnothwendigkeit and Its Ticklish Functions

Finally, and not easy to conceptualise within a normative framework, comes the idea of 'necessity'. Authors debating the role(s) of necessity in the nineteenth century saw it in a field of norms and thus in dialogue with the laws of war, and the customs of war.

Necessity was partly a general figure, which was discussed in an abstract manner in its relation to the codified laws of war. Necessity was evoked to define and enable the proper use of force: all military measures taken had to be necessary 'for the realisation of the purpose of war' (Oppenheim, 1906, p. 75). At the same time, certain positive regulations on the law of war, particularly in the *Hague Conventions* but also from the last decades of the nineteenth century, made explicit reference to 'necessity' in their provisions.[3] In those cases, 'necessity' was

[3] Examples in Porter (1914, pp. 91, 115, 196); *Geneva Convention* 1864, art. 4 (I); *Declaration of Brussels* 1874, arts. 13 g, 19 (railway); *Hague Convention* 1907, art. 54 (submarine cables).

explicitly addressed by positive law to limit obligations during wartime and in specific situations. As such, the principle of necessity had both a 'positive, expensive, violence-permitting role, and the negative, restrictive, violence-limiting role' (Kolb, 2013, p. 29).

Austrian international military lawyer Ferdinand Lentner made reference to 'Kriegsnothwendigkeit (Raison de guerre)' in a passage in which he promoted reckless warfare in favour of peace. Necessity, in other words, was a legitimation technique on different levels that brought other aspects into the normative debate. It could revocate other norms that were limiting and restraining warfare. It was limiting law's limitations. And in its most radical variant it was evoked not only in those cases which explicitly referred to it but in any regulation of warfare (Lammasch, 1917, pp. 5 f., 22). This was a specific, particularly militaristic understanding of 'necessity' and its effect was unleashing: the laws of war would lose their binding force (Oppenheim, 1906, p. 79).

3.3 Transnormative Constellations: Co-Operation, Co-Existence, and Collisions of Normative Orders

These normative entities existed only in theory and isolated ideal types. In practice (and I understand juridical debates in that sense as a kind of practice), they were not separate but engaged in complex interactions. It is quite clear that law and non-legal norms could engage in different constellations and variations. Addressing the same issue, they could co-operate, coexist or have conflicts with one another, which might be labelled as 'transnormative conflicts'.[4] I will focus particularly on one specific constellation, which is the collision of the attempts to juridify war with the idea of military necessity is a tool to revoke legal restrictions on warfare. But there were also other limits of the limitations which were restraining the abilities of international law in the field of warfare.

3.3.1 When Military Interests Trumped International Legal Provisions: Necessity versus Juridification

The debate about military necessity opposing juridification of war and warfare seems to have reached a high point in the years around 1900.

[4] I thank Sebastian M. Spitra (Vienna) for this proposal.

References to this discussion can be found in a range of international law textbooks throughout many European nations. In other words, not only the military is and was objecting to the juridification of war. It was also the international lawyers themselves who were critical about such restrictions and were calling for limits of the limitations. The intensity of the debate might be drawn back to several causes. Both perspectives, the legal and the military, had good reasons to underline their claims vigorously. International law was flourishing in those years. The nineteenth century had given birth to international law as an autonomous juridical discipline (Nuzzo and Vec, 2012). Before 1914, high (sometimes conflicting) hopes were addressed to this legal area. At the same time, nationalism, colonialism, and militarism promoted the mood for armed conflicts. The clash between legal and military claims thus took also place on normative levels when debating the role of 'necessity'.

Ferdinand Lentner stated in 1880 that international law, wherever it tries to restrict military operations, tactics, and freedom of acting would meet opposition and antipathy (Lentner, 1880, p. 18). And this is what brings the idea of military necessity into play. It was a doctrinal figure that could resolve the conflict between the legal restraints on warfare and the interests of the military to be free from such impositions. Westlake gave an account of this debate in his 1894 published *Chapters on the Principles of International Law* (Westlake, 1894, p. 241). The theoretical climax is the conflict of norms: '*Kriegsraison* embraces those cases in which, by way of exception, the laws of war ought to be left without observance'. Finally adding his own position, Westlake clearly stated that he was 'unable to approve of the distinction between *kriegsmanier* and *kriegsraison*' (Westlake, 1894, p. 241).

But this was not an undisputed position in the scholarly community. Some international lawyers viewed the idea of military necessity within hostile international relations less critically. Swiss international lawyer Rivier was subordinating international law provisions to the right of self-preservation: '*Dictées par l'humanité et l'intérêt bien entendu, les lois de la guerre restent subordonnées au droit essential de conservation*' (Rivier, 1896, pp. 241f). And he concluded: '*La nécessité de guerre peut excuser des rigueurs que les lois de la guerre condamnent. Elle prime les lois de la guerre*' (Rivier, 1896, p. 241). In other words, military interests trumped international legal provisions.

The vitality of the debate might have also been caused by the unconventional and unexpected rise of legal provisions in this field, which was seen for a very long time, if not free from legal provisions, at least determined by national control. Sovereignty was the source for any restrictions which were imposed on the state's own armies. But with the unprecedented rise of internationalism and international law, the field of force shifted away from national control.

3.3.2 *The Sovereign's Privileges: War and Warfare Excluded from Nineteenth-Century Constitutionalisation*

This idea that the principal power to impose regulations came from the sovereign was also expressed in the field of warfare during the nineteenth century. The right to resort to war was seen as a prerogative of the sovereign, and in the numerous monarchies across Europe it was one of the sovereign's privileges. Although many of them were constitutional monarchies, delicate aspects of the exterior relations were seen as the monarch's sovereign and exclusive rights. This had its premodern predecessors. Vattel announced in 1758: 'La puissance souveraine est donc seule en pouvoir de faire la guerre' (de Vattel, 1758, III 1, para. 4). Similar such statements can also be found in nineteenth-century international legal doctrine. But what did they imply? For a very long time, historiography supported the narrative of the 'free right of war'. According to that idea, sovereigns were free in their decision about warfare. Did that go beyond the widely read statement that war was 'not illegal' (Oppenheim, 1906, p. 57)? In fact, some pre-World War I statements from international lawyers support this impression (Heilborn, 1896, p. 332; similar: Heilborn, 1912, p. 23) and went further in their claims. How far that sovereign right went, however, is unclear. Recent publications are more cautious and question this narrative as a historical myth (Simon, 2018). In any case, one can imagine that such a right had its spill-over effects on other conceptualisations, such as the regulation of warfare. It can hardly be imagined that sovereigns were free in their decision of waging war but legally bound in methods and techniques of warfare.

3.3.3 *The Absolute Limits of International Legal Limitations: Denying the Law of War*

Another limitation of the limits of warfare came from a specific theoretical position. This position was mainly found in jurisprudence but also in philosophy and political theory. Its protagonists were labelled as the so-called deniers of international law.

3.3.4 'Deniers' as a (Polemic) Group Label

The most prominent of those intellectual authorities are often labelled as 'deniers of international law'.[5] This label only came up in the late nineteenth century; it was never a self-description but always an attribution from third parties, and it was always critical towards that position. Denial meant not necessarily that those authors were claiming that there is no normativity at all among nations. But they were constructing this normativity in a different way than the mainstream of nineteenth-century jurists and particularly international lawyers. In any case, the outcome was that they identified the basis of the provisions debated in morality, social customs or (most frequently) in domestic law and national sovereignty. German political author Rochau objected in principle to the assumption that power was subordinated to law (von Rochau, 1853, p. 3). A range of other writers across Europe were clearly against the idea that there was such a thing as a legal order among states. German philosopher Adolf Lasson or British legal scholar Thomas Erskine Holland belonged to that group.[6] Accordingly, in some cases the term 'international law'/'law of nations' was avoided.

3.3.5 Bringing State Sovereignty Back In: What Does 'Denying' the Laws of War Mean?

It is not easy to generalise the effects that such a construction had on the law of war. But from the jurist's point of view, it might be adequate to say that the capability of regulation was neglected or at least shifted to a national level and came back into the hands of the sovereign state. The German scholar Lasson came to the conclusion in 1871 that the law of war is just a type of good manners (Lasson, 1871, p. 78).

Instead of international legal obligations, state sovereignty came back into focus. Politically, that was the crucial point. If states lost their interest in a specific rule or a set of rules, they might be entitled, under such constructions, to revoke them: '*Der Staat also giebt sich selber die Regel und entbindet sich von ihr in höchster Instanz*' (Lasson, 1871, p. 79). 'Denying' the laws of war was another way of circumventing legal

[5] See the forthcoming manuscript by Viennese PhD student Paul Hahnenkamp, The Deniers of International Law (work in progress).

[6] '[I]t is impossible to regard those rules as "law" in the fullest sense, or as being in reality anything more than the moral code of nations' (Holland, 1880, p. 79).

obligations when they seemed inappropriate to specific actors in specific situations.

3.4 Collision Cases Before and After 1914: 'Not kennt kein Gebot?'

The previous sections of this article have illustrated that the attempts to regulate and restrict warfare in the field of IHL were opposed by a number of factors. The opposition and resistance came not only from the side of the military and from politicians but were also explicitly formulated by a number of international lawyers. To them, it seemed clear that the efforts to draw humanitarian limits to warfare also had their limitations (Huber, 1913, p. 359).

The years before the outbreak of World War I were characterised by efforts to manage political crisis within Europe in a diplomatic way, and the major European powers were relatively successful. However, in the summer of 1914, the raging mood for war was pushing reservations away. Now, the academic discussions about the clash between the limits of warfare, on the one hand, and the limitations of these limits, on the other, were, less than ever before, not a theoretical issue. Factors beside the results of the two Hague Conferences escalated the dynamics. The following section will discuss those conditions and the results in the field of IHL.

3.4.1 Total War: Politicisation of International Law

World War I has been characterised as the first total war. It is not necessary to decide on that claim, as it is clear that some features of that totality are easy to identify (primarily the inclusion and subordination of civil life to warfare). One aspect of this subordination can be labelled as politicisation, and this politicisation also affected international law. The international lawyers were definitely not apolitical before 1914, although some self-assessments might have supported this misinterpretation (Mälksoo, 2005). But with the beginning of the war, another tone came into their statements. Most publications were obviously supporting national positions and the political interests of their own governments which was already acknowledged by their contemporaries (Zoller, 1915, p. 3). In that sense, it is not true that the world war silenced the academic discourse. On the contrary, one might even say that it fuelled international law writing but in a very specific way. The international lawyers were publishing in favour of the interests of their governments, they were supporting the military actions by constructing historical and legal 'justification narratives' (see on that term: Forst, 2013). Norms of international law were subject to a process of reinterpretation.

3.4.2 Complexity Upgraded: Technological Progress beyond Legal Imagination – The Case of Poison Gas in Ypres 1915

But politicisation was just one factor dominating international law discourse. Another was the challenge presented by new technologies. The Hague Conferences had tried to regulate warfare, but an era of accelerated technological progress of inventions presented the actors with new challenges. The battlefields of World War I encountered aircraft bombs, poison gas, flamethrowers, and submarines (Hull, 2014, pp. 211ff.).

This is not to say that these new technologies were not regulated by the older provisions. Technology law regulations are often very abstract, not only in the field of military use but as well as civil use. However, it is quite clear that at least some of the inventions were beyond the imagination of the lawmakers of the last decades before 1914. In this constellation, international legal argumentation became particularly relevant. International lawyers could opt in their professional work for justification or dismissal of the use of certain technologies. As those technologies – one might think about the case of poison gas (Vec, 2017b) – were often not explicitly named in the treaties, jurists had to go back to more general rules. These rules were often debated on the level of principle rules, which brought fundamental aspects of international values and ethics to the academic stage. Unsurprisingly, debates premised on principle failed to achieve mutual understanding and agreement regarding (il)legality. On the contrary, the international lawyers were highly nationalised and disputed aggressively in their professional categories and legal terminology over the issues. In that combination with innovations without precedence, international law's restrictions displayed often toothless, diffuse legal clauses, and even enabled a 'technological march towards more destructive weaponry' (af Jochnik and Normand, 1994, p. 76).[7]

3.4.3 International Law: Alive, but Not Kicking

Nonetheless, it would be incorrect to claim that international law played no role during World War I. On the contrary, international law was a

[7] Accordingly, World War I was described as 'a war in which technology overtook the inherited rules of warfare' (Balfour, 2001, p. 121).

tool and a justification narrative of evident relevance. It was used to defend and attack the enemy in a different way to physical weapons. All belligerents were eager to justify their own actions as according to the standards of international law. And they were keen to accuse the enemy of violations as this would justify reprisals. Thus, international law (as well as diplomacy) did not only fail to prevent escalation, it was through its structure 'the outbreak and duration of the First World War' was further fuelled (Diggelmann, 2017, p. 107).

This pattern and discussion did not end in 1918 with the cease-fire or the peace treaties but continued for many years during the interwar period. International lawyers participated in political battles in the public sphere; they still shared the same grammar of international law, although their interpretations of norms and principles varied widely and hardly ever matched in cases of conflicts. This public sphere was restricted in many ways but most radical through legally enforced censorship. Open debates were impossible, critique restricted.

The aforementioned publications and strategies concerned mainly the will and wish of particular powers, addressing a domestic and international audience, often targeting neutral powers (Koellreutter, 1917/1918, p. 500). At the same time, it is not very clear what happened with internal political decision-making as it concerned international law considerations. It would be interesting to know more about decision-making in cases of weapon use whose legality was disputed. Unfortunately, such historical records rarely exist. However, it can be assumed that international law was not completely silenced in those years. It underwent a process of politicisation and nationalisation. It was, in other words, alive, but not kicking.

3.4.4 *Shift and Decline of Sources: Focus on Treaties, Wartime 'Necessity' Revocating Law*

The war had another effect on international law. The debates among international lawyers on the legality of warfare were not only instrumentalised by national interest, but they also had an impact on the use of sources of international law. The international lawyers were more inclined than ever to claim that certain treaties had lost their validity, and they identified a wide range of events which should have caused this change. Abandoning (specific) treaty regulations was in the national interest of governments. Instead of international perspectives, a prioritisation of national interests should legally take place. Authors like

German jurist Kohler would moralise international relations, declaring the wartime enemies as 'liars' and drawing the conclusion that treaties with such legal subjects would not hold any more (Kohler, 1916, p. 7). Specific treaties regulating wartime behaviour, in particular the results of the two Hague Conferences, were targeted. These represented the latest effort to codify international customary law. But now, in wartime, the achievements of these global regulatory efforts seemed disputed and not welcome any more. Through restrictive interpretation, it was argued that their coverage should be limited.

It is not surprising that these attempts were accompanied by even stronger efforts to renounce specific warfare limitations. Even less surprising was the recourse to 'military necessity' to achieve this. The debate about wartime necessity had always had its sympathisers. But after the beginning of World War I, theoretical mind play received practical relevance. Parties not willing to obey impositions on their warfare explicitly referred to the doctrine of 'military necessity'. Necessity could revocate, in this most radical interpretation, any ties, be they moral or legal.

It should be very clear that military necessity in this sense was informed by the writings of Niccolò Machiavelli (on necessity in early modern public law: Stolleis, 1988, pp. 92, 209). Accordingly, the main goal of any political acting should be self-preservation. Politicians or nations would be entitled to break promises, lie, and even to violate treaties and international law provisions if that would serve their interests. Necessity would be the doctrinal figure to realise goals and permit actions which otherwise would be interdicted by moral or legal restraints.

'Necessity' puts international law into question; military 'necessity' revocated the laws of war and abandoned the binding force of international treaty law (Mendelssohn-Bartholdy, 1927). Jurists like German Otto Koellreutter were promoting with explicit and sometimes even shocking wording that military and political considerations of utility should determine the validity of international legal provisions (Koellreutter, 1917/1918, p. 500). International law, claimed Koellreutter, should follow a different yardstick than domestic regulations. In other words, it was seen as the weaker legal structure and thus subordinated to national interest. From here, it is a short step to the before-mentioned label of denying international law. Fatal juridical traditions came together with the specific political and military situation. Koellreutter concluded that the validity of international legal norms was only guaranteed as long as the interests of states were not opposed to them (Koellreutter, 1917/1918, p. 500).

Such positions had their ideological forerunners in military thought, formulated years before World War I. In Germany, it was via the beforementioned notorious booklet from the Great General Staff (Historical Section), published in 1902 (Großer Generalstab. Kriegsgeschichtliche Abteilung I, 1902). Already the title is telling: 'Kriegsbrauch im Landkriege', which translates best as 'wartime customs in terrestrial war'. The authors, speaking for the military heads of Imperial Germany, conceptualised the restrictions on warfare explicitly as of a social custom quality or of 'moral value only' (Porter, 1914, p. 73; see further: Messerschmidt, 1983, p. 240). This was attentively read across Europe (Mérignhac, 1907; Bex, 1910, p. 157; af Jochnik and Normand, 1994, p. 64) and caused an outcry in other nations. There, readers tried to scandalise this conception. Translations soon appeared (von Bernhardi, 1914),[8] and the number of them – not accidentally – increased during the first years of World War I: the misguided conception of international law of the Germans should be a propagandistic weapon on the moral field. For Germany's enemies, this nefarious publication expressed the militarism, immorality, and denial of international law and provided further evidence of Germany's post-war guilt. German jurists tried to defend and reinterpret the statements made in 1902 (Cybichowski, 1912, p. 7), but that was less convincing. Additionally, they could not point to similar elaborations from foreign powers, which reinterpreted international law as mere social custom.

3.4.5 *Just a German Issue? Yes, but . . .*

American historian Isabel V. Hull is very clear about Germany's position towards international law after the beginning of World War I:

> The legal discussions of autumn 1914 inside Imperial Germany reveal no identification with international law and no sense that law might be, intrinsically, a good worth upholding or in Germany's interest to strengthen. On the contrary, it mostly appears either as an impediment to necessary action, or at most as a tool one might instrumentalise.
>
> (Hull, 2014, p. 239)

Reading the elaborations of the German military and some German international lawyers, one finds these assessments, which Hull traces back to fatal collective mentalities (Hull, 2005), pretty convincing.

[8] Publication de la section historique du grand etat-major allemande (1916).

Others have also highlighted a fatal elitist alliance against pacifism, democracy, and disarmament in Wilhelminian Germany (Messerschmidt, 1983, p. 239; af Jochnik and Normand, 1994, p. 63; Schlemmer, 2014, p. 37). But what about America and the other European powers? Politicisation and nationalisation also took place in other countries, for example in the societies of the wartime enemies. They also had their national discourses on international law and were publishing assessments about legality or illegality of warfare. The interesting question would be if and how those national styles differed. Was the contemptuousness of the law of war just a singularity and a German issue? And was the doctrine of wartime necessity only an instrument used by Imperial Germany?

This is an open and delicate question. Today's historians have to face the danger of national stereotypes, prolongations of wartime propaganda, and of overgeneralisations in such a field, especially in areas featuring too few sources. However, there are some indications that Germany's leading figures were more inclined than those of other countries to revoke international law by military necessity. A leading British international lawyer claimed that the doctrinal figure of military necessity within the law of war and the distinction of ordinary rules of war and what is exceptionally permitted was not familiar to the English doctrine. Westlake rejected this idea after having discussed it (Westlake, 1894, pp. 238, 241). When US Lieutenant Colonel Porter discussed the role of necessity for military law, he never upgraded it to an instrument to cancel legal provisions in principle (Porter, 1914, p. 95). Cybichowski stated in 1912 that French doctrine displays little sympathy for the – what he called – 'necessity law' (Cybichowski, 1912, p. 40). Some years ago, a German doctoral thesis pointed to implementation deficits of international law regulations particularly within the German military (Toppe, 2008, pp. 28, 30, 105).

On the other hand, it is also clear that promoting the idea of military necessity overruling international law did not only concern German international lawyers. The before-mentioned Alphonse Rivier was of Swiss nationality and clearly in favour of that idea. Cybichowski claimed that British and American lawyers would also support it (Cybichowski, 1912, p. 44). Four decades earlier, Jost Dülffer quoted in his book about the Hague Conferences clear confessions from prominent British politicians and militaries very much in favour of military efficiency as the most important principle (Dülffer, 1978, p. 76). Military efficiency was said to be able to outlaw international legal regulations. And already

Lassa Oppenheim pointed to the fact that not all German lawyers acknowledged that position (Oppenheim, 1906, p. 79).

3.4.6 *Summary: Narrating the Limits of Legal Regulations*

Coming back to the narratives of juridification, universalisation, and positivism in the law of war around 1900, the picture looks ambivalent. It is true that the predecessor of today's IHL, the law of war, had changed its face in the last decades of the nineteenth century. But the progress narrative often attached to it is misleading, primarily due to the failure to acknowledge the inherent complexity of this narrative. The juridification was said to humanise warfare, but already in that fundamental task, it also served to legitimate aggression, violence, and warfare (Simon, 2016, p. 508; von Bernstorff, 2018). International law's regulations not only restricted but also enabled mass violence. Additionally, attempts to limit warfare had severe limitations. Legal regulations could collide with other norms or be reinterpreted by them, like collective mentalities of the military, whereby some were in favour of reckless warfare as the best means to keep war short and human; peace would be best served through warfare. Similar effects emerged from ideas that were also in favour of unlimited, modern, technological warfare. Probably the most fundamental attack on international law's limits came from the idea of 'military necessity' in its most radical reading. Such military necessity was a tool to overrule any moral or legal bindings if needs were in favour of such an unlimited warfare. Interestingly, it was not only promoted by protagonists from the military and politicians but also from eminent international lawyers. Such writings and ideas were finally fuelled through World War I, which added violent militarism and nationalism to an already volatile mix. It initiated undercurrents and vibrant ideas of imperialism and colonialism, already existing before the summer of 1914. Juridification was further limited by racist and discriminatory ideas, which led to the exclusion of certain types of conflicts, particularly in colonial contexts, which were not seen as 'wars'. Moral attitudes and social customs also played a fatal role. Thus, pre-1914 international law was in some areas pretty far away from humanisation, universalism, and also from positivism. The contemporary enthusiasm about the law of war limiting the use of force did not recognise that regulating violence simultaneously legitimised it, and thus fashioned violence as a potential legitimation narrative.

The international lawyers played their role in these ambivalent and eventually disastrous developments; some of them were explicitly advocating 'military realism' (Messerschmidt, 1983, p. 244) and were apologists of power politics (Orakhelashvili, 2011, p. 454). Their self-perception, particularly before 1914, was misleading and sometimes an expression of a wishful thinking (Mälksoo, 2005). Their progress narratives on contemporary law of war had their dark sides and blind spots. Different from their assessment international law was not only limiting violence but relativising it and contributing to it (Diggelmann, 2017, p. 119).

References

Alexander, A. (2015). A Short History of International Humanitarian Law. *The European Journal of International Law*, 26(1), 109–38.

Balfour, S. (2001). Secret Wars in Forgotten Africa. *Journal of Romance Studies*, 1 (3), 121–31.

von Bernhardi, F. (1914). *Britain as Germany's Vassal. Together with Kriegsbrauch – The Customs of War.* Published by the German General Staff, Berlin, 1902, and Extracts from Regulations Adopted by the Hague Conference 1907 and Subscribed to by Germany, translated by J. Ellis Barker, London: Wm. Wawson & Sons Ltd.

von Bernstorff, J. (2018). The Use of Force in International Law before World War I: On Imperial Ordering and Ontology of the Nation-State. *The European Journal of International Law*, 29(1), 233–60.

Bex, J. (1910). *Essai sur l'évolution du droit des gens*, Paris: Librarie des Sciences Politiques & Sociales.

Bluntschli, J. C. (1868). *Das moderne Völkerrecht der civilisirten Staten als Rechtsbuch dargestellt*, Nördlingen: C. H. Beck'sche Buchhandlung.

Brooks, R. (2016). *How Everything Became War and the Military Became Everything. Tales from the Pentagon*, New York: Simon & Schuster.

Cybichowski, S. (1912). Der große Generalstab und das Völkerrecht. In Cybichowski, S., ed., *Studien zum internationalen Recht*, Berlin: F. Vahlen, 5–8.

Dahn, F. (1884). Das Kriegsrecht. Für den Tornister deutscher Soldaten 1870. In Dahn, F., ed., *Bausteine: gesammelte kleine Schriften; Reihe 5, Schicht 1: Völkerrechtliche und statsrechtliche Studien*, Berlin: Janke, 1–44.

Diggelmann, O. (2017). Beyond the Myth of a Non-Relationship. International Law and World War I. *Journal of the History of International Law / Revue d'histoire du droit international*, 19(1), 93–120.

Dülffer, J. (1978). *Regeln gegen den Krieg? Die Haager Friedenskonferenzen von 1899 und 1907 in der internationalen Politik*, Frankfurt am Main: Ullstein.

Endres, K. (1909). *Die völkerrechtlichen Grundsätze der Kriegsführung zu Lande und zur See*, Berlin: Decker.

Ferguson, A. (1792). *Principles of Moral and Political Science; Being chiefly a Retrospect of Lectures delivered in the College of Edinburgh*, Vol. II, Part II, Chap. IV, Sec. IV, Edinburgh: Creech & A. Strahan and T. Cadell.

Forst, R. (2013). Zum Begriff eines Rechtfertigungsnarrativs. In Fahrmeir, A., ed., *Rechtfertigungsnarrative. Zur Begründung normativer Ordnung durch Erzählungen*, Frankfurt am Main: Campus Verlag, 11–28.

García-Salmones Rovira, M. (2013). *The Project of Positivism in International Law*, Oxford: Oxford University Press.

Gong, G. W. (1984). *The Standard of 'Civilization' in International Society*, New York: Oxford University Press.

Grand état-major allemande. (1916). *Les lois de la guerre continentale*, translated to the French by Paul Carpentier, Paris: Librairie Payot & Cie.

Großer Generalstab. Kriegsgeschichtliche Abteilung I, ed. (1902). *Kriegsbrauch im Landkriege (Kriegsgeschichtliche Einzelschriften 31)*, Berlin: Ernst Siegfried Mittler und Sohn.

Halleck, H. W. (1866, reprinted 1872). *Elements of International Law and Laws of War*, Philadelphia: J. B. Lippincott & Co.

Heilborn, P. (1896). *Das System des Völkerrechts entwickelt aus den völkerrechtlichen Begriffen*, Berlin: Verlag von Julius Springer.

(1912). *Grundbegriffe des Völkerrechts*, Vol. I, Stuttgart: W. Kohlhammer.

Holland, T. E. (1880). *The Elements of Jurisprudence*, Oxford: Clarendon Press.

Huber, M. (1913). Die kriegsrechtlichen Verträge und die Kriegsraison. *Zeitschrift für Völkerrecht*, 7, 351–74.

Hull, I. V. (2005). *Absolute Destruction: Military Culture and the Practices of War in Imperial Germany*, Ithaca, NY: Cornell University Press.

(2014). *A Scrap of Paper. Breaking and Making International Law during the Great War*, Ithaca, NY: Cornell University Press.

af Jochnik, C. and Normand, R. (1994). The Legitimation of Violence. A Critical History of the Laws of War. *Harvard International Law Journal*, 35(1), 49–95.

Jouannet, E. (2012). *The Liberal-Welfarist Law of Nations: A History of International Law*, Cambridge: Cambridge University Press.

Kaldor, M. and Chinkin, C. (2017). *International Law and New Wars*, Cambridge: Cambridge University Press.

Keene, E. (2012). The Treaty-Making Revolution of the Nineteenth Century. *The International History Review*, 34(3), 475–500.

Kennedy, D. (2006). *Of War and Law*, Oxford: Princeton University Press.

Kleinschmidt, H. (2013). *Diskriminierung durch Vertrag und Krieg. Zwischenstaatliche Verträge und der Begriff des Kolonialkriegs in*

Völkerrechtstheorie, Militärtheorie und Praxis der internationalen Politik des 19. und frühen 20. Jahrhunderts, München: Oldenbourg.

Koellreutter, O. (1917/1918). Kriegsziel und Völkerrecht. Betrachtungen aus der Front. Abhandlungen. *Zeitschrift für Völkerrecht*,10, 493–503.

Kohler, J. (1916). Das neue Völkerrecht. Abhandlungen. *Zeitschrift für Völkerrecht*, 10, 5–10.

Kolb, R. (2013). The Main Epochs of Modern International Humanitarian Law since 1864 and Their Related Dominant Legal Constructions. In Mujezinović Larsen, K., Guldahl Cooper, C. and Nystuen, G., eds., *Searching for a 'Principle of Humanity' in International Humanitarian Law*, Cambridge: Cambridge University Press, 23–71.

Lammasch, H. (1917). *Das Völkerrecht nach dem Kriege (Publications de l'Institut Nobel Norvegien III)*, Kristiania: H. Aschehoug & Co.

Lasson, A. (1871). *Princip und Zukunft des Völkerrechts*, Berlin: Wilhelm Hertz.

Lentner, F. (1880). *Das Recht im Kriege. Kompendium des Völkerrechtes im Kriegsfalle. Dargestellt auf Grund der Brüsseler Deklaration vom 27. August 1874 über die Kriegssatzungen und Kriegsgebräuche*, Wien: L.W. Seidel & Sohn.

Liivoja, R. (2012). Chivalry without a Horse: Military Honour and the Modern Law of Armed Conflict. In Liivoja, R. and Saumets, A., eds., *The Law of Armed Conflict: Historical and Contemporary Perspectives*, Tartu: Tartu University Press, 75–100.

(2013). Law and Honour: Normative Pluralism in the Regulation of Military Conduct. In Klabbers, J. and Piiparinen, T., eds., *Normative Pluralism and International Law: Exploring Global Governance*, Cambridge: Cambridge University Press, 143–65.

Lorimer, J. (1883 and 1884). *The Institutes of the Law of Nations: A Treatise of the Jural Relations of Separate Political Communities*, 2 vols., Edinburgh: William Blackwood & Sons.

Lovrić-Pernak, K. (2013). *Morale internationale und humanité im Völkerrecht des späten 19. Jahrhunderts. Bedeutung und Funktion in Staatenpraxis und Wissenschaft*, Baden-Baden: Nomos.

Maine, H. J. S. (1888). Lecture VII: The Mitigation of War. In Maine, H. J. S., ed., *International Law*. A series of lectures delivered before the University of Cambridge 1887, New York: Henry Holt & Company.

Mälksoo, L. (2005). The Science of International Law and the Concept of Politics. The Arguments and Lives of the International Law Professors at the University of Dorpat/Iur'ev/Tartu 1855–1985. *British Year Book of International Law*, 76(1), 383–502.

de Martens, F. (1903). Préface. In Merignhac, A., ed., *Les lois et coutumes de la guerre sur terre d'après le droit international moderne et la codification de la Conférence de la Haye de 1899. Ouvrage précédé d'une lettre du ministre de la guerre et d'une préface par F. de Martens*, Paris: Librairie Maresque & Cie, Éditeurs.

Mendelssohn-Bartholdy, A. (1927). Kriegsnotwendigkeiten und Repressalien. Zwei Feinde des Völkerrechts. *Europäische Gespräche, Hamburger Monatshefte für Auswärtige Politik*, 6, 319–28.

Mérignhac, A. (1907). *Les théories du grand état-major allemand sur les lois de la guerre continentale mises en regard de la doctrine de la pratique des divers états et des décisions de la Conférence de La Haye de 1899. Conférence aux officiers sous les auspices de l'université & du commandement en chef du 17e corps d'armée*. Revue générale de droit international public, Vol. 14, Paris: A. Pedone, 197–239.

Messerschmidt, M. (1983). Völkerrecht und 'Kriegsnotwendigkeit' in der deutschen militärischen Tradition seit den Einigungskriegen. *German Studies Review*, 6(2), 237–69.

Neff, S. C. (2014). *Justice among Nations: A History of International Law*, Cambridge, MA: Harvard University Press.

Nuzzo, L. and Vec, M., eds., (2012). *Constructing International Law: The Birth of a Discipline*, Frankfurt am Main: Vittorio Klostermann.

Oppenheim, L. F. L. (1906). *International Law. A Treatise, Vol 2: War and Neutrality*, London: Longmans, Green, & Co.

Orakhelashvili, A. (2011). The 19th-Century Life of International Law. In Orakhelashvili, A., ed., *Research Handbook on the Theory and History of International Law*, Cheltenham: Edward Elgar, 441–55.

Pfizer, P. A. (1846). Art. 'Ewiger Friede'. In von Rotteck, K. and Welcker, C. T., eds., *Das Staats-Lexikon. Encyklopädie der sämmtlichen Staatswissenschaften für alle Stände*, 2nd ed., Vol. IV, Altona: Hammerich, 560–64.

Porter, J. B. (1914). *International Law, Having Particular Reference to the Laws of War on Land*, 2nd ed., Fort Leavenworth, KS: Press of the Army Service Schools.

Proudhon, P. J. (1861). *La guerre et la paix: Recherches sur le principe et la constitution du droit des gens*, Paris: E Dentu.

Rivier, A. (1896). *Principes du droit des gens*, Vol. II, Paris: Arthur Rousseau.

von Rochau, L. A. (1853). *Grundsätze der Realpolitik, angewendet auf die staatlichen Zustände Deutschlands*, Vol. 1, Stuttgart: K. Göpel.

Schlemmer, T. (2014). Pfadabhängigkeit, situative Kontingenz und 'Kriegsnotwendigkeit'. Deutsche Kriegführung und Verstöße gegen das Kriegsvölkerrecht 1914 bis 1918. In Schlemmer, T., Löhnig, M. and Preisner, M., eds., *Krieg und Recht – Die Ausdifferenzierung des Rechts von der ersten Haager Friedenskonferenz bis heute*, Regenstauf: H. Gietl Verlag & Publikationsservice, 25–47.

Schmitt, C. (1950). *Der Nomos der Erde im Völkerrecht des Jus Publicum Europaeum*, Cologne: Greven Verlag.

Simon, H. (2016). Das Recht des Krieges. *Rechtsgeschichte – Legal History*, 24, 508–10.
(2018). The Myth of Liberum Ius ad Bellum: Justifying War in Nineteenth-Century Legal Theory and Political Practice. *The European Journal of International Law*, 29(1), 113–36.
Simpson, G. (2007). *Law, War and Crime: War Crimes Trials and the Reinvention of International Law*, Cambridge: John Wiley & Sons.
Sluga, G. (2013). *Internationalism in the Age of Nationalism*, Philadelphia: University of Pennsylvania Press.
Stolleis, M. (1988). *Geschichte des öffentlichen Rechts in Deutschland. Band 1: Reichspublizistik und Policeywissenschaft, 1600–1800*, München: C. H. Beck.
Taylor, H. (1901). *A Treatise on International Public Law*, Chicago: Callaghan & Company.
Toppe, A. (2008). *Militär und Kriegsvölkerrecht. Rechtsnorm, Fachdiskurs und Kriegspraxis in Deutschland 1899–1940*, München: Oldenbourg.
de Vattel, E. (1758). *Le droit des gens, ou principes de la loi naturelle, appliqués à la conduite et aux affaires des nations et des souverains*, London.
Vec, M. (2006). *Recht und Normierung in der Industriellen Revolution*, Frankfurt am Main: Vittorio Klostermann.
(2017a). Sources in the Nineteenth Century European Tradition: The Myth of Positivism. In Besson, S. and d'Aspremont, J., eds., *Oxford Handbook on the Sources of International Law*, Oxford: Oxford University Press, 121–45.
(2017b). Challenging the Laws of War by Technology, Blazing Nationalism and Militarism: Debating Chemical Warfare before and after Ypres, 1899–1925. In Friedrich, B., et al., eds., *100 Years of Chemical Warfare. Research, Deployment, Consequences*, Berlin: Springer Verlag, 105–34.
Westlake, J. (1894). *Chapters on the Principles of International Law*, Cambridge: Cambridge University Press.
(1907). *International Law*. Part II: War, 1st ed., Cambridge: Cambridge University Press.
Whitman, J. Q. (2014). *The Verdict of Battle. The Law of Victory and the Making of Modern War*, Cambridge, MA: Harvard University Press.
Witt, J. F. (2011). The Dismal History of the Laws of War. *UC Irvine Law Review*, 1 (3), 895–911.
Ziegler, K. H. (2004). Zur Entwicklung von Kriegsrecht und Kriegsverhütung im Völkerrecht des 19. und frühen 20. Jahrhunderts. *Archiv des Völkerrechts*, 42 (3), 271–93.
Zoller, O. (1915). *Das Völkerrecht und der Krieg 1914/15*, Zürich: Verlag von Rascher & Cie.

4

Cultivating Humanitarianism

Moral Sentiment and International Humanitarian Law in the Civilising Process

RICHARD DEVETAK

> I sympathized, almost on cue, by which I mean achingly when the televised images of the carnage were strongest, and almost not at all when the story was absent from the evening news broadcasts.
>
> David Rieff (1995, p. 33)

Introduction

David Rieff's *Slaughterhouse* (1995) provides a powerful indictment of the West for its moral and political failure to save Bosnia from preventable slaughter. It is exemplary in the genre of war correspondence that combines insightful reportage and reflection with passionate argument and engaged judgement. As testimony to the events in Bosnia, Rieff's narrative is permeated by a range of feelings. Anger and frustration at the apparent indifference of the United Nations (UN) Secretary-General, Boutros Boutros-Ghali, to the genocidal destruction of Bosnia; sympathy for a people who had been abandoned, brutally victimised, and massacred; and despair for a world capable of maintaining such steadfast indifference in the face of ethnic cleansing. The West elected to do nothing, to stand by and watch as '[t]wo hundred thousand Bosnian Muslims died in full view of the world's television cameras, and more than two million other people were forcibly displaced' (Rieff, 1995, p. 23).

In Rieff's narrative, a notable victim of the Bosnian War – beyond the dead, the wounded, the traumatised, and the multicultural polity – was the conceit or, as he puts it elsewhere, 'fantasy' (Rieff, 2002, p. 42), that once Western publics and governments had a clear picture of what was transpiring in Sarajevo, they would feel compelled to take action. If only they could 'see on their television screens images of what a child who has just been hit by a soft-nosed bullet or a jagged splinter of shrapnel really looks like, or the bodies of citizens massacred as they queued for bread or water, then they would want their governments to do something' (Rieff, 1995, p. 216). It was believed that such pitiful and distressing images would stimulate sympathy in the West for the misfortune and suffering of besieged and victimised Bosnians – that the exposure of this unnecessary suffering would lead to political action.

But if any kind of military intervention to stop the slaughter was an option, the West 'chose to do *anything but* intervene' (Rieff, 1995, p. 13). The UN scrupulously maintained an impartial stand, refusing to amend or extend its mandate or be swayed by the impassioned pleas of Bosnian victims or witnesses. If any compassion was provoked by the images and stories, they nonetheless failed to move the West to action. Consistent with J. S. Mill's (1977, p. 130) description of the way comfortable civilised peoples like to keep human suffering out of sight, the preferred response in the West was to look away (Power, 2002, p. xvi).

Rieff understands that reliance on emotion and sentiment is inadvisable in politics. For although it is 'easy to mobilize, sentiment is almost the antithesis of real conviction' (Rieff, 1995, p. 42), the emotions lack constancy. They are fickle. Moreover, there are no guarantees that images and stories will elicit the 'proper' emotional responses, no guarantees that knowledge of, and sympathy for, the plight of suffering strangers will deliver a rescue. Despite appreciating sentimentality's fickleness, Rieff's narrative exploits its ambiguous moral power.

By its powerful affect, Rieff's captivating and tragic narrative heightens sympathy for the Bosnian people as it aims to indict the West for its moral and political failures, and it employs moral sentiment as a resource for political judgement. For Rieff, the experience of Bosnia negates any optimistic hope that international politics may be susceptible to moralisation or civilisation. In later reflections on humanitarianism, Rieff (1995, p. 1; 2002, pp. 10–11) would disparage the so-called 'moralization of international politics' and the 'revolution of moral concern' championed by liberals and human rights advocates such as Michael Ignatieff as a delusion.

Though we might expect international relations theories to make moral sentiment a central feature of enquiries into humanitarianism, this is generally not the case. This chapter surveys the rehabilitation of emotions and moral sentiment in political and international theory, with a view to examining the cultivation of sympathy as a normative and historical condition of the humanitarianism that has informed what is now known as international humanitarian law (IHL), the branch of public international law focused on the conduct of armed conflict (see Alexander, 2015). The history of IHL is often told as a story centred on the transition from *jus in bello* to the *Geneva Conventions* (Best, 1994). This makes sense, given that it is essentially concerned with the rules applying to conduct in war, as opposed to the *jus ad bellum*, the rules justifying a war. That is to say, IHL's rules are concerned to humanise or civilise war and reduce its barbarism, as far as possible, by giving protections to civilians and the war wounded. While such protections had long been part of the laws of war as expressed in the natural law theories from Grotius to Vattel (Best, 1983), it was not until the late nineteenth century that a flurry of multilateral agreements codified the laws of war (Best, 1994; Killingsworth, 2016). These codified laws of war could only be agreed because states were willing to recognise a common interest in the regulation of warfare; however, a growing moral sentiment to alleviate human suffering on the battlefield was also a crucial condition. This chapter does not attribute a direct causality to moral sentiment, rather, it argues that, then as now, as part of a broader 'civilizing process' (Elias, 1994; Linklater, 2016), moral sentiment has been an indispensable factor in pursuit of humanitarian action, including the concrete realisation in IHL of protections for both civilians and combatants. But moral sentiments are inherently ambiguous in their transference to the political domain and in their contribution to 'civilizing processes'.

The chapter develops in five parts. In the first, I survey the rehabilitation of emotions and the moral imagination in political theory. Emotions – ranging from love and compassion to fear, anger, and hatred – are not just ineradicable features of political life, they are increasingly seen as integral to ethical reasoning. In the second part, I explore the way international relations (IR) theorists have treated compassion as an 'emotional foundation' of cosmopolitanism and humanitarian government, redefining politics and IR through the language of moral sentiment and characterising the growth in humanitarian sentiment as part of the civilising process. The following part considers the revolution in moral sentiments associated with eighteenth-century moral and political thought. This serves as a reminder that the history of political thought contains resources for understanding how emotions such as sympathy are cultivated. The final part of the chapter analyses the way that moral sentiments such as sympathy and compassion were extended to the war wounded on battlefields in the nineteenth century, helping to give birth to IHL. In this respect, the chapter concurs with Linklater's (2016, p. 321) argument that the International Committee of the Red Cross (ICRC) and the development of IHL 'together represented a major step forward in globalizing the civilizing process' by reforming international society's attitude to the conduct of war and establishing standard-setting international legal conventions.

4.1 Rehabilitation of the Emotions in Political Theory: Sympathetic Sentiments and Moral Imagination

In recent years, we have witnessed a rehabilitation of emotions in the human and social sciences. It is a rehabilitation because the current resurgence of interest follows the eighteenth century's treatment of emotions in political thought. I return to the eighteenth century's treatment of emotions below, but first I highlight how recent exercises in political theory have explored the complex moral interdependence of politics and emotions in the attempt to understand how moral sentiments are cultivated and how they translate into politics.

Philosophers, historians, and social and political theorists alike have come to appreciate the powerful role of literature in cultivating the moral imagination and stimulating sympathy in the audience or reader. Martha Nussbaum, for example, the foremost contemporary moral and legal philosopher of emotions, draws heavily on literature as a source for understanding the structure of sympathy and compassion. Literary genres not only foreground 'generic human predicaments' (Muldoon, 2014, p. 161), but they are also instructive in revealing how integral emotions are to ethical and moral reasoning (Nussbaum, 2001, p. 1). One of Nussbaum's preferred genres to highlight how appeal to emotions can stimulate the audience's moral imagination, including the cultivation of sympathy and compassion, is Greek tragedy, where war often forms the backdrop to the drama.

In *Trojan Women*, for example, Euripides invites the audience to feel the terror of a city set aflame in war, where the enemy's citizens are raped, enslaved, or murdered. 'Compassion for the women of Troy should at least cause moral unease, reminding Athenians of the full and equal humanity of people who live in distant places, their fully human capacity for suffering', Nussbaum (2003, p. 11) explains. For the Greek audience to feel compassion, the Trojan women somehow had to appear familiar, 'so that Greeks could see their own vulnerability in them, and feel terror and pity, as for their own relations' (Nussbaum, 2003, p. 11).

In other words, to create feelings of sympathy, the emotional distance between the audience and the Trojan women had to be overcome. Vulnerability and suffering could then be recognised as universal human characteristics the audience shared with the play's Trojan women. Basic human emotions, Nussbaum suggests, will compel fellow-feeling and a sense of common humanity. As Paul Muldoon (2014, p. 158) glosses Nussbaum's position: 'the sight of others in pain is likely to elicit projects of helping because it puts people in mind of their own, all too human, vulnerability to suffering'.

The theoretical point for Nussbaum (2001, p. 3) is that emotions must be considered to form part of the human cognitive repertoire. They are not simply pre-cognitive or non-reasoning urges; they are thoughts or evaluative judgements. She thus distances herself from Stoic and Kantian philosophers who counterpose reason and emotion by viewing morality as 'a system of principles to be grasped by the detached intellect' (Nussbaum, 2001, p. 1). For Nussbaum, by contrast, emotions – and compassion in particular – hold not just cognitive but ethical import because of the way they can shape moral thinking. This moral thinking extends to beliefs about the suffering or misfortune experienced by others, which result in feelings of sympathy and compassion (Nussbaum, 2001, p. 306). Recognition of others' suffering is thus an act of cognition that can inform conduct and potentially shape humanitarian sentiments and political responses.

Nussbaum is here treating sympathy and compassion as straightforwardly positive political virtues. However, emotions can be ambivalent in their effects, as she and other political theorists have observed. First, they do not always expand the sense of fellow-feeling beyond the bounded community. They can be used to reify bounded communities and inoculate them against sympathy for outsiders, especially in the context of war where enemy civilians and combatants may be dehumanised as barbarians. Emotional investment in a sense of civilisational superiority was used by European empires to legitimise wars of conquest, dispossession, and annihilation, as well as to deny 'barbarians' rights to protection under laws of nature or nations or under laws of war (Wight, 1991; Keal, 2003; Kinsella, 2011, ch. 3; Linklater, 2016, ch. 6). In a peacetime context, we might also think of the way that populist and far-right nativist movements have fuelled and harnessed the anger of those who feel powerless and 'left behind' by socio-economic and cultural change (see Mishra, 2017; Müller, 2017), creating fractured and polarised societies. Conversely, anger is commonly treated by Christian and Graeco-Roman moral conventions as a dangerous emotion for its capacity to fuel and unleash violence. But, as Muldoon (2008) has argued, anger might also be morally legitimate in some circumstances. He argues that, so long as it is distinguished from resentment and revenge, anger can be redeemed in societies that are transitioning from apartheid or recovering from civil war. It has a kind of therapeutic effect, and for the victims it may be a condition of reconciliation with their erstwhile tormenters or enemies.

Second, as Hannah Arendt showed in her study *On Revolution* (2006, pp. 69–80), compassion can just as easily shade into pity. Her analysis of Herman Melville's *Billy Budd*, Jean-Jacques Rousseau, and the French Revolution indicts compassion – 'the capacity for suffering with others' (Arendt, 2006, p. 71) – because its overriding social concern with the suffering masses undermines the liberal political values of freedom, tolerance, and respect, and sets no limits on resort to violence in pursuit of the good or just (Ure and Frost, 2014, p. 4). What Arendt (2006, p. 86) calls 'the misplaced emphasis on the heart' as the source of political virtues like compassion created the French Revolution's 'fateful mood of suspicion' that saw 'intrigue and calumny, treachery and hypocrisy everywhere', and that led eventually to the guillotine and the Terror. That is why Arendt reached the conclusion that pity, taken as 'the spring of virtue, has proved to possess a greater capacity for cruelty than cruelty itself' (Arendt, 2006, p. 79, cited in Ure and Frost, 2014, p. 4). The point here is that compassion as a moral virtue may not necessarily translate into political virtue.

The moral ambivalence of emotions is teased out further by Muldoon. Through a close reading of Sophocles' Greek tragedy *Philoctetes* (2015), Muldoon (2014) argues that compassion can endanger the political demands of community just as much as it can sustain the ethical demands of humanity. The expert archer Philoctetes had been abandoned by Odysseus on the island of Lemnos a decade previously because of a festering wound suffered on the way to Troy, but when Odysseus learns from a prophet that Troy will only be defeated with the bow and arrow Heracles gave to Philoctetes, he hatches a plan to bring Philoctetes back into battle. Odysseus' purpose is strictly political and guided by military necessity: he wants to secure the services of Philoctetes and his magical bow and arrow in the war against Troy. But, knowing Philoctetes will be disinclined after a decade of isolation as a castaway, Odysseus uses Achilles' son Neoptolemus to trick the resentful Philoctetes into returning to the war. However, Neoptolemus' compassion for Philoctetes and guilt at the deceit get the better of him, and he reveals the plot to Philoctetes. In the end it is a *deus ex machina* that resolves the situation as the ghost of Heracles persuades Philoctetes to co-operate with Odysseus.

Philoctetes is particularly interesting because it exposes the tension between the ethical obligation to others and the ethical obligation to one's own political community when confronted with human suffering outside the usual rule-governed context of a polity (Muldoon, 2014, pp. 162–63) – in this case, one's own wounded soldier. On the surface, it would seem that Sophocles' contrast between Neoptolemus' compassion and honesty and Odysseus' cold and deceitful instrumentalism is meant to acclaim the former. However, Muldoon argues that while Neoptolemus' compassion may appear ethically unimpeachable, 'feelings of compassion are as likely to endanger the political as to ennoble it' (Muldoon, 2014, p. 169), because they may jeopardise the safety or even existence of the political community. For all its ethical virtue, as Muldoon's reading of *Philoctetes* and Arendt's analysis of the French Revolution suggest, compassion is not intrinsically a political virtue. Notwithstanding their political ambivalence, emotions remain pervasive elements in politics, not least because of their role in the formation of the moral imagination.

4.2 From Emotional Foundations to Civilising Processes: Moral Sentiment in International Relations

While emotions are ubiquitous in political life, until recently they have received surprisingly little attention from IR scholars, beyond studies in political psychology and foreign policy (Crawford, 2000; Bleiker and Hutchison, 2008). This section shows how IR theorists have rehabilitated the study of emotions, particularly to understand what might be called, following Emma Hutchison (2016, p. 23), 'the emotional foundations' of IR. More historically oriented scholars have shifted the focus to the way that international society has developed 'civilizing processes' based on moral sentiment.

Fear has a long history in politics and in the history of political thought (Robin, 2004). Its crucial political role has been well analysed by thinkers from Thucydides and Thomas Hobbes to twentieth-century political realists, such as Kenneth Waltz and Danilo Zolo. Fear and terror, together with anger and hatred, have once again assumed a central and obvious role in world politics after the 11 September 2001 terrorist attacks, where they are used as weapons by terrorists and governments alike to pursue political agendas (Devetak, 2005). A growing body of literature – from philosophy, cultural studies, and history to anthropology, sociology, and political theory – has drawn attention to the emotional power of fear to galvanise governmental programs and foreign policy agendas. But, as Neta Crawford (2000, p. 116) noted, studies of emotions in general had rarely, if ever, been given systematic theoretical treatment in IR. This neglect is usually explained by IR's investment in reason and rationality (Jeffery, 2014). That has changed in recent years with the advent of what some IR scholars refer to as 'the emotional turn', in which emotions are no longer counterposed to reason and are instead recognised as ineradicable and constitutive elements of social and political life.

Roland Bleiker and Emma Hutchison (2008, see also Hutchison and Bleiker 2014, and Hutchison 2016), together with Neta Crawford (2000, 2014), Jonathan Mercer (2005, 2014), and Renée Jeffery (2014), have pioneered IR's 'emotional turn'. They have argued that emotions lie at the heart of politics and that even rationality is inseparable from emotions. They have advanced these arguments on the basis of different theoretical grounds; some appeal to neuroscience for scientific validation, others to social theory and political philosophy. What they all share is a commitment to the notion that emotions matter in ways that IR has failed to investigate. One of the characteristic features of the emotional turn in IR has been the focus on 'good' emotions such as sympathy and compassion, and their capacity to promote humanitarian causes and cosmopolitan ethics.

One of the leading critical international theorists, Andrew Linklater, has reached beyond the natural law, Kantian, and Stoic intellectual influences of his earlier work to engage with emotions as the source of cosmopolitan ethical impulses. The point of this intellectual shift is to show that there are universal human impulses, namely emotions, that align with the ethical imperatives of deontological and dispassionate forms of moral reasoning without originating in abstract philosophy.

Rather than locate cosmopolitanism's moral foundations in abstract reason or 'disembodied selves', to use Toni Erskine's (2008, ch. 2) term, Linklater (2007, pp. 20–21) argues that they are better grounded in the 'socio-psychological commitments to empathy and sympathy, which are among the universal pre-requisites of social life'. Building on the premise that humanity shares a basic vulnerability to pain and suffering and a capacity to empathise with suffering strangers, Linklater (2007, p. 22) seeks to capitalise on globalisation's capacity to expand 'the boundaries of community by bringing distant suffering directly into the lives of onlookers', regardless of their national or geographical location. The global media's capacity to disseminate images of human suffering, he argues, invites a compassionate moral response (Linklater, 2007, p. 28). Onlookers cannot, or should not, remain morally indifferent to distant suffering when made aware of it. But as Rieff's account of the Bosnian War suggests, knowledge of distant suffering exposed and made public by the global news media is not sufficient to mobilise action (Keenan, 2002). For this reason, Linklater (2007, p. 24) concludes, compassion is a crucial human capacity that must be cultivated to implement the 'universal obligations' he derives from 'embodied cosmopolitan' theory. Interestingly, however, Linklater also suggests that guilt and shame might be just as essential to cosmopolitanism as compassion. His reasoning here is that sympathetic identification with distant suffering may not be sufficient to propel action. It might also be necessary for 'by-standers' to feel guilt or shame that they cannot alleviate the suffering or indeed may be indirectly responsible for it (Elias, 1994, p. 492; Linklater, 2007, p. 27).

Those feelings of shame and embarrassment were instrumental, according to Linklater (2016, p. 233), in delegitimising European practices such as colonialism and slavery. Colonial and racist attitudes and practices were redescribed as 'barbaric' and incompatible with an international society claiming to be 'civilized'. Linklater's concern is to emphasise the significance of a range of moral sentiments – from shame and embarrassment to sympathy and compassion – in the delegitimisation of slavery and the slave trade. Aware of growing public sympathy, 'abolitionists attempted to harvest support for their cause by drawing public attention to the particular brutalities suffered by female slaves' (Linklater, 2016, p. 254). Slavery had come to be seen as a barbaric practice, as a 'stain on "civilized" peoples . . . and as a symbol of the "moral backwardness of international society"' (Linklater, 2016, p. 252). The movement to abolish slavery was part of a wider social phenomenon in which knowledge of distant suffering was used to cultivate the moral sentiments of sympathy and compassion. These moral sentiments were also tied to the civilising process, in Norbert Elias' (1994) sense, and the conviction that cruel practices such as slavery were not just barbaric, but barbarising rather than civilising (Linklater, 2016, p. 257).

Similar accounts of civilising development in IR can be found in Michael Barnett's illuminating history of humanitarianism. Like Linklater, the key to Barnett's (2011, pp. 49–50) story is the 'revolution in moral sentiments and the emergence of a culture of compassion' that aspires to civilise international society. Following a well-told history,

Barnett traces the intellectual origins of humanitarianism back to the Latitudinarian divines of the late seventeenth century, who sought to combat 'stoic insensibility' and the pessimistic views of human nature prevalent in Puritan and Epicurean thinking with a more positive Christian ethic of care. Humanitarians 'wanted to save souls through acts of individual conversion and to build a more perfect, civilized, society' (Barnett, 2011, p. 54).

By the middle of the eighteenth century, so the narrative goes, the concept of humanity and the 'cult of the "man of feeling"' were firmly established in European society, even penetrating the pages of political thinkers. The unsentimental depiction of political life offered by Hobbes in *Leviathan* (1651) had given way to Smith's *Theory of Moral Sentiments* (1759). Older theories of natural law were now joined by a rival moral tradition, but both converged to generate a notion of humanity (Barnett, 2011, p. 51). Humanitarianism's origins cannot be reduced to intellectual evolution alone, of course. As Barnett (2011, pp. 51–52) explains, advances linked to 'an expanding market, urbanization, and modernization' were also necessary to create the conditions for moral sentiments to reshape society. But as Barnett (2011, p. 9) argues, humanitarianism is 'a creature of the world it aspires to civilize'; its commitment 'to release civilizing processes to reduce human suffering' cannot be separated from its colonial and paternalistic histories (Barnett, 2011, p. 30 and ch. 3).

Complementing Barnett's historical narrative, Craig Calhoun historicises humanitarianism by showing how the imperative to reduce human suffering has constantly changed in meaning and migrated and expanded its focus since its modern inception. Rather than issue out of a single origin, Calhoun (2008, p. 75) shows how it emerged out of an array of different religious and secular principles and practices advocated by eighteenth- and nineteenth-century reform movements, who drew, in different ways, upon ideas of Christian charity, the ethics and laws of war, and cosmopolitanism. This prepared the ground for humanitarianism's emergence in an array of religious and secular institutional practices and interventions aimed either at ending chronic patterns of suffering or saving lives in emergency situations. Humanitarianism was not simply the result of a series of abstract intellectual events; it grew out of concrete practices. What remained essential to humanitarianism, however, was the narrative genre that allowed authors to convey the suffering of distant strangers in compelling detail. As I show below, the same techniques that made the novel so popular in the eighteenth century – the cultivation of sympathy – are the same as that made the humanitarian narrative so influential in the nineteenth century.

The introduction of emotions or moral sentiments into the study of IR has allowed scholars to gain a better understanding of the way boundaries of community have expanded and contracted over time to facilitate or impede sympathy for distant human suffering. For Linklater, compassion is a crucial emotion underpinning the normative projects of cosmopolitanism and 'international harm conventions' (Linklater, 2011). Basic human vulnerabilities are universal, and so are the capabilities of sympathy and empathy, irrespective of distance from the suffering. What distinguishes Linklater's argument from other IR theorists of emotions is his historical approach; moral sentiments are proposed as constitutive *historical* features of a 'civilizing' international society. To that extent, his approach follows the path of well-known eighteenth-century thinkers such as David Hume and Adam Smith, and less well-known thinkers such as Sophie de Grouchy, among others, who linked moral sentiment to civilising processes. Returning to eighteenth-century concern with emotions and moral sentiments will enable us to acquire a better understanding of how and why moral sentiment came to exercise greater influence in civilising the political sphere and initiating a variety of humanitarian campaigns.

4.3 The Revolution in Moral Sentiments: Civility and Sympathetic Spectators

The eighteenth-century Enlightenment is typically portrayed as an Age of Reason, a time when thinkers reached for more abstract forms of knowledge and when rationalism was exulted. But recent histories have highlighted another facet of the Enlightenment: its preoccupation with feelings and sentiments (see Phillips, 2008). The great Scottish humanist, David Hume (2007, p. 266), had of course pushed back against rationalism by insisting that 'Reason is, and ought only to be, the slave of the passions'. To appreciate this alternative Enlightenment, we need to shake off the influence of nineteenth-century historiographies, shaped by Romanticism, which depicted eighteenth-century Enlightenment thinking exclusively as cold, abstract, rationalist philosophising. We need to expand our conception of the Enlightenment to include the literary novel, *belles lettres*, and history, as well as to recognise the significance of sentiment and civility in moral and political thought of the eighteenth century.

Writers of all kinds in the middle of the eighteenth century – from novelists to historians and moral philosophers – sought to make their narratives more vivid and dramatic so that readers would respond, and be affected, as if they were spectators live at the events or scenes being recounted. At the juncture of moral philosophy and belletrism, Scottish Enlightenment thinkers such as Lord Kames, Francis Hutcheson, Smith, and Hume reworked traditional humanist views about morality and history by proposing exercises in the moral imagination. This intellectual movement converged with the development of the novel to refocus the moral imagination on 'interior feelings', to use Denis Diderot's term (Hunt, 2007, pp. 27–28). The point was not simply to recognise the role of passions in human society but to stimulate the emotional or moral sensibilities of the reader so as to promote sympathetic identification with or attachment to others and to propel the civilising process.

As Lynn Hunt (2007, p. 39) explains, novels such as Richardson's *Pamela* (1740) and *Clarissa* (1747–48) and Rousseau's *Julie* (1761) reminded readers of the equal vulnerability to pain, misfortune, grief, and suffering, thereby creating 'a sense of equality and empathy through passionate involvement in the narrative'. Drawn into the world vividly and realistically constructed by the novelist, readers empathised with characters whose inner feelings and worldly struggles were revealed through the narrative (Laqueur, 1989, pp. 180–81; Hunt, 2007, ch. 1). Authors believed that by enlarging our sympathies through reading about the pain and suffering of others, we would cultivate our humanity and civility as feeling subjects (Phillips, 2008, p. 54; Festa, 2010, p. 7). In other words, both philosophical and literary writing became concerned with cultivating sympathetic comportment as an essential part of the civilising process.

Arguably the most significant contribution was Smith's *Theory of Moral Sentiments*. This was not a treatise of moral philosophy as we have come to understand the genre after Kant. More sociological and psychological than philosophical, it is concerned to refute philosophies of an egoistic human nature proffered by Hobbes Pufendorf, and Mandeville, among others. Although he was concerned with morality, Smith was not interested in transcendental moral truths of the kind that Aquinas or Kant pursued. Rather, following Hume, he accepted that morality was a fact of life and was concerned to understand the basic social processes by which moralities were produced and contributed to a 'civilized' society, that is, 'a society characterized by the disposition of civility' (Boyd, 2013, p. 444). Morality did not spring from a pure intellect or transcendental principles but from social interactions that shaped and cultivated the moral imagination. For Smith, morality is a social institution common to all cultures and societies, though the specifics of moral doctrine and conduct will vary across time and space (Haakonssen, 2002, p. xii). He wanted to demonstrate that we learn the rules or principles of morality not from abstract theoretical reflection but from everyday experience and the role of emotions in moral judgement and motivation. Smith's *Theory* is thus a radical departure from the rationalist treatises of natural law and subsequent Kantian critical philosophies that would come to exert such an enormous influence over twentieth-century normative theory. Long before the 'emotional turn' in IR, Adam Smith offered a thick description of the role of the imagination and moral sentiments in crafting the rules and laws of civilised societies.

Theory of Moral Sentiments opens with an account of sympathy – 'the emotion which we feel for the misery of others' (Smith, 2002, p. 11). This 'fellow-feeling', which leads us to 'weep even at the feigned representation of a tragedy' (Smith, 2002, p. 52), is a result of the moral imagination. To explain how moral sentiment is produced and cultivated out of sympathy, Smith (2002, p. 26) invoked the figure of an 'impartial spectator' who imaginatively projects himself into the situation of a person suffering misfortune. This act of imagination, whereby we place ourselves in another's situation as if we were to endure 'all the same torments' as the sufferer (Smith, 2002, p. 12), makes the emotion of sympathy possible. The impartial spectator gives rise to a form of self-problematisation designed to induce moral sentiments and conduct that would be approved by others in a civilised society.

The imagination is vital, but it depends on the presentation of a distressing scene to incite sympathy. Smith (2002, p. 26) says that the spectator must 'bring home to himself every little circumstance of distress which can possibly occur to the sufferer ... with all its minutest incidents'. Smith was not so naïve to believe that altruistic sympathy for the pain of others was easily achieved or constant. In a famous example, he conceded that the loss of a finger was likely to cause greater anguish than knowledge that millions of Chinese had perished in an earthquake (Smith, 2002, pp. 157–58). For Smith, and Hume (2007, p. 267), the question was how to enlarge sympathy so that 'the destruction of the whole world' would matter more to an individual than a cut to one's finger. But Smith (2002, p. 179) was well aware that, when it comes to IR, the same sentiments that attach an individual to their nation can animate 'hostile passions' towards foreign nations. As Richard Boyd (2013, p. 460) summarises, the 'flip-side of an otherwise benign sympathy for members of our own nation or group is animosity or resentment towards others'.

For Hume and Smith, this enquiry into the formation of moral sentiment was part of a broader study of the civilising process; understanding the ways in which individuals and societies form moral personalities, make judgements, and satisfy the moral needs of themselves and others in everyday, ordinary life. The capacity to generate an 'impartial spectator' thus became an element in Smith's regimen of moral self-problematisation, which is designed to cultivate fellow-feeling. An interesting extension of Smith's argument is to be found in Sophie de Grouchy's *Letters on Sympathy* (2019). Grouchy was a translator of Smith's *Theory of Moral Sentiments* and wrote an eloquent commentary published as an 'Afterword' to her translation. Her argument was that morality was a sensibility, a feeling that originated in the body through its own experience of pleasure and pain and depended on the imagination (de Grouchy, 2019, pp. 59–61, 80). When a level of civilisation had been achieved, this feeling or disposition was extended to the pain of others; it formed the basis of sympathy and a desire to relieve others of their troubles (de Grouchy, 2019, pp. 71–73). It was this sensibility that she wished to cultivate in order to reform social and political institutions.

4.4 Narrating the Horrors of War: The Humanitarian Cultivation of Sympathy

As shown above, eighteenth-century writers – whether authors of fiction or philosophical treatises – constructed narratives exploring inner feelings and the moral imagination for the purpose of civilising their societies. The cultivation of sympathy through narrative techniques continued into the nineteenth century as a new cluster of non-fictional narratives emerged that was concerned to generate civilising social and political reforms on the basis of sympathy (Laqueur, 1989). In a range of narrative texts, including medical case histories, autopsies, and parliamentary enquiries, detail became a 'sign of truth' (Laqueur, 1989, p. 177), evidence of the reality of suffering. One of the most notable features of this emergent genre of humanitarian narrative is the extraordinary detail into which it goes to relate stories of pain, suffering, misery, and death. Typically, these humanitarian narratives had focused on the suffering of the sick, the poor, the outcast. Much of the detail tended to focus on the body as the 'locus of pain', the evidence of suffering, and the source of sympathy (Laqueur, 1989, pp. 177, 195). According to Thomas Laqueur

(1989, p. 178), the genre of humanitarian narrative had the express purpose of arousing sympathy and compassion so that ameliorative action would become a moral imperative. We might thus describe humanitarian narratives as advocacy texts because of their reformist commitments.

In the nineteenth century what we might call 'sentimental humanitarianism' migrated to the theatre of war. The Romantic philhellenes of the early nineteenth century such as Lord Byron and Percy Bysshe Shelley had brought to the British public's attention the atrocities committed by the Ottoman Empire in the Greek War of Independence in the 1820s. They criticised Britain's neutrality, a position adopted for balance-of-power reasons, arguing that military intervention was necessary to defend liberty and civilisation against despotism and barbarism (Bass, 2008, p. 48). Greece held a unique place in the romantic British imagination for its claim as the origin of civilisation. British press coverage of the war tended to play down Greek cruelties and to highlight Ottoman atrocities, reinforcing the notion that this was a war in defence of civilisation against barbarism and solidifying sympathy for the 'civilized' nation (Bass, 2008, pp. 55–57, 71). Lord Castlereagh, who resisted 'counsels of the heart', plied a more realist strategy of statecraft as foreign minister, but even he admitted that 'humanity shudders' at the violence perpetrated by the 'fanatic and semi-barbarous' Ottomans (quoted in Bass, 2008, p. 63). What the British discourse on Greek liberation from Ottoman rule reveals is not just the emotional appeal of sympathy but the use of the 'asymmetrically opposed concepts' (Koselleck, 1985, p. 161) of civilisation and barbarism to justify an interventionary war. The asymmetrical counterconcepts of civility and barbarity continued to shape late nineteenth-century international law, including racist applications of the European 'standard of civilization' (Gong, 1984), but were also used in humanitarian narratives to highlight the barbarism of intra-European wars.

The classic nineteenth-century example of the humanitarian narrative is Henri Dunant's *Un souvenir de Solferino* [*A Memory of Solferino*] (1959), an advocacy text detailing the horrors of war and the spontaneous efforts of nurses and local women to tend to the battlefield wounded and dying. His narrative had been preceded by the writings of Florence Nightingale, Ferdinando Palasciano, Henri Arrault, and Jean-Charles Chenu, who had borne witness to the medical challenges posed by war and tabled proposals to governments and medical associations for improving wartime medical services. They argued that 'it was the duty of the state to reorganise its own military medical administration in order to provide soldiers with better diet, sanitation, and medical care' (Hutchinson, 1989, p. 564). Dunant demurred on the question of responsibility but like them sought to expand the circle of compassion to the battlefield's war wounded. His *Souvenir*, heavily invested with moral sentiment and morbid detail, was an exemplary and tremendously influential humanitarian narrative that helped pave the way for IHL.

Dunant was an evangelical Christian who had been involved in the League of Alms (Geneva), which was dedicated to providing spiritual and material comfort to the sick and poor. He was also a committed member of The Young Men's Christian Union. The enthusiastic commitment to philanthropy, charity, and compassion would have been developed in those contexts. But it was not until he encountered the horrors of war after the Battle of Solferino in June 1859 that he poured his moral sentiments into the detailed humanitarian narrative of an advocacy text. Dunant (1959, p. 4) described his eye-witness account of the bloody battle between French and Austrian troops and its aftermath at Solferino as 'personal impressions'. But this was not a narrative intended to glorify the liberation of Italy; rather, it was motivated by the overwhelming suffering experienced by injured and dying soldiers. The narrative recounted the battle in all its horrible details:

> Austrians and Allies trampling each other under foot, killing one another on piles of bleeding corpses, felling their enemies with their rifle butts, crushing skulls, ripping bellies open with sabre and bayonet. No quarter is given; it is sheer butchery; a struggle between savage beasts, maddened with blood and fury.
>
> (Dunant, 1959, p. 19)

The narrative also related the destructiveness of modern weaponry. If his general depiction of the slaughter was not enough, Dunant detailed the devastating consequences of the weaponry employed:

> The impact of a cylindrical bullet shatters bones into a thousand pieces, and wounds of this kind are always very serious. Shell-splinters and conical bullets also cause agonizingly painful fractures, and often frightful injuries. All kinds of splinters, pieces of bone, scraps of clothing, equipment or footgear, dirt or pieces of lead, often aggravate the severity of a wound and double the suffering that must be borne.
>
> (Dunant, 1959, p. 44)

Such scenes are repeated endlessly and at length to disturb the onlooker's moral imagination so as to stimulate sympathy for the wounded and dying and admiration for the volunteer nurses providing much-needed medical relief. Dunant's narrative compelled the onlooker to take notice. His assumption is that the scenes of horror will arouse in the reader sufficient sympathy to prompt remedial action for the suffering soldiers.

'But why have I told all these scenes of pain and distress, and perhaps aroused painful emotions in my readers?', Dunant (1959, p. 115) asked. 'Why have I lingered with seeming complacency over lamentable pictures, tracing their details with what might appear desperate fidelity?' His answer was another question: 'Would it not be possible, in time of peace and quiet, to form relief societies for the purpose of having care given to the wounded in wartime by zealous, devoted and thoroughly qualified volunteers?' (Dunant, 1959, p. 115). Dunant's proposal for a voluntary civil society organisation dedicated to the provision of medical relief in war zones garnered the support of influential and committed individuals such as the Genevan lawyer and philanthropist Gustave Moynier. Moynier, who had been involved in several reform movements, was chairman of a local charity, the Geneva Public Welfare Society, which agreed to drive forward Dunant's proposal. A year after publishing *Un souvenir*, Dunant's proposal became a reality with the establishment of the ICRC in 1863 (Boissier, 1985; Hutchinson, 1989).

Consistent with developments elsewhere in European societies, Dunant had realised that sympathy alone was insufficient if it could not be translated into effective treatment on the ground. An ethos of what Rebecca Gill (2007) calls 'calculated compassion' was required – an ethos prescribing 'rational intervention, neutral care and anonymity' in the provision of humanitarian assistance. Dunant acknowledged as much when he stated that the necessity for triage was 'akin to cold calculation', but the triage of determining who could be saved and who could not was essential if suffering was to be alleviated. Decisions had to be made. Nonetheless, he confessed:

> [Y]ou feel sometimes that your heart is breaking – it is as if you were stricken all at once with a sense of bitter and irresistible sadness, because of some simple incident, some isolated happening, some small unexpected detail which strikes closer to the soul, seizing on our sympathies and shaking all the most sensitive fibres of our being.
>
> (Dunant, 1959, p. 74)

Dunant (1959, p. 72) felt a sense of 'utter inadequacy'. Faced with horrific pain and suffering and insufficient resources for tending to the wounded and dying, Dunant realised that a better organised, more professional humanitarian service was needed. Here he differed from earlier humanitarians such as Nightingale, Palasciano, and Arrault who placed this responsibility on states; Dunant, by contrast, pitched for a voluntary civilian service. Nightingale responded to Dunant's humanitarian proposal by arguing that 'Such a society would take upon itself duties which ought to be performed by the government of each country' (quoted in Hutchinson, 1989, p. 566). In the end, Dunant's vision prevailed.

By depicting the brutality and horror of war so vividly, Dunant's narrative lays bare the resulting human torment and incites sympathy in the reader. The narrative is less concerned with historical objectivity than a form of witnessing that is grounded in compassion and a sense of civilised humanity. '[I]n an age when we hear so much of progress and civilization', Dunant (1959, p. 127) asks, 'is it not a matter of urgency, since unhappily we cannot always avoid wars, to press forward in a human and truly civilized spirit the attempt to prevent, or at least to alleviate, the horrors of war?' *Un souvenir de Solferino* may thus be understood as an 'advocacy text'; it makes an emotional appeal to onlookers' moral sentiments, seeking to harness their compassion so as to advocate for concerted humanitarian assistance on the battlefield as part of the civilising process.

Dunant's project thus combined a sense of moral and medical urgency with civilisational progress. In line with early modern natural law, it was an attempt to civilise or humanise war, not to eradicate it. 'For the very first time there was a convention [Geneva 1864] and a semi-official body [ICRC] that would regulate the conduct of war and the treatment of soldiers' (Barnett, 2011, p. 80). Not only could states now be held to account for their conduct in war, but protections were now extended to the war wounded and those administering medical relief. Critics since then have pointed to the limitations of both the *Geneva Conventions* and the ICRC (af Jochnick and Normand, 1994). But the achievement should not be underestimated. The Red Cross movement is now universally recognised by the society of states. This is in part because the Red Cross accommodates itself to the legitimacy of a world of states and partly because 'from the very beginning the ICRC's very existence and effectiveness depended on states' (Barnett, 2011, p. 81). As Dunant expressed it in a meeting of the ICRC, his *Souvenir* was based on the hope that 'the civilized Powers would subscribe to an inviolable, international principle', namely that 'all official and unofficial persons devoting themselves to the relief of victims of war' would be protected (International Committee for the Relief of the Wounded, 1863, p. 65).

It is perhaps no coincidence that the late nineteenth century saw a flurry of international treaty-making around the laws of war (see Best, 1994; Killingsworth, 2016). At roughly the same time that Dunant and the group of Genevan citizens and reformers were working on the ICRC, President Abraham Lincoln hired the émigré German professor of history and political economy from Columbia College, Franz Lieber, to draw up basic rules and principles to regulate the American Civil War. The 'Lieber Code' as it became known was signed into law by Lincoln as General Order No. 100 on 24 April 1863. This ordinance, which drew upon the European laws and customs of war, aimed to moderate the conduct of the opposed armed forces in the Civil War. Running through the Lieber Code was a set of expectations about the conduct of war based on the distinction between civilised nations and barbarous peoples; the former, Lieber declares, respect the rule that civilians should not deliberately be harmed (Lieber, 1863, §§ 22–25).

Other codifications of the laws of war arose during this period too, including the 1868 *St Petersburg Declaration*, the 1874 *Brussels Project of an International Declaration concerning the Laws and Customs or War*, and the Institute of International Law's 1880 manual on *The Laws of War on Land*. These were also followed by the 1899 and 1907 *Hague Conventions* (Best, 1994, p. 41). As David Kennedy (2004, pp. 246–48) explains, the codification of what were essentially diplomatic or military practices into legal rules was part of a broader effort to establish a single universal international law, albeit one in which colonial and racial prejudices often informed the distinction between civilised and uncivilised peoples.

These codifications were the earliest multilateral agreements banning certain weapons and affirming the principle that 'the necessities of war should yield to the requirements of humanity', as the *St Petersburg Declaration* put it, in order that 'the progress of civilization should have the effect of alleviating as much as possible the calamities of war' (quoted in Best, 1994, pp. 42–43; see also Crawford, 2018). These early declarations and conventions set out a path for IHL to develop further three fundamental principles: the principle of distinction between combatants and non-combatants, the principle of proportionality, and the principle of reducing unnecessary suffering. These constituted the legal framework for the humanitarian governance of war, but underlying assumptions about civility and barbarity or savagery were never completely absent from the developing laws of war throughout the early twentieth century (af Jochnick and Normand, 1994, pp. 62–77).

Conclusion

It is easy to hold IHL to exacting standards. Repeating Kant's famous dismissal of Grotius, Pufendorf, and Vattel as 'sorry comforters' who merely legitimised war, critics of IHL have often cleaved to a moral standard entirely removed from the morality of states. Indeed, the very notion of a morality of states is anathema to the moralising critics who see it as a flawed or incomplete morality. Yet, as mutable and peculiar as the morality of states may be, it has a history and legitimacy that is grounded in the practices of states in international society. The society of states possesses its own morality; one that permits states to wage war under certain circumstances – principally self-defence. Humanitarian imperatives have not made the society of states more moral, but they have changed the discourse of war used by states, the public, and interested civil society actors such as the ICRC. As Didier Fassin (2010, 2012) has argued extensively, what he calls 'humanitarian reason' has reconfigured IR by transforming governmental imperatives. It has introduced into the political sphere a new moral economy, suffusing politics with the language of suffering, compassion, assistance, and responsibility to protect (Fassin, 2012, pp. 1–2). By infiltrating governmental logics, this 'moralization of international politics' (Devetak, 2011) has modified the way states manage, regulate, and administer their own and foreign populations, including on the battlefield.

Emotions and moral sentiments are part and parcel of politics, and have been recognised as such since at least the eighteenth century. Since the late nineteenth century, the sympathy and compassion of onlookers helped to secure agreement from states that there were international humanitarian laws that should regulate their actions even in war. Protections should be afforded to injured soldiers as much as innocent civilians if states were to claim the status of being 'civilized'.

Not unlike Dunant, who wrote almost a century and a half earlier, Rieff sought to prick the conscience of spectators. For both writers, the scenes of human devastation they depicted were intended to excite sympathy or compassion for those afflicted by warfare, and to incite action. In Dunant's case, the formation of a voluntary civilian association dedicated to the medical care of injured soldiers; in Rieff's case, the intervention by armed forces to rescue or protect the civilian victims of war. Rieff's calls went unheeded. Distant onlookers were content to spectate and sympathise, but they and their governments were unwilling to risk their armed forces

(Rieff, 2002, pp. 36–37). Dunant's calls for reform were heeded; they shaped the development of the Red Cross, an organisation that has achieved global recognition in the 150 years since its establishment. In one case, appeal to moral sentiment proved successful; in the other, it failed, revealing the emptiness of Europe's and the West's claims to civilisation. Emotions and moral sentiment may be ineradicable features of international relations, but their capacity to translate into virtuous political action remains as politically ambiguous and contingent as ever.

References

Alexander, A. (2015). A short history of international humanitarian law. *European Journal of International Law* 26(1), 109–38.

Arendt, H. (2006). *On Revolution*, Harmondsworth: Penguin Books.

Barnett, M. (2011). *Empire of Humanity: A History of Humanitarianism*, Ithaca, NY: Cornell University Press.

Bass, G. J. (2008). *Freedom's Battle: The Origins of Humanitarian Intervention*, New York: Alfred A. Knopf.

Best, G. (1983). *Humanity in Warfare: The Modern History of the International Law of Armed Conflict*, New York: Columbia University Press.

(1994). *War and Law since 1945*, Oxford: Oxford University Press.

Bleiker, R., and Hutchison, E. (2008). Fear no more: emotions and world politics. *Review of International Studies* 30(3), 503–39.

Boissier, P. (1985). *History of the International Committee of the Red Cross: From Solferino to Tsushima*, Geneva: Henry Dunant Institute.

Boyd, R. (2013). Adam Smith on civility and civil society. In C. J. Berry, M. P. Paganelli, and C. Smith (eds.), *The Oxford Handbook of Adam Smith*, Oxford: Oxford University Press.

Calhoun, C. (2008). The imperative to reduce suffering: charity, progress, and emergencies in the field of humanitarian action. In M. Barnett and T. G. Weiss (eds.), *Humanitarianism in Question: Politics, Power, Ethics*, Ithaca, NY: Cornell University Press.

Crawford, E. (2018). The enduring legacy of the St Petersburg Declaration: distinction, military necessity, and the prohibition of causing unnecessary suffering and superfluous injury in IHL. *Journal of the History of International Law* 20(4), 544–66.

Crawford, N. (2000). The passion of world politics: propositions on emotions and emotional relationships. *International Security* 24(4), 116–36.

(2014). Institutionalizing passion in world politics: fear and empathy. *International Theory* 6(3), 535–57.

Devetak, R. (2005). The gothic scene of international relations: ghosts, monsters, terror and the sublime after September 11. *Review of International Studies* 31 (4), 621–44.

(2011). The moralization of international politics: humanitarian intervention and its critics. *Quaderni di Relazioni Internazionali* 14(May), 70–85.

Dunant, H. (1959). *A Memory of Solferino*, Geneva: International Committee of the Red Cross.

Elias, N. (1994). *The Civilizing Process: The History of Manners and State Formation and Civilization*, trans. Edmund Jephcott, Oxford: Blackwell.

Erskine, T. (2008). *Embedded Cosmopolitanism: Duties to Strangers and Enemies in a World of 'Dislocated Communities'*, Cambridge: Cambridge University Press.

Fassin, D. (2010). Heart of humaneness: the moral economy of humanitarian intervention. In D. Fassin and M. Pandolfi (eds.), *Contemporary States of Emergency: The Politics of Military and Humanitarian Interventions*, New York: Zone Books.

(2012). *Humanitarian Reason: A Moral History of the Present*, trans. Rachel Gomme, Berkeley: University of California.

Festa, L. (2010). Humanity without feathers. *Humanity* 1(1), 3–27.

Gill, R. (2007). The 'new humanitarian' ethos in Britain: 1870–1918. *Quatrième journée guerre et médecines*, 12 May, 1–9.

Gong, G. (1984). *The Standard of 'Civilization' in International Society*, Oxford: Clarendon Press.

de Grouchy, S. (2019). *Sophie de Grouchy's Letters on Sympathy: A Critical Engagement with Adam Smith's The Theory of Moral Sentiments*, trans. Sandrine Bergès, Oxford: Oxford University Press.

Haakonssen, K. (2002). Introduction. In *Adam Smith, The Theory of Moral Sentiments*, ed. Knud Haakonssen, Cambridge: Cambridge University Press.

Hume, D. (2007). *A Treatise of Human Nature: A Critical Edition*, ed. David Fate Norton, Oxford: Oxford University Press.

Hunt, L. (2007). *Inventing Human Rights: A History*, New York: W. W. Norton & Company.

Hutchinson, J. F. (1989). Rethinking the origins of the Red Cross. *Bulletin of the History of Medicine* 63, 557–78.

Hutchison, E. (2016). *Affective Communities in World Politics: Collective Emotions after Trauma*, Cambridge: Cambridge University Press.

Hutchison, E., and Bleiker, R. (2014). Theorizing emotions in world politics. *International Theory* 6(3), 491–514.

International Committee for the Relief of the Wounded (1863). Minutes of the Meeting of the Sub-Committee of the Society for the Relief of Combatants Wounded in Time of War, held on 17 Feb 1863. *International Review of the Red Cross* (23), 65–67.

Jeffery, R. (2014). *Reason and Emotions in International Ethics*, Cambridge: Cambridge University Press.

af Jochnick, C., and Normand, R. (1994). The legitimation of violence: a critical history of the laws of war. *Harvard International Law Journal* 35 (1), 49–95.

Keal, P. (2003). *European Conquest and the Rights of Indigenous Peoples: The Moral Backwardness of International Society*, Cambridge: Cambridge University Press.

Keenan, T. (2002). Publicity and indifference (Sarajevo on television). *PMLA* 117 (1), 104–16.

Kennedy, D. (2004). *The Dark Sides of Virtue: Reassessing International Humanitarianism*, Princeton, NJ: Princeton University Press.

Killingsworth, M. (2016). From St Petersburg to Rome: understanding the evolution of the modern laws of war. *Australian Journal of Politics and History* 62 (1), 100–15.

Kinsella, H. (2011). *The Image before the Weapon: A Critical History of the Distinction between Combatant and Civilian*, Ithaca, NY: Cornell University Press.

Koselleck, R. (1985). *Futures Past: On the Semantics of Historical Time*, trans. Keith Tribe, Cambridge, MA: MIT Press.

Laqueur, T. (1989). Bodies, details, and humanitarian narrative. In Lynn Hunt (ed.), *The New Cultural History*, Berkeley: University of California Press.

Lieber, F. (1863). *Instructions for the Government of Armies of the United States, in the Field*, New York: van Nostrand.

Linklater, A. (2007). Distant suffering and cosmopolitan obligations. *International Politics* 44(1), 19–36.

(2011). *The Problem of Harm in World Politics: Theoretical Investigations*, Cambridge: Cambridge University Press.

(2016). *Violence and Civilization in the Western States-Systems*, Cambridge: Cambridge University Press.

Mercer, J. (2005). Rationality and psychology in international politics. *International Organization* 59, 77–106.

(2014). Feeling like a state: social emotion and identity. *International Theory* 6 (3), 515–35.

Mill, J. S. (1977). Civilization. In *Essays on Politics and Society*, ed. J. M. Robson, Toronto: University of Toronto Press and Routledge Kegan Paul.

Mishra, P. (2017). *Age of Anger: A History of the Present*, New York: Picador.

Muldoon, P. (2008). The moral legitimacy of anger. *European Journal of Social Theory* 11(3), 299–314.

(2014). *Philoctetes* and the politics of rescue. In Michael Ure and Mervyn Frost (eds.), *The Politics of Compassion*. London: Routledge.

Müller, J.-W. (2017). *What Is Populism?*, Harmondsworth: Penguin Books.

Nussbaum, M. C. (2001). *Upheavals of Thought: The Intelligence of Emotions*, Cambridge: Cambridge University Press.

(2003). Compassion and terror. *Daedalus* 132(1), 10–26.

Phillips, M. S. (2008). On the advantage and disadvantage of sentimental history for life. *History Workshop Journal* 65, 49–64.

Power, S. (2002). *'A Problem from Hell': America and the Age of Genocide*, London: Flamingo.

Rieff, D. (1995). *Slaughterhouse: Bosnia and the Failure of the West*, London: Vintage.

(2002). *Bed for the Night: Humanitarianism in Crisis*, London: Vintage.

Robin, C. (2004). *Fear: The History of a Political Idea*, Oxford: Oxford University Press.

Smith, A. (2002). *The Theory of Moral Sentiments*, ed. Knud Haakonssen, Cambridge: Cambridge University Press.

Sophocles (2015). Philoctetes. In *Oedipus the King and Other Tragedies*, trans. Oliver Taplin, Oxford: Oxford University Press.

Ure, M., and Frost, M. (2014). Introduction. In M. Ure and M. Frost (eds.), *The Politics of Compassion*, London: Routledge.

Wight, M. (1991). Theory of Mankind: 'Barbarians'. In G. Wight and B. Porter (eds.), *International Theory: The Three Traditions*, Leicester: Leicester University Press.

5

Limits to the Scope of Humanity as a Constraint on the Conduct of War

TIM MCCORMACK, SIOBHAIN GALEA, AND DANIEL WESTBURY

5.1 The Emergence of Humanity as a Constraint on the Conduct of War

International humanitarian lawyers often claim that the rules of international humanitarian law (IHL), whether the body of rules regulating the conduct of hostilities or the body of rules establishing minimum standards of protection for different categories of victims of armed conflict, are a balancing act between two key overarching principles: humanity and military necessity.[1] So, for example, the rule on distinction, the prohibition on indiscriminate attack, the rule on proportionality, and the rules on precautions in, and from, attack are all carefully balanced between these two overarching principles. The articulation of the rule on proportionality most explicitly encapsulates an obligation on the military decision-maker to balance these two overarching principles: Article 51(5)(b) of *Additional Protocol I*, for example, codifies the rule and prohibits 'an attack which may be expected to cause incidental loss of civilian life, injury to civilians, damage to civilian objects, or a combination thereof, which would be excessive in relation to the concrete and direct military advantage anticipated'. The military decision-maker is obliged to assess the anticipated direct and concrete military advantage from attacking the intended military object against the expected loss of civilian lives, civilian injury and/or damage to civilian property – arguably the quintessential example of attempting to strike a balance between military necessity and humanity (see e.g. Neuman, 2004).

Martti Koskenniemi coined the descriptor 'the gentle civilizer of nations' for the role and contribution of international law in his book

[1] For one of the most explicit and compelling articulations of this position, see Schmitt (2010).

by that title emanating from his 1998 Sir Hersch Lauterpacht Memorial Lectures (Koskenniemi, 2004). Although Koskenniemi did not focus on the development of IHL as his key *indicium* of civilising influence, the notion of humanity as a constraint on the conduct of hostilities was fundamental to the emergence of IHL. The purported *raison d'être* for the early push for multilateral agreement on legal constraints on the conduct of war was the introduction of a 'gentle civilizer' in the maelstrom of war; at least that is how the orthodox interpretations of the origins of IHL would have us understand the motivation behind the push for multilateral regulation of the conduct of war.

The origins of the notion of humanity as a legal constraint on the conduct of war is well-trodden ground. Within the global Red Cross and Red Crescent Movement, we honour the role of Henri Dunant, the unlikely *génevois* merchant banker who wrote up his observations of the aftermath of the Battle of Solferino and of his mobilisation of a civil humanitarian relief effort for hundreds of wounded combatants lacking basic medical treatment, food, and shelter.

In his memoir, *Un souvenir de Solferino*,[2] Dunant called for the creation of an impartial humanitarian relief organisation that would be able to provide basic medical assistance so palpably absent at Solferino (Dunant, 1959). As a consequence of his call and the contemporary political receptiveness to it, the International Committee of the Red Cross (ICRC) was established in 1863 and, the following year, the 1864 *Geneva Convention* was adopted – the very first multilateral treaty regulating conduct in war. This was a relatively rudimentary treaty with just two pages of text incorporating the principal obligation for States Parties to respect, and to ensure immunity from attack for, hospitals, medical vehicles, medical personnel, and the wounded in war. For present purposes though, the substance of the 1864 Convention is less significant than the claimed motivation behind Dunant's initiative. He challenged the notion that war by its very nature inevitably constitutes a humanitarian black hole. In the final pages of *Un souvenir de Solferino*, Dunant asserted that:

> Humanity and civilization call imperiously for such an organization as is here suggested. . . . [I]n an age when we hear so much of progress and

[2] Originally published in French in 1862. Now readily available in electronic form in English and in other languages at: https://shop.icrc.org/e-books/un-souvenir-de-solferino.html. The English language translation from the original French was first provided by American Red Cross in 1939 and is now reproduced by the International Committee of the Red Cross with permission of the American Red Cross.

> civilization, is it not a matter of urgency, since unhappily we cannot always avoid wars, to press forward in a human and truly civilized spirit the attempt to prevent, or at least to alleviate, the horrors of war?
>
> (Dunant, 1959, pp. 126–27)

It is easy for those of us associated with the International Red Cross and Red Crescent Movement to silo the Battle of Solferino and the emergence of IHL, and to naively assume that somehow or other Dunant was a lone humanitarian beacon shining a light in the darkness of mid-nineteenth-century human depravity. Dunant's statement above, 'in an age when we hear so much of progress and civilisation' implies a broader context – one which could broadly be defined as a general rise of humanitarianism – particularly throughout the nineteenth century. It is overly simplistic to disaggregate developments emerging out of the aftermath of the Battle of Solferino and the subsequent establishment of the ICRC in isolation from that general and prevalent geo-political environment. The then world's political leadership would hardly have been as receptive to Dunant's call but for the context in which it was pitched. Analysis of the prevailing context in which Dunant promoted his proposal is important to understand the receptivity to it. But those who label themselves IHL lawyers have tended to mythologise Dunant's motivations and his achievements, and it is also important to present a more nuanced and accurate account: particularly to explain the limits of who he intended as the beneficiaries of 'humanity' as a constraint on the conduct of war.

One key contemporary manifestation of a growing humanitarianism was the movement to abolish slavery – the so-called Abolitionist Movement – which reached its zenith in the nineteenth century. The insatiable thirst for workers to fuel labour-intensive industries, such as tobacco, sugar, coffee, cotton, and precious metals (particularly gold), drove a massive increase in the trans-Atlantic slave trade to the Americas during the eighteenth century. In the two British colonies of Virginia and Maryland in 1680, for example, there were fewer than 5,000 African slaves combined. By the time of US independence in 1776, the number of African slaves in those two former colonies alone had increased by more than 4,000 per cent to over 200,000 (Ferrell, 2006, p. 4). The Abolitionist Movement in the UK, led by British Quakers and the so-called 'Clapham Sect' of Anglican reformers (including William Wilberforce and Henry Thornton), campaigned for decades to witness the formal abolition of the slave trade throughout the British Empire with the enactment of the *Slave Trade Act 1807*. The reformers continued to campaign and, twenty-six years later, celebrated the enactment of the *Slavery Abolition Act 1833* in the UK. Neither of those legislative milestones ended the de facto reality of slavery in the British Empire, but they did constitute significant breakthroughs transforming the UK from a major global user of slaves to a leading international opponent of the practice.

On the other side of the Atlantic Ocean, both pre- and post-American Independence, Quakers led the abolitionist movement against formidable opposition. Claudine Ferrell claims that by the 1830s–50s, slavery was so deeply embedded in 'virtually every aspect of American life' that:

> . . . [A] full range of economic, social, political, constitutional, religious, historical, anthropological, gendered and biological assumptions and opinions confronted them. The result was that the abolitionists themselves were seen as the threats to the nation. In the new republic, concepts of liberty, individualism, progress and God's will inspired slavery's opponents, just as they guided slavery's supporters.
>
> (Ferrell, 2006, p. 5)

Assertions of the right to exercise ownership over other human beings divided opinion in the United States so fundamentally as to constitute the principal catalyst for the secession of the Confederate States from the Union and the outbreak of the Civil War (see McPherson, 1995, pp. 29–51). Abraham Lincoln had been elected President in 1860 against the express wishes of the southern States because of his anti-slavery policies. Following his election, Lincoln refused to commit to a political compromise which may have preserved the Union by allowing the Confederate States an exemption to maintain slavery (McPherson, 1995, pp. 29–31). The Confederacy rejected Lincoln's position, and thousands of Americans lost their lives in the ensuing conflagration.

Two years into the Civil War, in 1863, coincidentally the same year in which the ICRC was established, President Lincoln unilaterally promulgated the Lieber Code regulating the conduct of Union forces in the Civil War (U.S. War Department, 1863).[3] Burrus Carnahan provides the following analysis of the Code's significance:

> Drafted by an academic intent on drawing general principles of human morality from empirical evidence, and issued by a President determined

[3] The Code is named after its principal author, Francis Lieber, who was then a scholar at Columbia College (now University) in New York City. A copy of the text of the Code is accessible at: https://ihl-databases.icrc.org/ihl/INTRO/110.

> to found his policies on human reason, the Lieber Code may be considered the final product of the eighteenth-century movement to humanize war through the application of reason. From this standpoint, the Lieber Code's greatest theoretical contribution to the modern law of war was its identification of military necessity as a general legal principle to limit violence, in the absence of any other rule.
>
> (Carnahan, 1998, p. 213)

Article 14 of the Lieber Code includes the following definition: 'Military necessity as understood by modern civilized nations, consists in the necessity of those measures which are indispensable for securing the ends of the war, and which are lawful according to the modern law and usages of war.' Although the respective efforts of Henri Dunant and Francis Lieber were not informed or influenced by the other (Roberts, 2019, p. 184), both figures shared similar reactions to the horrors of war and to the importance of constraints on the conduct of armed forces of civilised nations in war. However, as Sir Adam Roberts has observed, Dunant's approach was far narrower in scope (the 'minimalist' right of combatants to medical treatment and immunity from attack) than Lieber's (a 'maximalist' codification of a wide range of military actions) (Roberts, 2019, p. 195).

Far from a permissive concept, Lieber's notion of military necessity was of constraint in the conduct of war. Article 15 of the Code explains in some detail examples of legitimate military objectives, and Article 16 provides examples of excesses not justified by any military necessity:

> Military necessity does not admit of cruelty – that is, the infliction of suffering for the sake of suffering or for revenge, nor of maiming or wounding except in fight, nor of torture to extort confessions. It does not admit of the use of poison in any war, nor of the wanton devastation of a district. It admits of deception, but disclaims acts of perfidy; and, in general, military necessity does not include any act of hostility which makes the return to peace unnecessarily difficult.

Despite this conceptualisation of military necessity as a constraint on the conduct of war, Confederate leaders not only dismissed reciprocal application of the Code to their own forces but, as Carnahan explains, also used the Code as propaganda. Carnahan cites correspondence from the Confederate Secretary of War, James Seddon, to the Confederate Agent for Exchange of Prisoners, Colonel Robert Ould, claiming that:

> [I]n this code of military necessity . . . the acts of atrocity and violence which have been committed by officers of the United States and have

> shocked the moral sense of civilized nations are to find an apology and defense. . . . They cannot frame mischief into a code or make an instituted system of rules embodying the spirit of mischief under the name of a military necessity.
>
> (Carnahan, 1998, pp. 217–18)[4]

How intriguing that Secretary Seddon would appeal to the very 'moral sense of civilised nations' that Lieber and Lincoln relied upon to draft and to promulgate the Code respectively as a basis to attack it (and the application of the Code's provisions to military operations undertaken by Union Forces). The terminology here was not limited to the US Civil War context. The Martens Clause in the preamble to the 1899 *Convention (II) with Respect to the Laws and Customs of War on Land* [*Hague Convention*], for example, incorporates very similar language: 'the usages established between civilised nations, from the laws of humanity and the requirements of the public conscience'. Confederate leaders were not prepared to reciprocally apply the Code's restrictions and made no attempt to emulate the Lieber Code with their own written restrictions on the conduct of military operations. However cynical Seddon's comments though, the criticism is ubiquitous. The claim of civility – that military operations have been undertaken consistently with the laws and customs of war and/or with the constraints dictated by the public conscience of civilised nations – inevitably invites the critique that the claim is in reality a fig-leaf for barbarity.[5]

[4] Carnahan explains that the correspondence is reproduced in Hartigan (1983, p. 120).

[5] One of the more articulate recent critiques of this kind is by af Jochnick and Normand (1994). The authors followed up the general critique of IHL with a critical case study of US military operations in the 1990 Gulf War (Normand and af Jochnick, 1994). Sir Adam Roberts has published a recent critique of 'myths' surrounding both the Lieber Code and the 1864 *Geneva Convention*. Sir Adam claims of the Lieber Code:

> [I]t would be wrong to see the main purpose of the Lieber Code as wholly on the side of moderation in war. Any code of the laws of war is likely to assume that the killing of active enemy soldiers is legitimate. Indeed, it is a problem of the laws of war that they can be seen as compatible with industrial-scale killings of soldiers on the battlefield. The Lieber Code was drawn up at a time when the [US Civil] war was becoming more mechanised and more intense. Its provisions were far from being completely opposed to the move towards total war.
>
> (Roberts, 2019, p. 169)

5.2 Humanity as a Manifestation of 'Progressive Civilisation'

Fans of Dunant, and of his promotion of humanity as a constraint on the conduct of war, can easily overlook early understandings of limitations to the intended protective scope of this emerging notion. For both Dunant and his audience of political leaders, the constraining influence of humanity in war was inextricably linked to notions of progressive civilisation. In the passages quoted above from the final pages of *Un souvenir de Solferino*, Dunant is explicit about this link: '*Humanity and civilization* call imperiously for such an organisation as here called for' and then 'In an age when we hear so much of *progress and civilization*, is it not a matter of urgency . . . to press forward in a *truly civilized spirit*?' (Dunant, 1959, p. 127). Article 14 of the Lieber Code reflects a similar understanding on the part of both Lincoln as promulgator and Lieber as drafter: 'Military necessity, as understood by *modern civilized nations*'. Even Confederate Secretary Seddon drew on precisely the same inextricable link to condemn and to discredit the Lieber Code: 'the acts of atrocity and violence which have . . . *shocked the moral sense of civilized nations*' (Carnahan, 1998, pp. 217–18, emphasis added).

Modern sensitivities readily lead to an assumption that the notion of 'humanity' in war could only have been intended to benefit all humankind affected by armed conflict, without discrimination. Any such assumption is fallacious. Dunant's belief that expressions of humanity in war were a manifestation of progressive civilisation was restricted to war between 'civilised' sovereign nations. States Parties to the 1864 *Geneva Convention* were not bound by the treaty's provisions in armed conflict with states not party to the *Convention*, nor in non-international armed conflicts against non-state armed groups, and certainly not in armed conflicts waged against 'savages'.

Frédéric Mégret describes the exclusion of 'uncivilised' peoples from the protective scope of humanity as a constraint on the conduct of war as IHL's 'original sin' and makes the powerful observation that:

> There is a past that international humanitarian law would rather forget, but which is coming back to haunt it. This is a past that bears the shameful mark of racism and colonialism. It is a past that hardly ever gets more than a passing reference in the literature, probably because it is viewed as having been largely transcended, but also partly because it does not fit the overwhelmingly progressist narrative of international humanitarian law. Although the above description may overstate the case, there is no doubt that this is a past that is very real – and maybe even present.
>
> (Mégret, 2006, pp. 265, 268)

Dunant was of course a product of his time. Frédéric Mégret helps dismantle the tendency to mythologise Dunant's humanitarian motives. Dunant had extensive colonialist business interests in Algeria and was seeking to expand them. Mégret refers to Dunant's 'project for a *Société internationale universelle pour la rénovation de l'Orient*', which he described thus: *une nouvelle croisade par la civilisation*, included the establishment of commercial *comptoirs* in Constantinople, the construction of a harbour in Jaffa and a railway to Jerusalem' (Mégret, 2006, p. 270). It is clear that Dunant was not alone in demonstrating what we now see as significant contradictions. Mégret explains that others involved in the historical development of IHL were also steeped in the colonial enterprise with shared racist and paternalistic views of 'uncivilised savages' including Gustave Moynier, Friedrich von Martens, and Sir John Charles Ardagh (Mégret, 2006, p. 270).

On the other side of the Atlantic Ocean, the Lieber Code had been promulgated to regulate conduct of the Union Forces in the US Civil War (a non-international armed conflict in contemporary parlance). Although the Confederate Army did not represent another sovereign state, Lincoln hoped for reunification and had a vested longer-term interest in his military forces exercising restraint to better facilitate reconciliation in the aftermath of war (provided Union forces prevailed of course). Article 16 of the Code, cited above, explicitly referred to the motivation of facilitating reconciliation post-war: 'military necessity does not include any act of hostility which makes the return to peace unnecessarily difficult'.

It was one thing for the Code to apply to the conduct of the Union Army in their exchange of hostilities with the Confederates, but neither Lieber nor Lincoln ever intended that the same Union Army apply the Lieber Code in their military operations against America's indigenous peoples. Eric Ringmar's analysis is insightful:

> As for the Native Americans, their destiny was to be subdued. To Lieber this was an inevitable consequence of the progress of civilization, and, on the whole, hardly regrettable. With such an underlying mentality, it is no wonder that Lieber's laws of war never applied to Native Americans. The Indians were not, like the Spanish or Confederate *guerilleros*, temporarily, and misguidedly, descending into savagery; they really were 'savages', constitutionally and irredeemably. With Indians no compromises were possible, at least not regarding matters of *jus in bello*. This is consequently where we find the limits of international humanitarian law. . . . International law, as it developed in the nineteenth century, was

> formulated by and for civilized, Christian states inhabited by Europeans and their descendants. During the American Civil War these connections were of course particularly close. The Confederate enemy consisted of their 'brothers', people the war was supposed to bring back into the Union. ... Fighting non-Europeans, and non-Americans, was quite a different matter.
>
> (Ringmar, 2009, p. 56)

Read Dee Brown's *Bury My Heart at Wounded Knee* (1970) and weep over the shocking and recurrent accounts of deceit, of betrayal, and of the dehumanising of Native Americans as one massacre after another drove the indigenous tribes off their traditional lands. In the prevailing view of the invaders, these natives did not fight with any 'decency':

> Instead they routinely captured, scalped, and tortured their enemies; they disregarded cease-fires and flags of truce, acted treacherously and employed underhanded tactics. Most strikingly, they made no distinction between soldiers and civilians. To a savage – civilians – including women and children – are all legitimate targets.
>
> (Ringmar, 2009, p. 56)

John Fabian Witt analyses the reasons for such 'terrifyingly ferocious forms of violence' in the frontier wars with Native Americans. Witt's argument is that the related but slightly different notions that 'non-Christians fell outside the boundaries of the laws of war' or that 'savage peoples were not entitled to the law of war's civilizing protections' provide inadequate explanations. His view is that while the norms of warfare were not irrelevant to these wars, 'the norms that existed collided with one another' so spectacularly that they generated intense revulsion for the opposing party's *modus operandi* and escalating, uncontrolled violence ensued (Witt, 2011, p. 903).

The Native Americans also stood in the way of access to land and to resources. Killing them to ensure the safety, security, and prosperity of settlers was deemed a necessity and an inevitability to facilitate the 'manifest destiny' of the new Americans to spread over the entire continent and subdue it (see Pratt, 1927). Some of that killing was perpetrated by settlers themselves. Much of it also happened at the hand of the US Army. Clearance of the land west of the Mississippi occurred during the 1820s, 1830s, and right through to the late 1870s – throughout the entirety of the Civil War and beyond it. 'Progressive civilisation' in this particular context manifest not in humanitarian constraint but in eradication and in the insatiable thirst for settlement to open up access to land and to resources.

It is wrong to single out America here. Lyndall Ryan's mapping of massacres in Australia's frontier wars is as significant to Australia's national understanding of the brutal history of colonial interaction with its indigenous peoples as it is harrowing in the extent of armed violence across the continent.[6] Ryan's *Tasmanian Aborigines: A History Since 1803* (2012) details the interactions between colonial settlers and the indigenous peoples of Van Diemen's Land. The descriptions of the hunting down and wanton slaughter of indigenous peoples across the colony, particularly during the 1820s and 1830s, are appalling. Aboriginal peoples were never extended humanity in the colonial violence to which they were subjected, and that violence was so overwhelming as to result in the near annihilation of Aboriginality in the colony (Ryan, 2012).[7] Social Darwinism influenced the purported justification that the Aboriginal people of Van Diemen's Land were not only an obstacle to the settlement enterprise but that in their 'savage' state they were sub-human and doomed to extinction. Lyndall Ryan explains that:

> [T]he British settlers initially invoked eighteenth-century religious and scientific beliefs in 'savagery' and 'fatalism' to explain the near extinction of what they believed were at least 6,000 – 8,000 Tasmanian Aborigines within a generation of invasion. This explanation enabled the settlers to justify their genocidal behaviour by claiming that the Aborigines themselves were responsible for their near demise by virtue of their 'innate inferiority' and inability to 'compete successfully with Europeans'
>
> (Ryan, 2012, p. xix, citing Cove, 1995, pp. 44–45).

This 'othering' of Tasmania's Aboriginal people, excluding them from any tempering or restraining influence of the emerging laws of war, is a shameful aspect of the history of Tasmania and Australia. The killings were of such magnitude as to exemplify the attempted extermination of another race. Raphael Lemkin, the Polish scholar who coined the label 'genocide' to describe the intentional destruction of a group of people on the basis of race, cited the slaughter of the Aborigines of Tasmania as a

6 An online interactive national map is accessible at: https://c21ch.newcastle.edu.au/colonialmassacres/map.php. The ongoing project has only detailed massacres in eastern and central Australia to date and is yet to complete the required research to map massacres in Western Australia.

7 We Tasmanians are fortunate that, through great resilience, a remnant of our Aboriginal people survived on islands in Bass Strait and faithfully passed on their cultural, linguistic, spiritual, and legal traditions to successive generations. Aboriginal culture is thriving in Tasmania as a consequence and our society is the richer for it.

leading case study in support of his calls for multilateral criminalisation of such conduct (see e.g. Curthoys, 2005, pp. 162–69).

Given the comprehensive and brutal colonial history in Van Diemen's Land/Tasmania, the contemporary thriving of indigenous culture in the island state is an incredible testament to collective resilience and determination. Australia's frontier wars and those in the United States were not considered 'wars' because of a refusal to acknowledge any equivalence in combatant status. The great irony here is that the legal justification for lack of application of constraints by the colonisers was the 'savagery' of the natives who fought without any chivalry or respect for decency. And yet, in the waging of wars of annihilation, the self-identifying 'civilised' peoples descended into their own savagery. Mégret characterises it this way:

> Ironically, what came to haunt European nations was not the warfare of the 'savages', as had been feared. Rather, it was the West's own savageness, revealed to itself in the process of repressing the colonial 'other'. Wars of colonization kept alive the savagery within that the laws of war were supposed to have expunged. . . . In the end, it was less the 'savages' who were 'civilized', than the 'civilized' who 'savaged' themselves, through no responsibility other than their own.
>
> (Mégret, 2006, p. 294)[8]

[8] In his rush to downplay the significance of organised armed resistance on the part of the Aborigines, Keith Windschuttle perpetuates this interpretation of the status of the frontier conflict in Van Diemen's Land. He asserted that the Tasmanian Aborigines did:

> not wage war themselves. That is, though one side waged war, there was not a state of war between the parties. . . . Hence, even though the British used military tactics and methods themselves, the lack of reciprocation by the Aborigines meant the two were not linked by anything that deserves the title warfare. In short, the Black War is a misnomer and the orthodox school of Aboriginal history is mistaken. There was no frontier war in Van Diemen's Land.
>
> (Windschuttle, 2002, pp. 197–98)

Windschuttle's disparagement of the 'orthodox school of Aboriginal history' is particularly referring to Henry Reynolds who has arguably done more than any other single historian to explain the scale and the intensity of Aboriginal resistance to colonial invasion and dispossession. In his most recent book, *Tongerlongeter: First Nations Leader and Tasmanian War Hero* (2021, p. 100), Reynolds and his co-author, Nicholas Clements, describe the 'most violent period of frontier war in Australia's history, and the stiffest armed resistance ever mounted by Indigenous people' between 1828 and 1830 in Van Diemen's Land.

This restrictive scope of application of the emerging notion of humanity was not unique to constraints on the conduct of war. The abolition of slavery and subsequent emancipation were both dramatic achievements but did not result in suffrage for former slaves (McPherson, 1995, p. 26). In the United States, the Fifteenth Amendment to the US Constitution extended suffrage to non-white men and freed male slaves in 1870, but it took decades for the suppression of these rights through so-called 'Jim Crow Laws' in southern US States to be declared unconstitutional by the US Supreme Court (Schmidt Jr, 1982). In Australia where, despite accepting Aboriginals into the military in World War I and conscripting them in World War II, it was not until the Constitutional referendum in 1967 that Section 127 of the Australian Constitution was repealed, allowing Aboriginals to be counted in the national census (see Attwood and Markus, 2007).[9]

The limitations on scope of application of the emerging notion of humanity as a constraint on the conduct of war are confirmed in the subsequent development of IHL. The exemplar for the exclusion of 'uncivilised savages' from the protective scope of the emerging laws of war was the British insistence on the right to develop different ammunition for use in its colonial wars against these 'others'. Mégret describes this as 'one of the most notable yet forgotten cases of double standards in the history of international law' (Mégret, 2006, p. 277).

5.3 Prohibiting Exploding and Expanding Bullets

The 1864 *Geneva Convention* was followed just four years later by the *St Petersburg Declaration* (*Declaration Renouncing the Use, in Time of War, of Explosive Projectiles under 400 Grammes Weight*, 1868) a prohibition on exploding bullets (or more specifically 'any projectile of a weight below 400 grammes, which is either explosive or charged with fulminating or inflammable substances'). This was the first ever multilateral instrument to prohibit a category of weapons. The Russian military had developed a bullet which exploded on contact with a hard substance.

[9] The authors discuss popular misunderstandings of the referendum as giving Aboriginal People the vote, granting Aboriginal People equal citizenship and/or repealing racially discriminatory laws.

It was originally invented in 1853 to destroy ammunition wagons, but in 1867 it was modified to explode on contact with a soft substance (Higgins, 1909, p. 25). It was clear that potential anti-personnel application could inflict horrific wounds.

The Russian War Minister persuaded his government to regulate the use of such bullets (Higgins, 1909, p. 25). This was probably driven by concern about the morale of the Russian forces once technology spread and explosive bullets were used against Russian soldiers (Kalshoven, 2016, pp. 94, 96). Consequently, Czar Alexander II called an international conference of military delegates in St Petersburg to negotiate a treaty prohibition (Higgins, 1909, p. 25). The text of the Preamble to the ensuing *Declaration* reveals a great deal about the motivation, or at least the ostensible motivation, for the treaty:

> That the progress of civilization should have the effect of alleviating as much as possible the calamities of war;
> That the only legitimate object which states should endeavour to accomplish during war is to weaken the military forces of the enemy:
> That for this purpose, it is sufficient to disable the greatest possible number of men;
> That this object would be exceeded by the employment of arms, which uselessly aggravate the sufferings of disabled men or render their death inevitable:
> That the employment of such arms would therefore be contrary to the laws of humanity.

Here again, consistent with Dunant's call in *Un Souvenir de Solferino*, we read the proposition that 'the progress of civilisation' should manifest in humanity in war (Dunant, 1959, pp. 126–27). Notice that in 1868 the notion of humanity as the key *indicium* of progressive civilisation had morphed from a somewhat nebulous concept in 1864 to the 'laws of humanity' just four years later. International humanitarian lawyers understandably focus on these aspects of the Preamble to the *St Petersburg Declaration* as evidence of the growing multilateral commitment to the legal regulation of the conduct of war. However, the text of the Preamble to the *Declaration* exposes the inherent restrictions to the scope of the new humanitarian protections:

> The contracting parties engage mutually to renounce in case of war amongst themselves the following category of weapons. This engagement is compulsory only upon the contracting or acceding parties in case of war between two or more of themselves. It is not applicable to non-contracting parties. It will also cease to be compulsory from the moment

> when in a war between contracting parties a non-contracting party shall join one of the belligerents.

So, the emerging 'laws of humanity' only applied to some and not to others. In one sense, the proposition in this paragraph of the *Declaration* is entirely consistent with the fundamental principle of treaty law that a treaty's provisions only bind States Parties to the treaty in their relations with other States Parties (*Vienna Convention on the Law of Treaties*, arts. 26, 34). But the final paragraph in the Preamble to the *Declaration* refers to the pre-existing 'laws of humanity', suggesting that the states negotiating the text of the *Declaration* accepted the existence of a broader customary international legal norm prohibiting certain categories of weapons causing particularly egregious injuries.[10] There is an inherent inconsistency in the principles here, and it seems that the narrower, exclusionary, principle of treaty law was the prevalent one in the latter half of the nineteenth century.

Perhaps one of the most spectacular examples of precisely this inconsistent application of humanity as a constraint in the nineteenth century transpired in the final decade. In 1895, the British Raj in the Chitral Campaign in India was deeply concerned by the inefficacy of the standard bullet used in the .303 calibre rifle. This bullet was known as the Mark II (Spiers, 1975, p. 4). Commentators reported that 'natives' wounded by the Mark II were able to quickly receive hospital care and recover from multiple wounds (Spiers, 1975, p. 4). The Ordnance Department in India developed and tested a bullet based on one used in big-game hunting at an ammunition factory in Dum Dum, in northern India (northeast of Calcutta) (Spiers, 1975, p. 3). This bullet had a rounded nose which was not covered by a full metal jacket, leaving it to expand on impact with a human target – the so-called Dum Dum bullet.

These bullets were used to grotesque effect against Indian fighters in the Chitral Campaign. The Ordnance Department continued its development process – this time a bullet with a depression in its tip which also expanded on impact with the human body. This depressed tip round was known as Mark IV. The United Kingdom was a State Party to the *St Petersburg Declaration* prohibiting explosive bullets, and so the

[10] In their study of customary international law, the ICRC cited the preamble of the *St Petersburg Declaration* as evidence of state practice for the rule of customary international law prohibiting means and methods of warfare which are of a nature to cause superfluous injury or unnecessary suffering (Henckaerts and Doswald-Beck, 2005, vol. II, ch. 1, rule 70).

development of hollow point and depressed tip rounds, designed to flatten and spread within the human body, seemed incompatible with those treaty obligations.

There is, of course, a technical distinction between a round that explodes and a round that flattens and spreads within soft human tissue. Expansion is not explosion. But in offering a technical legal argument distinguishing between a round which explodes on contact with soft tissue and a round that expands on contact with soft tissue the counter-argument is obvious. It is not just the letter of the law but also the spirit of it that is relevant here. Whether a bullet explodes or expands on contact with soft tissue, the likelihood of fatality increases dramatically (compared to a 'normal' full metal jacket round) (see e.g. Sykes Jr, Champion and Fouty, 1988, p. 619). If an exploding bullet causes death or, at least, useless aggravation of suffering, such that the bullet violates a legal norm, so should a bullet which expands or flattens easily.

Surgeon Major-General J. B. Hamilton of the British Army claimed that the demands of small colonial warfare warranted this deviation (the creation of the Dum Dum bullet) from the standard issue in European armaments (rounds with full metal jackets) (Spiers, 1975, p. 7). The enemies who Britain encountered were not armies from the European States Parties to the *St Petersburg Declaration*, but 'fanatical natives, savages and barbarians. Civilized man is much more susceptible to injuries than savages. The savage, like the tiger, is not so impressionable and will go on fighting even when desperately wounded' (Hamilton, 1898).

Lord Lansdowne, the British Secretary of State for War, recommended to the cabinet that Britain manufacture and keep stock of two kinds of ammunition: 'with the intention (which we can keep to ourselves) of using the expanding bullet when we have to deal with savages, or with an enemy who is himself using an expanding bullet' (Spiers, 1975, p. 7).

Ultimately the suggestion was opposed by the Ordnance Department. Logistically, it would be too difficult to store and direct the two different stocks of ammunition to different forces (Spiers, 1975, p. 7). This pragmatic approach took precedence over more moral and legal reasons, including that to discriminate in such a way might appear morally, if not legally (not an international armed conflict with a State Party to the *Hague Declaration Concerning Expanding Bullets*), repugnant.

Just a few years after these new bullets had been developed and the British had offered their justifications for the necessity for such rounds, Czar Nicholas II, Alexander's successor, sent a circular letter to 'civilised nations' requesting an 'international discussion' to ensure: 'to all peoples the benefits of a real and durable peace, and above all, of putting an end to the progressive development of the present armaments' (Eyffinger, 1999, p. 17).

Queen Wilhelmina of the Netherlands offered to host these discussions, resulting in the first Hague International Peace Conference of 1899 (Eyffinger, 1999, p. 39). There were three themes of the conference: the Peaceful Settlement of Disputes, Arms Control and Disarmament, and The Laws of War (Higgins, 1909, pp. 76–77). Proposals for the Conference included, in the second of those three themes, Arms Control and Disarmament, a prohibition on Dum Dum bullets: bullets which expanded or flattened easily in the human body and which, as a consequence, inflicted needlessly cruel injuries (Higgins, 1909, pp. 76–77).

This proposal was adopted as the *Hague Declaration Concerning Expanding Bullets* (Higgins, 1909, p. 21). Twenty-three national delegations were present for the first Hague Peace Conference in 1899. Twenty of them voted in favour of the prohibition on expanding bullets. The United States and Britain voted against the prohibition and Portugal abstained from the vote (Scott, 1920, pp. 276–79). In opposing the prohibition the British delegate, Sir John Ardagh, argued for the right to 'use projectiles of sufficient efficacy against savage populations' (*The Proceedings of the Hague Peace Conference*, 31 May 1899, p. 343). A number of delegates strongly opposed the British stance in debate immediately prior to the vote on prohibiting Dum Dum bullets. For example, the Russian Assistant Secretary-General to the Conference, Arthur Raffalovich, said Ardagh's ideas were: 'contrary to the humanitarian spirit which dominates this end of the nineteenth century. It is impermissible to make a distinction between a savage and a civilised enemy; *both are men who deserve the same treatment.*' (*The Proceedings of the Hague Peace Conference*, 31 May 1899, p. 343; this approach was also endorsed by the President of the Chamber, the Belgian Auguste Beernaert, p. 344.)

These Russian sentiments appear inclusive but even for the Russians, and all other delegations voting for the prohibition, it was only ever expected that the prohibition would apply to wars involving other States Parties to the treaty. Article II of the *Hague Convention*, also adopted at the Conference, stated this limitation explicitly: 'The provisions contained in the Regulations ... are only binding on the Contracting Powers, in case of war between two or more of them' (*Hague Convention*, art. II).

There is a real sense in which the apparent aberration of the British position on Dum Dum bullets reflected a more widespread acceptance that the emergent prohibitions were limited in their scope. The British applied their exclusionary approach within two months of the end of the Hague Peace Conference by disregarding the *Hague Convention* in the Boer War. The Boer republics were not signatories to the *Hague Convention*, and so it was arguable that the Convention did not apply to British Forces fighting against their Boer opponents as a matter of treaty law. Sir John Ardagh conceded that the British were bound by the *Convention* in so far as it reflected the laws and customs of war (Spies, 2001, pp. 170–71),[11] but that position did not manifest in any constraints in military operations against Boer opponents. In the course of the Boer War, the British violated the *Hague Convention* so grievously as to motivate one commentator to characterise operations as constituting 'a more blatant disregard for the customs of war than had previously been evinced in modern times' (Surridge, 2012, p. 608).

British (and Commonwealth, including Australian) Forces established concentration camps for old people, women, and children (Pretorius, 2010, pp. 35–36); engaged in widespread destruction of homes, farms, crops and livestock; perpetrated extensive pillaging (Miller, 2010, p. 325); and summarily executed prisoners (Hobhouse, 1902, p. xv).[12] Native African fighters received even harsher treatment at the hands of the British and Commonwealth Forces than did the Boers (Miller, 2010, pp. 315–16; Surridge, 2012, p. 616). Little statistical information is available on native combatants, but historical research on British attitudes on the application of the *Hague Convention* to the ethnic Boers is telling.

In the asymmetric fight, the Boers resorted to tactics we would today consider guerrilla warfare. In response to this, the British commander, Lord Kitchener, responded by burning farms, confiscating livestock, and developing notorious concentration camps for the families of guerrilla fighters (Miller, 2010, p. 317). It appears that, at the very least, the conduct of the British campaign violated Articles 45, 46, and 47 of the *Regulations* annexed to the *Hague Convention*, and their respective prohibitions

[11] However, some British commentators thought the British army was not bound by the outcomes of the Conference: see Miller (2010, p. 315). The *Hague Convention* did also not enter into force until 4 September 1900.

[12] On the complicity of colonial governments in Australia as well as of individual Australian soldiers in the perpetration of serious and recurrent violations of the law of war, see Reynolds (2016, pp. 187–96).

against pillage, respect for private property, and compulsions of oaths of allegiance from occupied populations (Miller, 2010, p. 317).

While the *Hague Convention*, acknowledged as an authoritative expression of the *jus in bello* by the British, condemned looting and pillage in the strongest terms, 'the sense of the need for a prohibition against looting to distinguish civilized warfare from barbarism holds up less well to the extent the British considered the Boers inherently barbaric' (Miller and Miller, 2019, p. 189). Both the Boers and the Indian natives in the Chitral Campaign were seen as 'barbarous' – in contrast to the 'civilised' signatories of the *Hague Convention*. These lingering attitudes at the outset of the early development of IHL perhaps explain, at least in part, the reticence to develop the law applicable to non-international armed conflicts.

5.4 Two World Wars and Changing Attitudes to the Notion of Humanity as a Constraint

The protracted nature of World War I and the scale of destruction and loss of life exploded a myth about the progress of civilisation in Europe. In the 'War to End All Wars' supposedly 'civilised' European powers went to war with each other in a conflagration so extensive that its geographic spread was vast and its toll of dead and wounded unprecedented. Despite the reverberant shockwaves around the world in response to the horrors of the war and to the scale of the devastation resulting from it, the machinations of international law responded slowly.

It is true that the establishment of the League of Nations in the aftermath of the war, an unprecedented attempt to create a multilateral institution to prevent the outbreak of another global conflagration, was a bold and innovative, even though ultimately unsuccessful, approach to the attainment of world peace. It is also true that the Allied Commission on Responsibility for the War moved into previously uncharted territory with the proposal for Allied High Tribunals to try nationals of defeated Central Powers for their alleged international crimes (Commission on the Responsibility of the Authors of War and on Enforcement of Penalties, 1920, p. 117). But these proposed tribunals, which failed to eventuate for political reasons (see Bass, 2000, pp. 58–146), were only to be empowered to prosecute some categories of international crime (war crimes and what we now refer to as the crime of aggression) and not other atrocities (specifically not crimes against humanity). The Allied Commission on Responsibility for the War discussed the possibility of trying Ottoman defendants for massacres of the Armenian people. Both the United States and the Japanese delegates to the Commission on Responsibility argued against any such possibility on the basis that crimes against humanity did not exist as a category of international crime: conduct directed against another sovereign nation was properly the subject of international law, but the ways in which a sovereign nation treated its own population was not regulated by international law (see Bassiouni, 1992, pp. 168–73).

The Allied failure post-World War I to establish Allied High Tribunals to hold German and Ottoman defendants to account was not repeated in the aftermath of World War II. German and Japanese approaches to war, particularly the invasion and subsequent occupation of one country after another in the European and Pacific theatres of the War respectively, elicited unshakeable Allied resolve to ensure accountability – at least for the senior political, military, and industrial leadership of both defeated Axis Powers. The perpetration of the Holocaust was so shocking that, in contrast to the position of the Allied Commission on Responsibility for the War following World War I, crimes against humanity were included as a separate category of crimes in the Nuremberg and Tokyo Charters,[13] and, as a consequence, a number of German defendants at Nuremberg were convicted of this offence for their involvement in the Holocaust.[14]

The Nuremberg and Tokyo Trials were certainly significant and unprecedented events in the development of international criminal law, but they were conducted in a broader context of an increasing commitment to effective multilateralism. The conduct of World War II, devastating as it was for civilian populations – particularly those the subject of military occupation and/or aerial bombing campaigns – provided the catalyst for a remarkable period of international institution building and the making of international law. It is, of course, tragic that it took a second global conflagration to create circumstances conducive to concerted change, but it is also staggering to reflect on what was achieved in the circumstances of that immediate post-War environment. The

[13] Philippe Sands captures the significance of Sir Hersch Lauterpacht's contributions to the Prosecution case, particularly the submissions of Sir Hartley Shawcross, the British Prosecutor at Nuremberg (Sands, 2016, pp. 289–93).

[14] Sixteen of the twenty-two accused at Nuremberg were convicted of Crimes Against Humanity. For details of the judgments against each of the accused see: The Avalon Project, *Judgment of the International Military Tribunal*, with links to each of the judgments against the individual accused at: https://avalon.law.yale.edu/subject_menus/judcont.asp.

creation of the United Nations in 1945, the Nuremberg and Tokyo Trials from 1945 (when the Nuremberg Trial commenced) through to 1948 (when the Tokyo Judgment was handed down; *United States of America v Araki (1948)*), the *Convention on the Prevention and Punishment of the Crime of Genocide* of 1948, the UN General Assembly's Universal Declaration of Human Rights of 1948 (contrast the orthodoxy of international law prior to World War II with the very first operative provision of the Universal Declaration that 'All human beings are born free and equal in dignity and rights'; UN General Assembly Resolution 217A (III), 1948), and the *Geneva Conventions* of 1949 (and particularly Common Article 3 regulating the conduct of non-international armed conflict).

These developments in the aftermath of World War II initiated a process of transformation of the notion of humanity not only as a tempering influence on the behaviour of states but also as an increasing source of legal obligation. Now the obligation to demonstrate humanity extends beyond the conduct of war to international human rights law and the regulation of a sovereign state's treatment of its own nationals, its own minorities, its prisoners, its terrorists, and its asylum seekers. In addition, humanity as a constraint in the conduct of war now extends to the legal regulation of non-international armed conflicts and ostensibly extends its protections not only to the civilian population but also to all fighters in an armed conflict regardless of allegiance, race, ethnicity, nationality, or any other defining characteristic. But is that outcome actually achieved?

5.5 Challenges to the Efficacy of the Constraining Effect of Humanity

It is right to expose, and to attempt to explain, the restrictions on the scope of humanity as a constraint on the conduct of war so readily understood and accepted in the nineteenth century and so easily misunderstood and overlooked in contemporary times. It is also appropriate to acknowledge progress since to redress some of those inherent restrictions and to broaden the scope of application of the protections of IHL. But any sense of ultimate achievement should be challenged for two key reasons.

First, recurrent and abhorrent disregard of basic legal obligations of humanity in contemporary armed conflicts exposes a gaping chasm between legal obligations and the lack of effective implementation and enforcement of egregious violations. The Syrian catastrophe, now in its twelfth year, is one glaring example, but so too are the expulsion of the Rohingya from Myanmar and the armed conflict in Yemen. The list of current armed conflicts characterised by blatant disregard for humanity as a constraint on the conduct of hostilities is extensive. Imagine assessing the *vox populi* on the streets of Aleppo or Raqqa or Homs and asking residents what they think of international law and its constraining influence on the conduct of war. It is hard to envisage anyone affected by one or other of the multiple Syrian armed conflicts (see Gill, 2016) arguing for the efficacy of international law as a constraining influence delivering a protective effect for the millions of Syrian victims. International humanitarian law has not served that benighted population well as a gentle civiliser in the conduct of armed hostilities. Then US Secretary-General Ban Ki-moon called the inaugural World Humanitarian Summit in 2016 and pleaded with States not to accept what he described as 'the erosion of humanity',[15] which he rightly claimed is so tragically prevalent in the world's contemporary armed conflicts.

One critical question in response to recurrent egregious violations of IHL, especially in the absence of substantive responses from the international community, is the extent to which the practice undermines the strength of the normative regime. The ICRC has been rightly agitated and concerned about the threat to normative standards in armed conflict as a consequence of the extent of abuse and violation of the basic rules of IHL (see e.g. UN News, 31 October 2015).[16] It is a significant challenge to shore up multilateral support for the legal regime and to ensure that those parties to armed conflict intent on egregious violations of the law are condemned and their responsible personnel held to account.

Secondly, the suggestion that nineteenth-century racist colonial exclusions from the protective constraints of an emerging IHL have been remedied through subsequent developments in the law, particularly the legal regulation of the conduct of non-international armed conflicts, is fallacious. We have our own contemporary exclusions from the protections of IHL all too redolent of inceptive approaches in the nineteenth century.

[15] Ban Ki-moon issued his plea multiple times in the lead-up to the world Humanitarian Summit (see e.g. Ki-Moon, 2016; UN Regional Information Centre for Western Europe, 2016).

[16] The ICRC (2009, p. 7) has separately claimed that:

> As the guardian of humanitarian law, the ICRC takes measures to ensure respect for, to promote, to reaffirm and even to clarify and develop this body of law. The organization is particularly concerned about possible erosion of international humanitarian law and takes bilateral, multilateral or public steps to promote respect for and development of the law.

Frédéric Mégret, for example, critiques the approach of the Bush Administration to its self-declared Global War on Terror – particularly the labelling of al Qaeda fighters as 'unlawful combatants'. The Bush Administration had applied IHL for the purposes of permitting the targeting of al Qaeda 'terrorists' in the course of military hostilities while simultaneously arguing that none of the protections of IHL applied once the 'terrorists' were in physical custody. The Bush Administration argued that Common Article 2 of the *Geneva Conventions* did not apply to al Qaeda fighters because al Qaeda was not a sovereign nation-state and that Common Article 3 also did not apply to al Qaeda because the US armed conflict with al Qaeda was 'of an international character'. Common Article 3 only applies to armed conflicts 'not of an international character' (occurring on the physical territory of a single State), and the Bush Administration argued that the armed conflict with al Qaeda was of an international character because the United States would prosecute that armed conflict wherever in the world it identified al Qaeda fighters. Here was a classic case of 'othering' – an attempt to create a category excluded from the protective constraints of IHL.

The plurality of the US Supreme Court in *Hamdan* rejected this Administration's argument and decided, instead, that there is no gap in IHL protections between Common Articles 2 and 3 of the *Geneva Conventions*:

> The Court of Appeals thought, and the Government asserts, that Common Article 3 does not apply to Hamdan because the conflict with al Qaeda, being 'international in scope' does not qualify as a 'conflict not of an international character'. . . . That reasoning is erroneous. The term 'conflict not of an international character' is used here in contradistinction to a conflict between nations. . . . In context, then, the phrase 'not of an international character' bears its literal meaning . . . 'betwixt nation and nation'.
>
> (*Salim Ahmed Hamdan v Donald Rumsfeld et al.*, 2006, pp. 67–68)

The adverse decision of the plurality in *Hamdan* did not prevent the Bush Administration from pursuing its exclusionary approach to its treatment of detainees in the Global War on Terror.[17] Some detainees remain in indefinite military detention at Guántanamo Bay more than twenty years later.

[17] Following the *Hamdan* decision, the Bush Administration gained Congressional enactment of the 2006 *Military Commissions Act* which sought to 'remedy' by legislative means the exclusion of al Qaeda detainees from the protections of IHL.

Again, it is wrong to single out the United States here and to imply that no other supposedly 'civilised' Western nation engages in a process of 'othering' to exclude the protective constraints of humanity to specific categories of people. There are multiple blind spots, prejudices, and 'othering', and it would be naïve to pretend otherwise. Just as we judge nineteenth-century racist colonial attitudes, future generations will judge contemporary attitudes, values, and assumptions that facilitate exclusions from the protections of the law.

References

Attwood, B., and Markus, A. (2007). *The 1967 Referendum: Race, Power and the Australian Constitution*, 2nd ed., Aboriginal Studies Press.

Bass, G. (2000). *Stay the Hand of Vengeance: The Politics of War Crimes Tribunals*, Princeton University Press.

Bassiouni, M. C. (1992). *Crimes against Humanity in International Criminal Law*, Martinus Nijhoff.

Brown, D. (1970). *Bury My Heart at Wounded Knee*, Holt, Rinehart & Winston.

Carnahan, B. M. (1998). Lincoln, Lieber and the laws of war: the origins and limits of the principle of military necessity. *American Journal of International Law*, 92, 213–31.

Commission on the Responsibility of the Authors of War and on Enforcement of Penalties (1920). Report presented to the Preliminary Peace Conference 29 March 1919. *American Journal of International Law*, 14(1/2), 95–154.

Convention on the Prevention and Punishment of the Crime of Genocide, opened for signature 9 December 1948 (entered into force 12 January 1951) 78 UNTS 277.

Convention (II) with Respect to the Laws and Customs of War on Land, opened for signature 29 July 1899 (entered into force 4 September 1900).

Cove, J. J. (1995). *What the Bones Say: Tasmanian Aborigines, Science and Domination*, Carleton University Press.

Curthoys, A. (2005). Raphaël Lemkin's 'Tasmania': An Introduction. *Patterns of Prejudice*, 39(2), 162–69.

Declaration Renouncing the Use, in Time of War, of Explosive Projectiles under 400 Grammes Weight, opened for signature 29 November 1868, [1901] ATS 125 1 (entered into force 11 December 1868) (*St Petersburg Declaration*).

Dunant, H. (1959). *A Memory of Solferino*, International Committee of the Red Cross.

Eyffinger, A. (1999). *The 1899 Hague Peace Conference: The Parliament of Man, the Federation of the World*, Kluwer Law International.

Ferrell, C. L. (2006). *The Abolitionist Movement*, Greenwood Press.

Gill, T. D. (2016). Classifying the conflict in Syria. *International Law Studies*, 92, 353–80.

Hamilton, J. B. (1898). The evolution of the Dum Dum bullet. *British Medical Journal*, 1, 1250–51.

Hartigan, R. S. (1983). *Lieber's Code and the Law of War*, Precedent Publishing.

Henckaerts, J.-M. and Doswald-Beck, L., eds. (2005). *Customary International Humanitarian Law*, Cambridge University Press, vol. 2, ch. 1 (rule 70).

Higgins, A. P. (1909). *The Hague Peace Conferences and Other International Conferences Concerning the Laws and Usages of War: Texts of Conventions with Commentaries*, Cambridge University Press.

Hobhouse, E. (1902). *The Brunt of the War and Where It Fell*, Methuen & Company.

International Committee for the Red Cross (2009). *The ICRC: Its Mission and Its Work*.

af Jochnick, C. and Normand, R. (1994). The legitimation of violence: a critical history of the laws of war. *Harvard International Law Journal*, 35, 49–95.

Kalshoven, F. (2016). The history of international humanitarian law treaty-making. In R. Liivoja and T. McCormack, eds., *The Routledge Handbook on the Law of Armed Conflict*, Routledge.

Ki-moon, B. Opening Remarks to Member States on Preparations for the World Humanitarian Summit. Speech delivered at UN Headquarters, New York, 4 April 2016.

Koskenniemi, M. (2004). *The Gentle Civilizer of Nations: The Rise and Fall of International Law 1870–1960*, Cambridge University Press.

McPherson, J. M. (1995). *The Struggle for Equality: Abolitionists and the Negro in the Civil War and Reconstruction*, Princeton University Press.

Mégret, F. (2006). From 'savages' to 'unlawful combatants': a postcolonial look at international law's 'other'. In A. Orford, ed., *International Law and Its Others*, Cambridge University Press.

Miller, S. M. (2010). Duty or crime? Defining acceptable behaviour in the British army in 1899–1902. *Journal of British Studies*, 49, 311–31.

Miller, S. M. and Miller, J. (2019). Moral and legal prohibitions against pillage in the context of the 1899 Hague Convention and the South African War. *War in History*, 26(2), 185–203.

Neuman, N. (2004). Applying the rule of proportionality: force protection and cumulative assessment in international law and morality. *Yearbook of International Humanitarian Law*, 7, 79–112.

Normand, R. and af Jochnick, C. (1994). The legitimation of violence: a critical analysis of the Gulf War. *Harvard International Law Journal*, 35, 387–416.

Pratt, J. W. (1927). The origin of 'manifest destiny'. *The American Historical Review*, 32(4), 795–98.

Pretorius, F. (2010). The white concentration camps of the Anglo-Boer War: a debate without end. *Historia*, 55, 34–49.

The Proceedings of the Hague Peace Conference, First Commission: Third Meeting on 31 May 1899.

Reynolds, H. (2016). *Unnecessary Wars*, NewSouth Publishing.

Reynolds, H., and Clements, N. (2021). *Tongerlongeter: First Nations Leader and Tasmanian War Hero*, NewSouth Publishing.

Ringmar, E. (2009). Francis Lieber, terrorism and the American way of war. *Perspectives on Terrorism*, 3(4), 52–60.

Roberts, A. (2019). Foundational myths in the laws of war: the 1863 Lieber Code, and the 1864 Geneva Convention. *Melbourne Journal of International Law*, 20, 158.

Ryan, L. (2012). *Tasmanian Aborigines: A History since 1803*. Allen & Unwin.

Salim Ahmed Hamdan v Donald Rumsfeld et al., 528 U.S. 557 (2006), no. 05.184, 29 June 2006.

Sands, P. (2016). *East West Street: On the Origins of Genocide and Crimes against Humanity*, Weidenfeld & Nicholson.

Schmidt Jr, B. C. (1982). Principle and prejudice: the Supreme Court and race in the progressive era. Part 1: The Heydey of Jim Crow. *Columbia Law Review*, 82, 444–524.

Schmitt, M. N. (2010). Military necessity and humanity in international humanitarian law: preserving the Delicate Balance. *Virginia Journal of International Law*, 50(4), 795–839.

Scott, J. B. (1920). *The Proceedings of the Hague Peace Conference*, London.

Spies, S. B. (2001). The Hague Convention of 1899 and the Boer Republics. In F. Pretorius, ed., *Scorched Earth*, Cape Town.

Spiers, E. M. (1975). The use of the Dum Dum bullet in colonial warfare. *The Journal of Imperial and Commonwealth History*, 4(1), 3–14.

Surridge, K. (2012). An example to be followed or a warning to be avoided? The British, Boers and guerrilla warfare, 1900–1902. *Small Wars & Insurgencies*, 23, 608–26.

Sykes Jr, L. N., Champion, H. R. and Fouty, W. J. (1988). Dum-dums, hollow-points, and devastators: techniques designed to increase wounding potential of bullets. *The Journal of Trauma*, 28, 618–23.

United Nations General Assembly Resolution 217A (III), UN GAOR, 3rd session, 183rd plenary meeting, UN Doc A/810 (10 December 1948).

United Nations News. Ban, Red Cross Chief Express Concern Over 'Brazen and Brutal' Erosion of Respect for Humanitarian Law, 31 October 2015.

United Nations Regional Information Centre for Western Europe We Will Not Accept the Erosion of Humanity which we see in the World Today, 5 April 2016.

United States of America v Araki (Judgment) (International Military Tribunal for the Far East, 4 November 1948). In N. Boister and R. Cryer (2008). *Documents on the Tokyo International Military Tribunal: Charter, Indictments and Judgments*, Oxford University Press, p. 79.

U.S. War Department (1863). General Orders No. 100, 24 April 1863.

Vienna Convention on the Law of Treaties, opened for signature 23 May 1969 (entered into force 27 January 1980) 1155 *UNTS* 331.

Windschuttle, K. (2002). *The Fabrication of Aboriginal History: Volume I, Van Diemen's Land 1803–1847*, Macleay Press.

Witt, J. F. (2011). The dismal history of the laws of war. *University of California Irvine Law Review*, 1, 895.

6

The State, Civility, and International Humanitarian Law

MATT KILLINGSWORTH

Introduction

This chapter has three interrelated aims: first, to identify the relationship between the modern nation-state, international humanitarian law (IHL), and notions of civility; second, through a historical exploration of the relationship between military necessity, proportionality, and discrimination in IHL, to make the argument that the claimed shift from sovereignty to humanitarianism is not as complete as often argued, and that, rather, *raison d'état* continues to be a motivating factor informing constraint during combat; and, third, through an exploration of the 'standard of civilisation', to identify how this relationship informs discord between the universal underpinnings of contemporary IHL, and ongoing violations of the law. The chapter will conclude by proposing that the oft-maligned concept of a 'standard of civilisation' remains valuable in exploring continuities of double standards as they relate to protections afforded by the modern laws of war.

With this in mind, this chapter will be presented in three parts. Section one will offer a brief overview of the evolution of modern IHL, including a discussion on the degree to which contemporary IHL represents a safeguarding of 'politico-military interests ... aimed in particular at satisfying the requirements of the Great Powers and, to some degree, those of lesser states' (Cassese, 2014, p. 6). The second section will then trace the evolution of the four core principles of IHL, assessing the degree to which, according to Georg Schwarzenberger (1971, p. 171), the laws of war are an attempt to balance the needs of war with standards of civilisation. Following, the third section, engaging primarily with the English School of International Relations, will discuss the concept of a 'standard of civilisation', identifying the degree to which characterising actors as 'civilised' or 'barbarian' informs perceptions of who should be afforded protections under IHL.

6.1 The State, War, and IHL

For much of the modern era, the evolution of attempts to limit war via international law has been intrinsically linked with the evolution of the modern nation-state. This is not to deny pre-modern constraints on warfare, informed variously by notions of chivalry and customary rules of war. Nonetheless, contemporary IHL finds its genesis in the post-Enlightenment epoch, when the European state-system started to establish itself as the dominant form of political organisation. Concurrently, this period also bears witness to the increasing crystallisation of contemporary conceptions of the international, and a symbiotic relationship whereby states legitimated themselves via their membership of international legal institutions, and the emergence of an international society of states in which order was increasingly underpinned by the doctrine of sovereignty, whereby states 'increasingly sought to base their legal obligations on clearer, more precise, more formal and, most of all, more consensual foundations' (Armstrong, Farrell and Lambert, 2012, p. 61). In this respect, and elaborated on below, the modern laws of war, articulated as either IHL or the law of armed conflict (LOAC), are best understood as a historical balancing process between attempts to regulate the conduct of hostilities between belligerents and the self-perceived rights of states to use conflict to achieve desired ends.

The state's emergence as the dominant form of political organisation was due in part to its capacity, over time, to monopolise the use of violence, which it did in two, interrelated ways. First, as the war-making endeavours of European sovereigns expanded, and the cost of waging war dramatically increased, smaller, decentralised administrative units proved incapable of managing this new enterprise. The increasingly centralised state proved itself more adept at raising the capital required for this new militarism but also, as Charles Tilly (1992, p. 68) identifies, the states' increased capacity for raising revenue and streamlining administrative capacities enabled it to 'monitor, control and monopolise the effective means of violence'. Second, through a long historical process, the modern state was able to successfully disarm competitors (Thomson, 1994, p. 4). The disarming of non-state actors, sometimes through bargains struck with societal groups, but mostly via a long and bloody struggle, was a process which ended through 'Violence being shifted from the non-state, economic and international realms of authority into the state, domestic and political realms of authority . . . the transformation entailed the states' monopolisation of the authority to deploy violence beyond its borders *and* the state's acceptance of violence emanating from its territory' (Thomson, 1994, p. 4; emphasis in original).

In the pre-modern period, war existed as a form of spectator sport, with a set of rules that existed more as mutual obligations on warring parties than law, as such:

> The 'rules of the game' that constituted the laws of war at this time, however, were of little relevance to the feudal pheasants that constituted the foot soldiery of European armies, nor were they believed to be of any application to wars against *uncivilised enemies* – infidels and primitive peoples.
>
> (Turns, 2010, p. 822; emphasis added)

In this respect, up until the middle of the nineteenth century, attempts to restrain the use of force during conflict existed mainly as customary rules, often agreed to among warring (European) parties and, most importantly, generally existing without consistent punishments for violations of said rules and customs. Nonetheless, it would be incorrect to assume that war was fought without any boundaries or restrictions. As John Keegan (2001, p. 26) notes,

> War may have got worse with the passage of time, but the ethic of restraint has rarely been wholly absent from its practise ... Even in the age of total warfare when war was considered normal condition, and the inherent right of sovereign state presided, there remained taboos, enshrined in law and thankfully widely observed.

Not until the creation and subsequent crystallisation of the European state-system do we start to see what we now recognise as modern international law.[1] Beginning in the middle of the nineteenth century, this is a period that bears witness to a flurry of treaties aimed at restraining behaviour during conflict, the number and significance of which was staggering, especially when one considers the historically sclerotic advances up to then (Killingsworth, 2016).

This period also bears witness to a shift towards 'humanitarian' laws of war. David Turns (2010, p. 822) argues that this was informed by two factors: first, the increased human suffering during war, caused by a

[1] Martii Koskenniemi (2009, p. 142) elaborates on this point, arguing that what he calls the 'long nineteenth century' bears witness to a complicated amalgam of events that constitute European modernity – 'the formation of the nation-state, the tension between sovereignty and liberal individualism, influence of technology and economic growth on state power, secularism, rationalism and belief in progress as a lingua franca between international elites' – all of which international law is an outgrowth of.

combination of the rapid advances in military technology and inadequate military medical facilities; and, second, increased reporting of the battlefield. Similarly, Dieter Fleck (2021, pp. 28–29) argues that French Revolutionary Wars of the eighteenth and nineteenth centuries, reflecting ideas first espoused by Jean-Jacques Rousseau, were a catalyst for the establishment of laws that aimed to reduce unnecessary suffering. It is also generally established that Henri Dunant's *Un Souvenir de Solferino*, in which Dunant described the horror of witnessing the suffering of 40,000 Austrian, French, and Italian soldiers wounded on the battlefield of Solferino (1859), served as an important catalyst in the establishment of humanitarian focused laws of war. Indeed, Dunant's experience led him to play a leading role in the establishment of the International Committee of the Red Cross (ICRC), which was to become 'a promoter and custodian of the humanitarian idea and the primary initiation for its transition into international humanitarian law' (cited in Meyer and McCoubrey, 1998, p. 69).[2]

The 1856 *Paris Declaration Respecting Maritime Law* is generally cited as the first 'open ended, multilateral treaty i.e. the first treaty which, according to its terms, was open to accession by other states'. Subsequent treaties, however, are arguably more important. The first of these, the 1868 *St Petersburg Declaration Renouncing the Use, in Time of War, of Explosive Projectiles Under 400 Grammes Weight* is notable for two reasons that relate to fundamental principles of IHL. First, it is generally acknowledged as the first multilateral agreement banning the use of a particular weapon in warfare. Second, it articulates two ideas that subsequently underpin the fundamentals of modern IHL; military necessity and proportionality: 'The only legitimate object which States should endeavour to accomplish during war is to weaken the military forces of the enemy' and 'for this purpose it is sufficient to disable the greatest possible number of men' (*St Petersburg Declaration Renouncing the Use, in Time of War, of Explosive Projectiles Under 400 Grammes Weight*, 2000, p. 55). Although not specifically mentioning non-combatants, this, combined with the affirmation that 'the necessities of war ought to yield to the requirements of humanity', establishes a precedent upon which subsequent codified IHL seek to constrain warfare through distinctions between combatant and non-combatant.[3]

[2] For a critical examination of this traditional narrative, see Alexander (2015).

[3] For more on the importance of the *St Petersburg Declaration* to modern IHL, see Crawford (2018, pp. 544–66); and Dill and Shue (2012).

The relative success of the St Petersburg Conference paved the way for the second set of substantive, pre-World War I treaties – the so-called Hague Conventions of 1899 and 1907. While representatives from the twenty-six states that attended the first Hague Conference failed to reach concrete agreements on arms limitations, they did, in the shape of the *Convention on the Laws and Customs on War on Land*, conclude the first general codification of laws of land war in the form of a multilateral treaty (Roberts, 1994, p. 121). The final act of the 1899 Conference was agreement on the need for a further conference, which was subsequently held in 1907. Building on the pattern of the first, there was once again no general agreement on arms limitation. However, with a substantially increased state representation, authors and commentators are in general agreement that the thirteen conventions adopted in 1907, when considered alongside the 1880 Oxford Manual of the Laws and Customs of War and the 1899 *Hague Conventions*, represented a high-water mark in codified attempts to limit warfare. Taking this argument one step further, Christian Reus-Smit (1999, p. 142) argues that the Hague Conferences should be regarded as more than merely an instance of emerging multilateralism, but rather, serving as examples of judicial interpretations of the law, a step in the realisation of a civilised polity 'and thus a desirable feature of a society of civilised states'.

Despite being a period in which 'the law of war entered its epoch of highest repute' (Best, 1980, p. 129), the turn to positivism did not reconcile the tension between emerging humanitarian concern in warfare, and the historic predilection of military necessity as informed by *raison d'état*. Indeed, Geoffrey Best refers to this period as the 'militarisation of the humanitarians' (Best, 1980, p. 143), and Robert Kolb (2013, pp. 38–39) argues that the *Hague Conventions*, through their marginal concern with civilians and their protections, remained primarily military law (as opposed to humanitarian law); 'it was a special law for the combating forces rather than a general law protecting persons in general'. While Kolb's criticism is not incorrect, it does underestimate the degree to which the *Hague Conventions* 'define an extensive and detailed list of persons to be protected in various ways' (Johnson, 2000, p. 431). Thus, in agreeing with Rues-Smit and James Johnson, it is argued here that we see in both the *St Petersburg Declaration* and the *Hague Conventions* not only the emergence of positivist IHL but also the development of international law premised on humanitarian concerns, albeit law that continued to reflect the prevailing ideals of sovereignty and independence, and as such a continued, if only tacit, understanding that states could continue to conduct their military operations as informed by effective ends.

The onset of World War I and the subsequent devastation halted the pre-World War enthusiasms for further codification of laws designed to limit warfare.[4] The mood following the end of World War II, however, was discernibly different. Policy makers, scarred by two world wars and the Great Depression, set about the construction of a new, liberal world order, underpinned by the idea of 'never again', to be realised through the establishment of multilateral institutions. The United Nations stands as the most obvious representation of this post-war order, but of greater significance with regard to IHL are the four 1949 *Geneva Conventions* (and the subsequent 1977 *Additional Protocols*).[5]

The four *Geneva Conventions* of 1949 and the two 1977 *Additional Protocols* form the cornerstone of IHL. Their aim is 'to protect those not or no longer taking part in hostilities, as well as to limit the use of violence to the extent necessary to defeat the enemy' (Pothelet, 2018, p. 353). Notably, the *Geneva Conventions* do not address the means of waging war – this is covered by so-called Hague law. However, with the adoption of the two 1977 *Additional Protocols*, the distinction between Hague and Geneva law has essentially disappeared (Solis, 2010, p. 83). Universally ratified, the four 1949 *Geneva Conventions* are binding on all states, and most of their provisions are also acknowledged as existing as customary international law, the significance of which was highlighted in the International Court of Justice's (ICJ) *Nicaragua* judgment: 'an obligation to [respect the Conventions] does not derive from the Conventions themselves, but from the general principles of humanitarian law to which the Conventions merely give specific expression' (*Nicaragua v U.S.*, 1986, para. 220).

International humanitarian law (a term that has only assumed popular usage since after the end of World War II), as a body of international law that seeks to place restraints on the use of armed violence in conflict, is the culmination of a centuries-long process. The next section, via a discussion on the evolution of the concept of military necessity, will

4 In an interesting aside, Roberts (1994, p. 125) points out that 'ghastly as all this carnage of the land battles was, for the most part it was not contrary to the laws of war'.

5 The UN Charter's prohibition against the use of force, for the French lawyer Georges Scelle, meant that a declaration of war could no longer be anything more than 'a cynical admission of the intention to perpetrate the crime of war' (cited in Neff, 2005, p. 336). However, Article 2(4) should be understood primarily as a *jus ad bellum* codification – the UN Charter provides very little with regards to restrictions on conduct during war.

establish the argument that one of the central characteristics of IHL is that it continues to allow states to conduct wars constrained by *raison d'état*, and not humanitarian concerns.

6.2 Core Principles of IHL (with a Focus on Military Necessity)

The UK Ministry of Defence's (2004, p. 21) *Manual on the Law of Armed Conflict* notes that while much customary IHL has been codified into treaty form, there remain four fundamental principles that underly the law of armed conflict: 'military necessity, humanity, distinction, and proportionality'.[6] Indeed, at the very core of IHL is the balance between competing considerations, most starkly between military necessity and humanity. This section will explore each of the core principles identified, explain how they relate to each other, and, as identified in the introduction, explore the controversial nature of military necessity.

6.2.1 Distinction

For Solis (2010, p. 251), 'distinction is the most significant battlefield concept a combatant must observe'. Similarly, it has been qualified by the ICJ as one of the 'intransgressible principles of international customary law' and is to be seen as one of the 'cardinal principles' of IHL (cited in Heinsch, 2018, p. 307).

The first codification of discrimination, albeit being somewhat vague, occurs in the Lieber Code (1863), which required unarmed citizens to be spared 'as much as the exigencies of war will admit' (cited in Heinsch, 2018, p. 308). Further codified in the 1907 *Hague Regulations*, distinction was not properly codified until the 1977 *Additional Protocols* (*Additional Protocol I*, 1997, art. 48; *Additional Protocol II*, 1997, art. 13).

At its core, the principle of distinction provides that parties to an armed conflict must 'at all times distinguish between the civilian population and combatants and between civilian objects and military objectives and accordingly shall direct their operations only against military objectives' (Sassòli, Bouvier and Quintin, 2014). As Robert Heinsch (2018, p. 308) identifies, the principle recognises only two categories to be

[6] The ICRC identifies the Fundamental Principles of IHL as: 'the principle of humanity; the principle of distinction between civilians and combatants, and between civilian objects and military objectives; the principle of proportionality; and the principle of military necessity', available at https://casebook.icrc.org/glossary/fundamental-principles-ihl.

distinguished under IHL, civilians and combatants; while combatants can be lawfully targeted to achieve military advantage, civilians must not be targeted or made the object of attack. A further aspect of the principle, relating to objects rather than persons, stipulates 'the parties to the conflict must at all times distinguish between civilian objects and military objects. Attacks may be directed only against military. Attacks must not be directed against civilian objects' (Henckaerts and Doswald-Beck, 2005, p. 25). Elaborating on its importance, the ICRC (1987b) notes of *Additional Protocol I*, Article 48:

> It is the foundation on which the codification of the laws and customs of war rests: the civilian population and civilian objects must be respected and protected in armed conflict, and for this purpose, they must be distinguished from combatants and military objectives. The entire system established in the Hague in 1899 and 1907 and in Geneva from 1864 to 1977 is founded on this rule of customary law.

Nonetheless, while simple at its core, the principle of distinction, due primarily to the changed nature of armed conflict – including the rise in the number of non-international armed conflicts (NIAC), in which civilians more often take part in hostilities – has become increasingly difficult to apply (Heinsch, 2018, p. 308). Furthermore, as Gary Solis (2010, p. 257) argues, using the bombing of the Al Firdos bunker during the first Gulf War (1991), and citing the International Criminal Tribunal for the Former Yugoslavia (ICTY) ruling in *Prosecutor v Blaškić*, in practice, the violation of the distinction principle requires 'the act to be committed wilfully, "intentionally in the knowledge . . . that civilians or civilian property were being targeted"'(cited in Solis, 2010, p. 257). As Solis points out, the term 'wilfully' incorporates recklessness but excludes simple negligence, meaning the death of those not actively partaking in hostilities can, to a certain degree, be more easily justified.

6.2.2 Proportionality

The principle of proportionality is codified in *Additional Protocol I*, Article 51, which defines as indiscriminate 'an attack which may be expected to cause incidental loss of civilian life, injury to civilians, damage to civilian objects, or a combination thereof, which would be excessive in relation to the concrete and direct military advantage anticipated' (cited in Ghezzi, 2018, p. 577). *Additional Protocol I*, Article 57(2) further requires that:

> an attack shall be cancelled or suspended if it becomes apparent that the objective is not a military one or . . . that the attack may be expected to cause incidental loss of human life, injury to civilians, damage to civilian objects, or a combination thereof, which would be excessive in relation to the concrete and direct military advantage anticipated.
>
> (cited in Solis, 2010, p. 273)

As Maddalena Ghezzi (2018, p. 578) identifies, 'the definitions of "excessive" and "military advantage" are necessarily subjective and open to debate'. However, arguments suggesting that Article 51 authorises any sort of attack, so long as it does not cause excessive loss or damage in relation to the military advantage expected, are refuted by the ICRC (1987b):

> In order to comply with the conditions, the attack must be directed against a military objective with means which are not disproportionate in relation to the objective, but are suited to destroying only that objective, and the effects of the attacks must be limited in the way required by the Protocol; moreover, even after those conditions are fulfilled, the incidental civilian losses and damages must not be excessive.

Nonetheless, there are still challenges in the application of the proportionality principle: 'The law is not clear as to the degree of care required of the attacker and the degree of risk he must be prepared to take . . . there may be occasion when a commander will have to accept a higher level of risk to his own forces in order to avoid or reduce collateral damage to the enemy's civilian population' (Rogers, 2000, pp. 165–69).

Again, returning to the main argument of this chapter, IHL exists as an uncomfortable compromise between the protection of civilians and the military ends of belligerent states.

6.2.3 *Humanity*

The meaning of the principle of humanity, as Matthew Cross (2018, p. 396) notes, 'may at first be thought self-evident; a matter of common sense'. But as Nobuo Hayashi (2016, p. 93) points out, this is not always the case, noting that 'humanity' has been defined:

> as a notion that 'forbids the infliction of suffering, injury, or destruction not actually necessary for the accomplishment of legitimate military purposes', as synonymous with the prohibition of superfluous injury and unnecessary suffering; an equivalent to the Martens Clause; and a vehicle through which international human rights law has made its way into the regulation of armed conflicts.

Both Solis (2010, p. 270) and Cross (2018) make the compelling argument that humanity is perhaps best understood when considered in its relationship with military necessity: 'to some extent, the two concepts are mirror images, each qualifying the other. The principle of humanity does not absolutely forbid the use of force and the infliction of human suffering, but it does, at least, establish that such conduct is exceptional' (Cross, 2018, p. 396).

The now famous Martens Clause, appearing for the first time in the Preamble of the 1899 *Hague Convention*, is generally assumed to provide the legal basis for the principle of humanity, and has subsequently been adopted and reinforced in the 1949 *Geneva Conventions* and the 1977 *Additional Protocols*:

> Until a more complete code of the laws of war has been issued, the High Contracting Parties deem it expedient to declare that, in cases not included in the Regulations adopted by them, the inhabitants and the belligerents remain under the protection and the rule of the law of nations, as they result from the usages established among civilized peoples, from the laws of humanity and the dictates of public conscience.
>
> (cited in Solis, 2010, p. 53)

Furthermore, it is possible to identify impacts of the principle of humanity in other aspects of codified IHL, including the prohibition on certain weapons, including Dum Dum bullets and poisonous gasses; it is also possible to identify the impact of the principle of humanity in the *Rome Statute of the International Criminal Court*, which includes among its crimes arbitrary punishment, torture, and unlawful deportation or transfer or unlawful confinement (see United Nations, 1998).

However, as Cross (2018, p. 397) reinforces, the 'Martens approach' must be treated with caution:

> It does not mean that humanity trumps positivist law. In particular, there seems to be little support in state practice for the view that the principle of humanity can be called upon to limit conduct which is permitted by positive rules of IHL. For example, if rules of IHL permit an attack to be made, and the attack does not employ weaponry which is prohibited by positive rules of IHL, it remains controversial, in the least, to suggest that the attacker is nonetheless obliged to prioritise the weapon's effects on the target . . . in their choice of lawful weapon.

The above quote highlights the core tension with laws designed to bound the use of force, competing with state's historically informed, and self-anointed, right to use force when it serves its interests.

6.2.4 Military Necessity

According to Michael Schmitt (2010, p. 796), 'no principle is more central to IHL, nor more misunderstood than military necessity. It has been proffered to both justify horrendous abuses during armed conflicts, and to impose impractical and dangerous restrictions on those who fight'. And returning to a theme introduced above, IHL is generally understood to be a product of reconciliation demands of military necessity and humanitarian considerations. For Yoram Dinstein (2015), 'if military necessity were to prevail completely, belligerent parties would have full freedom of action with a view to winning a war; if humanitarian considerations were the only guide to the conduct of hostilities, the waging of war would become impossible by dint of the death, injury and suffering that unavoidably accompany it'.

Military necessity, as defined by the United States, 'is that principle which justifies those measures not forbidden by international law which are indispensable for securing the complete submission of the enemy as soon as possible' (cited in Solis, 2010, p. 258). As with all the fundamental or core principles identified here, numerous expressions of the principle of military necessity can be found in treaty and customary international law. Perhaps most famously, the 1863 Lieber Code states: 'Military necessity, as understood by *modern civilised nations*, consists in the necessity of those measures which are indispensable for securing ends in war, and are lawful according to the modern law and usages of war' (cited in Solis, 2010, p. 258, emphasis added). More recently, the preamble of the 1907 *Hague* Convention identified the aims of the treaty being to 'diminish the evils of war as far military requirements permit', and Article 54 of the *Hague Regulations* states that underwater power and communications cables between occupied and neutral territories are not to be seized or destroyed 'except in the case of absolute necessity' (cited in Crowe and Western-Scheuber, 2013, p. 52).

While not codified in the 1949 *Geneva Conventions* or the 1977 *Additional Protocols*, part III of the fourth 1949 *Geneva Convention* allows parties to 'take such measures of control and security in regard to protected persons as may be necessary as part of the war', and Article 54 of *Additional Protocol I* provides that civilian crops or livestock may not be removed except by parties in their own territory 'where required by imperative military necessity' (cited in Crowe and Western-Scheuber, 2013, p. 53).

As discussed in the first section of this chapter, the modern laws of war, described as either IHL or LOAC, are the result of a centuries-long process. As such, and as elaborated on above, while humanitarian concerns are relatively new, without necessarily describing them as such, there existed forms of distinction and proportionality in pre-modern attempts to restrain battlefield conduct. Similarly, military necessity has always been a consideration during conduct – but at different times in history, the term has meant different things. The degree to which competing understanding of the term 'military necessity' might inform contemporary perceptions of the principle necessitates a discussion on the evolution of the term.

Notions of military necessity appear in the seventeenth-century writings of Dutch jurist Hugo Grotius; writing at the time of the Thirty Years War, Grotius notes 'all engagements which are of no use in obtaining a right, or putting an end to war, but have as their purpose a mere display of strength … are incompatible with both the duty of a Christian and with humanity itself' (Grotius, 1995, pp. 743–44). Even as relatively late as 1814, US Supreme Court Chief Justice John Marshall observed, 'that war gives to the sovereign full rights to take the persons and confiscate the property of the enemy wherever found, is conceded' (cited in Solis, 2010, p. 260).

Arguably the most infamous expression of necessity overriding any restraint on conduct during war was the doctrine of *Kriegsraison geht vor Kriegsrecht* (necessity in war overrules the manner of warfare), mostly often shortened to *Kriegsraison*. In the late nineteenth and early twentieth centuries, a number of German theorists proposed the idea that 'the elevation of necessity over legal norms was justified when the sole means of avoiding severe danger was to violate the law, or when compliance with the law might jeopardise the conflicts ultimate objectives' (Schmitt, 2010, p. 797); it was subsequently endorsed by military leaders and politicians between 1871 and 1945 (Solis, 2010, p. 266).

As both Schmitt and Solis observe, *Kriegraison* never gained wider traction, and whatever legitimacy the doctrine might have had was extinguished in *The Hostage Case* where the American Military Tribunal noted:

> Military necessity permits a belligerent, subject to the laws of war, to apply any amount and kind of force to compel the complete submission of the enemy with the least possible expenditure of time, life and money … It permits the destruction of life of armed enemies and other persons whose destruction is incidentally unavoidable by the armed conflicts of the war … but it does not permit the killing of innocent inhabitants for purposes of revenge or the satisfaction of a lust to kill. The destruction of

> property to be lawful must be imperatively demanded by the necessities of war. Destruction as an end in itself is a violation of international law. . . . We do not concur in the view that the rules of warfare are anything less than they purport to be. Military necessity or expediency do not justify a violation of positive rules. International law is prohibitive law.
>
> (*United States v List, 1948*)

Similarly, Cassese (1979, p. 481), commenting on the success of the Diplomatic Conferences that completed *Additional Protocol I* and *Additional Protocol II*, observed:

> The Protocol places primary emphasis on humanitarian demands and, indeed, in many respects subordinates military exigencies to such demands. On this score, the Protocol markedly departs from the customary law, which in general tends to put military necessity on the same footing as humanitarian demands.

Of the four principles of IHL discussed here, military necessity is the principle that most clearly reflects the historically developed right, as discussed above, of states to determine the conduct of military affairs to suit their own defined ends. While subsequent developments in the laws of war have sought to constrain states' behaviour, and indeed 'the means to achieve military victory are not unlimited' (UK Ministry of Defence, 2004, p. 23), the concept of 'whatever it takes', and the related notion that states still feel relatively comfortable defending the actions of their armed services through references to national interest or *raison d'état*, retain some salience. One of the reasons for this, as argued here, and reinforced by Michael Schmitt (2010, p. 798), is historical: 'the historical underpinnings of military necessity as a justification for the divergence from the absolute protection of civilians and civilian objects during armed conflict are carried through and reflected in the entire body of IHL.'

The priority given to the state's capacity to use force in the name of the 'national interest' was also evident in the ICJ's (1996, p. 263) Advisory Opinion regarding the use of nuclear weapons:

> the threat or use of nuclear weapons would generally be contrary to the rules of international law applicable in armed conflict . . . however, in view of the current state of international law . . . the Court cannot conclude definitively whether the threat or use of nuclear weapons would be lawful or unlawful in an extreme circumstance of self-defence, in which the very survival of the state would be at stake.

Yoram Dinstein (2004, p. 78) notes that 'the last sentence is most troublesome. The linkage between nuclear weapons and "extreme circumstances" ... is hard to digest; it appears to be utterly inconsistent with the basic tenet that [IHL] applies equally to all belligerent states, irrespective of the merits of their cause'.

In a similar vein, Amanda Alexander (2015, p. 129), writing about the 1991 Gulf War, argues that there was:

> a widespread perception that the legal regime governing the Gulf War was not really a humanitarian law. The central principle of the *jus in bello* was not humanity but, rather, the principle of military necessity ... What was clear ... was that it was a permissive principle that allowed almost any action if it could be justified by military necessity. It amounted to nothing more than a prohibition on the direct or negligent targeting of civilians.

Commentating on the destruction of an electricity facility that killed hundreds of civilians during the same conflict, Judith Gardam and Michell Jarvis (2001, p. 834) also argue that:

> The conduct of hostilities in the Gulf conflict indicates that the concept of 'excessive casualties' was restricted to that context. In other words, the military advantage always outweighed the civilian casualties as long as civilians were not directly targeted and care was taken in assessing the nature of the target and during the attack itself. The impact of the practice of states such as the United States and its coalition partners on the formation of custom is considerable and cannot be overlooked. It seems inevitable that the concept of proportionality as a customary norm is limited to the situations outlined above.

Again reinforcing the shifting balance between humanity and necessity highlighted above, Alexander (2015, p. 135) argues that by the time of NATO's 1999 intervention in Kosovo, the equilibrium had shifted back to the humanitarian principle of IHL:

> When civilians were killed, their deaths were not blamed on the inadequacy of the law but, rather, on the failure of NATO to apply the law properly. When lawyers sought better protection for civilians, they called for better adherence to the law – they did not suggest that better laws were required. In this way, international humanitarian law was cemented not only as the governing regime of *jus in bello* but also as a respected and prestigious regime.

It is argued here that the War on Terror, primarily fought in Afghanistan and Iraq since the 2001 terrorist attacks on the United States, has again shifted the equilibrium towards the principle of military necessity. Several arguments can be made to this end.

First, as evinced by comments from Marcus Luttrell (cited in Solis, 2010, pp. 108–9, emphasis added), a US Navy SEAL veteran of

Afghanistan combat, the asymmetrical nature of the War on Terror means that the restraints prescribed by IHL are regarded by fighting persons not only as unfair but also dangerous to the lives of soldiers:

> These terrorist/insurgents know the rules . . . they are not their rules, they are our rules, the rules of Western countries, *the civilised side of the world.* And every terrorist knows how to manipulate them in their own favour . . . they know we are probably scared to shoot them, because we get charged with murder . . . The truth is, in this kind of terrorist/insurgent warfare, no one can tell who's a civilian and who's not. So what's the point of framing rules that cannot be comprehensively carried out by anyone? Rules that are unworkable, because half the time no one knows who the goddamned enemy is, and by the time you find out, it might be too late to save your own life. . . . Nothing's fair in war, and occasionally the wrong people do get killed. It's been happening for about a million years. Faced with the murderous cutthroats of the Taliban, we are not fighting under the rules of Geneva IV Article 4. We are fighting under the rules of Article 223.556 mm – that's the calibre and bullet gauge of our M4 rifle.

As a SEAL, Luttrell would have been trained not only in the particulars of IHL but also its importance in ensuring, in the words of Michael Walzer (2000, p. 42), that war remains 'distinguishable from murder and massacre' by applying restrictions on the reach of battle. His rejection of several core principles of IHL, but particularly humanity, echoes those concerns noted by Alexander with regard to the 1991 Gulf War above, where military personnel view necessity as the most important principle of IHL. Furthermore, and in relation to the second argument made in this chapter (and elaborated on further below), Luttrell's comments about IHL being the law of civilised peoples are enlightening. By dehumanising the opposition, and tacitly identifying them as barbarian, Luttrell is subsequently denying terrorist groups the protections that IHL, more so in its customary form, provides all belligerents during combat.

The second set of case studies that demonstrate the degree to which the equilibrium in IHL has shifted towards military necessity are more political in nature. The first concerns the decision by former US President Donald Trump to pardon and reinstate Special Operations Chief Edward Gallagher over the wishes of the Pentagon, and the second concerns comments with regard to possible violations of IHL by former Australian SAS soldier Ben Roberts-Smith.

With a focus on Gallagher's 2017 deployment in Iraq, SEALs in his platoon told commanders and Navy investigators that they saw him shoot civilians and murder a wounded captive with a hunting knife, among other misconduct. Gallagher was subsequently found not guilty of first-degree murder of a captive ISIS fighter and attempted murder of civilians in Iraq but was convicted of posing for photos with the teenage captive's dead body (Philipps, 2019). The Navy then attempted to both demote Gallagher and remove him from the SEALs, decisions that were both blocked by President Trump. In October of 2019, in response to the Navy's announcement that they would be investigating claims of war crimes, Trump tweeted, 'We train our boys to be killing machines, then prosecute them when they kill!' (cited in Buzbee, 2019). Announcing the decision to block Gallagher's removal from the SEALs, Trump tweeted, 'The Navy will NOT be taking away Warfighter and Navy Seal Eddie Gallagher's Trident Pin. This case was handled very badly from the beginning. Get back to business!' (cited in Philips et al., 2019). As identified above, Trump's actions, as the Commander in Chief of the US military, provide further evidence of the shift away from the humanity principle of IHL, towards one more focused on military necessity.

The second political example of this shift concerns comments made by the Director of the Australian War Memorial, Brendon Nelson, regarding accusations of war crimes against Ben Roberts-Smith: 'I do not doubt that . . . bad things have happened. But as far as I'm concerned, unless there have been the most egregious breaches of laws of armed conflict, we should leave it all alone. War is a messy business' (cited in McDougall and Bachelard, 2019). Although perhaps more subtle than Trump, Nelson, while not explicitly referring to military necessity, is invoking a long-discredited 'fog of war' defence, which in turn prioritises necessity over the other three core principles of IHL.

Exploring modern interpretations of the principle of military necessity, starting with the *St Petersburg Declaration*, and working our way through to the War on Terror, it is clear that the law, the impact it has on belligerents, and the way that it is interpreted by political and military elites have evolved over time. Based on the evidence identified above, it is argued here that in our current epoch, the principle of military necessity is holding sway over the principle of humanity.

Nonetheless, as Dinstein (2015) observes, this is certainly not to argue that the laws of war have been rendered useless:

> An equilibrium between military necessity and humanitarian considerations underlies every norm of the law of international armed conflict,

> whether customary in nature, or drawn up in treaty form. Each norm reflects the equilibrium in a different fashion. At times it appears that military necessity has trumped humanitarian considerations. On other occasions, the opposite seems to be the case. Either way, the solution chosen by the framers of the treaty – or consolidated in the general practice of states – must be viewed as binding on contracting parties, or on the entire international community, in the very form in which it is constructed.

Rather, IHL is a compromised body of law in which states, through a historically attained right to use force as they see fit, frame this self-anointed right through either tacit or explicit reference to the principle of military necessity.

6.3 IHL and the 'Standard of Civilisation'

The 'standard of civilisation' concept, while having deep roots in international law, is also a key concept of the English School of International Relations, primarily as a tool (albeit contested) with which to explain the expansion of European international society in the late nineteenth and early twentieth centuries. Its strong association with colonial attitudes and practices means that while appropriate to use it when looking at pre-1945 international society, its usefulness as an analytical tool for contemporary world politics is generally regarded as limited.

In agreeing with Barry Buzan (2014, p. 577), and taking up his challenge to 'raise the profile of the "standard of civilisation" not just in its historical work, but also in its analysis of the post-colonial world', it will be argued here that the concept remains valuable in exploring continuities of double standards as they relate to protections afforded by the modern laws of war.

Civilisation, a term coined in the eighteenth century, came to be associated in its nineteenth-century usage with the idea of progress 'and the theory that nations advance through different stages of development' (Obregon, 2012, p. 917). Europeans increasingly came to use the term as a comparative 'other', believing they were 'endowed with an advanced level of social complexity, in opposition to "barbarous" nations, who could possible acquire civilisation if they conformed to certain values, or "savages", who were condemned to never access it' (Obregon, 2012, p. 917). Indeed, as Andrew Linklater (2016, p. 394) suggests, 'The idea of civilisation was regarded as having a transcendent quality that provided an image of a future political condition in which European peoples reached a higher state of civilisation by eradicating unnecessary suffering in warfare.'

In terms of giving rise to the European 'standard of civilisation', the adjective 'civilised', and its counter concept 'uncivilised' (or 'barbarian'), found its way into the writings of publicists, as well as judicial decisions and treaties. The two terms 'described and evaluated peoples, nations or states in their relation to sovereignty . . . the civilised, those endowed with civilisation, were recognised as proper subjects of international law. The uncivilised, those lacking civilisation, were left outside international law' (Obregon, 2012, p. 918). Thus, the standard of civilisation 'supported a partly racist taxonomy of "savage, barbarian and civilised" as a way of classifying the non-European world in relation to Europe' (Bowden, 2005, p. 1) and became the means by which people or states were admitted or barred from the international society of states (Buzan, 2014, p. 578).[7]

Although never codified as such, Gerrit Gong's (1984, pp. 14–21) criteria for a state to be civilised, and thus be accepted into international society, is the most widely cited; non-western states needed to (1) guarantee basic rights, as understood in the west, for foreign nationals; (2) have an organised and efficient political bureaucracy with capacity for self-defence; (3) have a domestic system of courts and codes, and adhere to international law; (4) have diplomatic institutions in order to engage in international relations; and (5) conform with Western mores, norms, and customs.

Not identified by Gong but nonetheless a further element that underpinned the emergence of a standard of civilisation was 'the increasing dominance of positive over natural law in western thinking and practise during the 19th century' (Buzan, 2014, p. 579). While natural law assumed the equality of humans under the sight of God, positive international law, emanating from sovereign states, was explicitly the law of civilised European states (see Koskenniemi, 2001, pp. 73–75, 99–116). Thus, as Schwarzenberger (1955, p. 222) identifies, 'the generation of pre-1914 international lawyers was fully justified in regarding international law as a powerful civilising agency'.

[7] See also Yang (2014, p. 679), who argues that the standard of civilisation, as it developed in the nineteenth century, was developed to practically protect 'European life, liberty and property in a culturally different and potentially hostile non-European world', and philosophically protect 'how to determine which non-European countries deserved legal recognition and legal personality in international law informed exclusively by the European tradition and civilisation'.

The degree to which such a standard ever existed is debated but is also unimportant. As Edward Keene (2002, p. 117) identifies, 'we need to appreciate the importance of the idea of civilisation not merely as a standard for regulating the entry of new states in international society, but also for validating an entirely different set of legal rules and political institutions in its own right'. Arguing that the existence of a standard to govern entry into the 'community of international law' did not exist in the nineteenth century, Martii Koskenniemi (2001, pp. 134–35) nonetheless acknowledges that the '*language of a standard*' existed, 'which gave the appearance of fair treatment and regular administration to what was simply a conjectural policy' (emphasis in original). Thus, as identified by Keene and Koskenniemi, the belief in a standard of civilisation by European and Western powers permitted them to exclude those who did not meet the expectations of the standard from the protections afforded by the newly forming body of international law.

As highlighted above, the link between the idea of civilisation and humanitarian laws of war goes back at least as far as the *St Petersburg Declaration*, which contended that in the relations between 'civilised nations', it was essential to identify the moment at which the 'necessities of war ought to yield to the requirements of humanity' (Linklater, 2016, p. 394). Similarly, the Lieber Code and Martens Clause both famously refer to 'civilised nations';[8] the Lieber Code, in defining military necessity, suggests that the law is both the product of, and applicable only to, civilised nations; somewhat similarly, although more explicitly, the Martens Clause also assumes protections for non-combatants to have evolved only from interactions between civilised nations. Indeed, 'the 19th century codification of the laws of war distinguished between insiders and outsiders of international society, with the former subject to rules that determined the scope of legitimate violence, not least that it should be discriminate and proportional, and the latter considered to be outside such rules' (Buzan, 2014, pp. 580–81; see also Sylvest, 2005; Pejcinovic, 2013).

While blatant distinctions between 'civilised and 'barbarian' have since disappeared, David Fidler (2000, pp. 388–89) notes that 'the rejection of the "standard of civilisation" as a driving force of international law has been more apparent that real'. Indeed, the cases identified and discussed above suggest the standard still exists when making determinations about protections afforded by IHL. For example, if one acknowledges the tacitly

[8] Linklater notes further that the Lieber Code 'was derived not from any existing legal text but from the core beliefs and practices of 'civilisation' (Linklater, 2016, p. 392).

Christian underpinnings of the concept as it developed in the nineteenth century, it clearly applies in considering Alexander's observations that predominantly non-Christian Iraqi belligerents were denied protections under the modern laws of war. Likewise, the language used by Luttrell tacitly identifies the Taliban as 'barbarian', and thus not 'worthy' of the same protections as 'civilised' belligerents.

Indeed, it is suggested here that as evinced by a number of the quotes above, the 'standard of civilisation', and the degree to which states represent the 'civilised', continues to remain an informant of who should be afforded protections by IHL, and in turn, a concept by which we can continue to understand the gulf between the (universal) humanitarian underpinnings of IHL, and violations of the laws of war.

Conclusion

Through an exploration of the relationship between the state and war, and a study of the way in which the modern laws of war are a culmination of a centuries-long process, this chapter has argued that IHL exists as a compromise between the state's historically informed and self-anointed right to use force to serve its political ends (as informed by *raison d'état*), and humanitarian concerns as they developed since the late nineteenth century. This chapter also argued that if one understands IHL as an equilibrium between the competing principles of humanity and military necessity, at various times throughout recent history the nature of this equilibrium has shifted, and, based on recent events discussed above, in the current epoch, military necessity is the dominant principle. Finally, via a brief discussion on the relationship between IHL and civility, it was argued here that distinctions of 'civilised' and 'barbarian' continue to inform protections afforded by IHL. Importantly, none of this is to argue that IHL is either redundant, nor that it offers little to no protection for civilians or civilian objects during conflict; rather, it is to provide a *via media* interpretation of IHL that lies between somewhat naïve expectations of humanitarian war, and conflict with restraint.

References

Alexander, A. (2015). A short history of international humanitarian law. *The European Journal of International Law* 26(1), 109–38.

Armstrong, D., Farrell, T. and Lambert, H. (2012). *International Law and International Relations*, 2nd ed., Cambridge: Cambridge University Press.

Best, G. (1980). *Humanity in Warfare*, London: Weidenfeld & Nicholson.

Bowden, B. (2005). The colonial origins of international law: European expansion and the classical standard of civilisation. *Journal of the History of International Law* 7, 1–24.

Buzan, B. (2014). The standard of civilisation as an English school concept. *Millennium: Journal of International Studies* 42(3), 576–94.

Buzbee, S. (2019). Trump undercuts his military leadership – and dishonors troops who uphold our values. *The Washington Post*, 24 November 2019 (online).

Cassese, A. (1979). A tentative appraisal of the old and the new humanitarian law of armed conflict. In A. Cassese, ed., *The New Humanitarian Law of Armed Conflict*, Naples: Editoriale Scientifica.

(2014). Current challenges to international humanitarian law. In A. Clapham and P. Gaeta, eds., *The Oxford Handbook of International Law in Armed Conflict*, Oxford: Oxford University Press.

Crawford, E. (2018). The enduring legacy of the St Petersburg Declaration: Distinction, military necessity, and the prohibition of causing unnecessary suffering and superfluous injury in IHL. *Journal of the History of International Law* 20, 543–66.

Cross, M. (2018). Humanity. In D. Djukic and N. Pons, eds., *The Companion to International Humanitarian Law*, Leiden: Brill.

Crowe, J. and Western-Scheuber, K. (2013). *Principles of International Humanitarian Law*, Oxford: Edward Elgar.

Dill, J. and Shue, H. (2012). Limiting the killing in war: Military necessity and the St. Petersburg assumption. *Ethics & International Affairs* 26(3), 311–33.

Dinstein, Y. (2004). *The Conduct of Hostilities under the Law of International Armed Conflict*, Cambridge: Cambridge University Press.

(2015). Military necessity. In *Max Planck Encyclopedia of International Law* (online).

Fidler, D. (2000). A kinder, gentler system of capitulations? International law, structural adjustment policies, and the standard of liberal, globalised civilisation. *Texas International Law Review* 35(3), 388–89.

Fleck, D. (2021). Historical development and legal basis. In D. Fleck, ed., *The Handbook of International Humanitarian Law*, 4th ed., Oxford: Oxford University Press.

Gardam, J. and Jarvis, M. (2001). *Women, Armed Conflict and International Law*, The Hague: Brill.

Ghezzi, M. (2018). Proportionality. In D. Djukic and N. Pons, eds., *The Companion to International Humanitarian Law*, Leiden: Brill.

Gong, G. (1984). *The Standard of Civilisation in International Society*, Oxford: Clarendon Press.

Grotius, H. (1995). *De Jure Belli Ac Pacis*, vol. 2, Francis W. Kelset (trans.), Buffalo, NY: William Hein.

Hayashi, N. (2016). Basic principles. In T. McCormack and R. Liivoja, eds., *Routledge Handbook of the Law of Armed Conflict*, New York: Routledge.

Heinsch, R. (2018). Distinction. In D. Djukic and N. Pons, eds., *The Companion to International Humanitarian Law*, Leiden: Brill.

Henckaerts, J.-M. and Doswald-Beck, L. (2005). *Customary International Humanitarian Law*, vol. 1, Oxford: Oxford University Press.

International Committee of the Red Cross (1987a). Commentary of 1987 Basic Rule, para. 1863.

International Committee of the Red Cross (1987b). Commentary of 1987 Protection of the Civilian Population, para. 1863.

International Court of Justice (1996). Advisory Opinion on the Legality of the Threat or Use of Nuclear Weapons, ICJ Rep., p. 263.

Johnson, J. (2000). Maintaining the protection of non-combatants. *Journal of Peace Research* 37(4), 421–48.

Keegan, J. (2001). *War and Our World*, New York: Vintage Books.

Keene, E. (2002). *Beyond the Anarchical Society: Grotius, Colonialism and Order in World Politics*, Cambridge: Cambridge University Press.

Killingsworth, M. (2016). From St Petersburg to Rome: Understanding the evolution of the modern laws of war. *Australian Journal of Politics and History* 62 (1), 100–15.

Kolb, R. (2013). The main epochs of modern international humanitarian law since 1864 and their related dominant legal constructions. In K. Mujezinović Larsen, C. Guldahl Cooper and G. Nystuen, eds., *Searching for a 'Principle of Humanity' in International Humanitarian Law*, Cambridge: Cambridge University Press.

Koskenniemi, M. (2001). *The Gentler Civiliser of Nations: The Rise and Fall of International Law, 1870–1960*, Cambridge: Cambridge University Press.

(2009). The legacy of the nineteenth century. In D. Armstrong, ed., *Routledge Handbook of International Law*, New York: Routledge.

Linklater, A. (2016). *Violence and Civilisation in the Western States-Systems*, Cambridge: Cambridge University Press.

McDougall, C. and Bachelard, M. (2019). Shining the spotlight: Why we reported that Ben Roberts-Smith was under investigation. *The Age*, 27 September 2019 (online).

Meyer, M. A. and McCoubrey, H., eds. (1998). *Reflections on Law and Armed Conflicts. The Selected Works on the Laws of War by the late Professor Colonel G.I.A.D. Draper, OBE*, The Hague: Kluwer Law International.

Military and Paramilitary Activities in and against Nicaragua (Nicaragua v U.S.), Merits, Judgment, ICJ Reports 1986, 14, 27 June 1986.

Neff, S. (2005). *War and the Law of Nations: A General History*, Cambridge: Cambridge University Press.

Obregon, L. (2012). The civilised and uncivilised. In B. Fassbender and A. Peters, eds., *The Oxford Handbook of the History of International Law*, Oxford: Oxford University Press.

Philipps, D. (2019). Navy SEAL Chief accused of war crimes is found not guilty of murder. *New York Times*, 2 July 2019 (online).

Philipps, D., Baker, P., Haberman, M. and Cooper, H. (2019). Trump's intervention in SEALs case tests Pentagon's tolerance. *New York Times*, 30 November 2019 (online).

Pejcinovic, L. (2013). *War in International Society*, Abingdon: Routledge.

Pothelet, E. (2018). Geneva Conventions. In D. Djukic and N. Pons, eds., *The Companion to International Humanitarian Law*, Leiden: Brill.

Protocol Additional (I) to the Geneva Conventions of 12 August 1949, and Relating to the Protection of Victims of International Armed Conflicts, Geneva, 8 June 1977 (entered into force 7 December 1978) 1125 UNTS 3 (*Additional Protocol I*).

Protocol Additional (II) to the Geneva Conventions of 12 August 1949, and Relating to the Protection of Victims of Non-International Armed Conflicts, Geneva, 8 June 1977 (entered into force 7 December 1978) 1125 UNTS 609 (*Additional Protocol II*).

Roberts, A. (1994). Land Warfare: From Hague to Nuremberg. In M. Howard, G. Andreopoulas, and M. Shulman, eds., *The Laws of War: Constraints on Warfare in the Western World*, New Haven, CT: Yale University Press.

Rogers, A. V. P. (2000). Zero casualty warfare. *International Review of the Red Cross* 837, 165–81.

Reus-Smit, C. (1999). *The Moral Purpose of the State: Culture, Social Identity and Institutional Rationality in International Relations*, Princeton, NJ: Princeton University Press.

Sassòli, M., Bouvier, A. and Quintin, A. (2014). *How Does Law Protect in War?* International Committee of the Red Cross, available online at https://casebook.icrc.org/glossary/distinction.

Schmitt, M. (2010). Military necessity and humanity in international humanitarian law: Preserving the delicate balance. *Virginia Journal of International Law* 50(4), 796–839.

Schwarzenberger, G. (1955). The standard of civilisation in international law. *Current Legal Problems* 8(1), 212–34.

(1971). *International Law and Order*, New York: Praeger.

Solis, G. (2010). *The Law of Armed Conflict: International Humanitarian Law in War*, Oxford: Oxford University Press.

St Petersburg Declaration Renouncing the Use, in Time of War, of Explosive Projectiles Under 400 Grammes Weight (2000). In A. Roberts and R. Guelff, eds., *Documents on the Laws of War*, 3rd ed., Oxford: Oxford University Press.

Sylvest, C. (2005). International law in nineteenth-century Britain. *British Yearbook of International Law* 75, 9–70.

Thomson, J. (1994). *Mercenaries, Pirates and Sovereigns*, Princeton, NJ: Princeton University Press.

Tilly, C. (1992). *Coercion, Capital and European States, AD 990–1992*, Cambridge, MA: Blackwell.

Turns, D. (2010). The law of armed conflict (international humanitarian law). In M. Evans, ed., *International Law*, 4th ed., Oxford: Oxford University Press.

UK Ministry of Defence (2004). *The Manual of the Law of Armed Conflict*, Oxford: Oxford University Press.

United Nations (1998). The Rome Statute of the International Criminal Court, available at www.icc-cpi.int/resource-library/documents/rs-eng.pdf

United States v List ('The Hostage Case'), Case No.7 (19 February 1948), reprinted in *Trials of War Criminals Before the Nuremburg Military Tribunals Under Control Council Law No.10*, p. 1230.

Walzer, M. (2000). *Just and Unjust Wars*, 3rd ed., New York: Basic Books.

Yang, Y. (2014). The standard of civilisation redux: Towards the expansion on international society 3.0?. *Millennium: Journal of International Studies* 42(3), 674–96.

7

Operationalising Distinction in South Sudan

Humanitarian Decision-Making about Military Asset Use*

REBECCA SUTTON

Introduction

This chapter focuses on one of the central tenets of international humanitarian law (IHL), the principle of distinction. The principle of distinction sets up two entities, the civilian and the combatant, and organises the relationship between them. The aim of this discussion is to investigate the operational reality of this principle in contemporary armed conflicts.

In the enduring scholarly and practitioner debates on IHL's principle of distinction, the focus is routinely placed on questions of who is who in the conduct of hostilities. That is, who is participating in war fighting versus who is a protected civilian (van Engeland, 2011, ch. 4). This chapter engages in a variation on the distinction debate that shifts the gaze to a new group of actors: the international actors who intervene in, and respond to, armed conflicts globally. It focuses in particular on the interactions of international humanitarian actors (Red Cross, United Nations (UN) and non-governmental organisations (NGOs)) and actors belonging to the UN Mission in South Sudan (UNMISS). In this account, members of the UN mission are split into two simple groupings: the terms 'peacekeeper' and 'peacekeeping forces' refer to the uniformed battalions, and 'civilian staff' refers to UNMISS civilian staff such as those working in the Political Affairs or Human Rights divisions.[1]

* The political situation in Sudan and South Sudan is in almost constant flux. The information in this chapter about the use of POC sites and UN peacekeeping measures was correct at the time of writing, but will have most likely changed.

[1] A point that will be made later in the discussion is that, like UN civilian staff, these peacekeeping forces will also generally be entitled to civilian protection under IHL.

Understanding the role law plays in the delineation of relationships between these international actors is crucial – particularly in light of the push for coherence and integration in UN, European Union (EU), and North Atlantic Treaty Organization (NATO) interventions globally.

Grounded in the socio-legal tradition and situated as part of the growing trend of empirical approaches to international law, this chapter draws on original fieldwork findings from South Sudan. The discussion illuminates how international humanitarian actors invoke 'distinction' in their interactions with others, focusing specifically on the day-to-day operational dilemmas that humanitarian actors face with respect to the use of military assets. Moving away from questions of legal compliance, it will be proposed that international humanitarian actors are producing a vaunted IHL rule through their everyday practices and interactions.

7.1 The Civilian in International Humanitarian Law

The traditional separation of military and civilian spheres is codified in IHL as the principle of distinction. This principle is one of IHL's most treasured tenets. It has been described as foundational for the whole system of IHL (Escorihuela, 2011, p. 319) but equally as an idea that is perilously fragile (Kinsella, 2011, p. 3). This principle requires parties to a conflict to distinguish between the civilian population and combatants, as well as between civilian objects and military objectives (Article 48 of *Additional Protocol I* to the *Geneva Conventions* of 1949). In terms of targeting concerns, the implication of civilian status is that one is thereby shielded from direct attack – so long as one does not directly participate in hostilities – while a combatant is deemed a legitimate military target. For the sake of simplicity, this chapter will treat the principle of distinction as though it applies equally in international and non-international armed conflicts as a matter of customary international law (Eritrea-Ethiopia Claims Commission, 2005).

Following Foucault, Kinsella proposes that IHL's principle of distinction should be understood as a relationship: one that 'puts into operation differences that are, at the same time, its conditions and its results' (Kinsella, 2011, p. 6). Taking a cue from this, the present discussion adopts a relational approach. As a consequence, the focus theoretically and empirically is on the boundaries between actors rather than on bounded groups (Desmond, 2014, p. 551). Rather than looking at humanitarian actors in isolation, the discussion attends to their interactions with other international actors to better understand how struggles over distinction arise.

As a backdrop to the exploration that follows, it is helpful to conceptualise the principle of distinction in IHL as a shell. More specifically, it is a set of two shells, with IHL doctrine providing little more than the (ostensibly hard) outer casing of the civilian and combatant entities. The shell motif is particularly fitting in the case of the civilian, as it is an entity that lacks precise legal definition. That is, IHL's civilian is designed in a manner that may be described as residual, negative, or derived: a civilian is simply anyone who is not a combatant (McDonald, 2004, p. 8). It is important to recognise that this negative IHL definition of the civilian is no mistake or mere oversight. For those who developed the Additional Protocols in Geneva in the 1970s, the intention was to grant legal protection in war expansively to all those who are not combatants.

The striking lack of content of the civilian shell has increasingly attracted the attention of scholars, who have pursued the civilian through various avenues (Alexander, 2007; Kinsella, 2011; Garbett, 2015). It will be proposed here that the everyday practices of international actors in armed conflict also serve as a site where IHL's civilian is constituted, produced, and disseminated.

7.2 The Field Research

This chapter is part of a wider research study that employs qualitative methodology and takes an inductive, grounded theory approach (Corbin and Strauss, 2008). In terms of epistemology, this study is closer to the interpretive end of the positivist–interpretivist spectrum; it aims not for explanation so much as for understanding (Macionis and Gerber, 2011, p. 33). This discussion is informed by field research conducted by the author in South Sudan in August and September 2015. Visits were made to the capital, Juba, in Central Equatoria state; Bor, in Jonglei State; and Bentiu, in Unity State. In addition to observation, interviews were conducted in and around the Protection of Civilians (PoC) sites where Internally Displaced Persons (IDPs) reside. A total of 113 individuals were interviewed, with 55 serving as key informants and the rest as participants in focus group discussions. Of these interviewees, 48 individuals were working for the UN mission, humanitarian NGOs, and other international agencies; the present discussion draws primarily on interviews conducted with these international actors. These empirical findings are enriched by the author's previous visits to South Sudan between 2010 and 2014, and two years of lived experience as head of mission for a humanitarian NGO in Sudan from 2009 to 2011. To protect confidentiality, the identity of all respondents has been anonymised.

7.3 Background on Conflict and Intervention in South Sudan

With the aim of providing necessary contextual background, a brief overview of the conflict in South Sudan and the ensuing international response will now be conducted.

Between 1983 and 2005, Sudan was engulfed in violent conflict. The two main parties were the Sudan People's Liberation Movement/Army (SPLM/A) and the Sudanese government, based in Khartoum (Fenton and Loughna, 2013, p. 5). The official end to the conflict was signalled by the signing of the Comprehensive Peace Agreement (CPA) in 2005. This agreement provided, among other things, for a future referendum on Southern Sudanese independence (Fenton and Loughna, 2013, p. 5). In July 2011, the Republic of South Sudan came into being, following a referendum in which 99 per cent of voters in Southern Sudan chose independence (Fenton and Loughna, 2013, p. 5).

In order to oversee the implementation of the peace ushered in by the CPA in 2005, the multi-dimensional integrated UN Mission in the Sudan (UNMIS) had been installed with its headquarters in Khartoum (UNSC Resolution 1590, 2005). This mission was officially replaced following independence in 2011, when UNMISS was introduced (UNSC Resolution 1996, 2011). Authorised under Chapter VII of the UN Charter, this integrated mission's mandate is to 'consolidate peace and security and to help establish conditions for development' in South Sudan (UNSC Resolution 1996, 2011).

The jubilation that greeted South Sudan's independence was short-lived, and in December 2013 there was a serious spike in armed violence, as fighting broke out between different factions of the SPLA (Blanchard, 2016). This conflict took on an ethnic dimension, pitting the Dinka and the Nuer, the country's two main ethnic groups, against each other. Following the outbreak of violence in December 2013, the UN Security Council (UNSC) reinforced UNMISS and 'reprioritised' its robust PoC mandate, as well as its human rights monitoring activities, support for the delivery of humanitarian assistance, and oversight of the implementation of the Cessation of Hostilities agreement (UNSC Resolution 2155, 2014). In connection with the December 2013 violence, tens of thousands, and eventually hundreds of thousands, of IDPs sought refuge at UNMISS bases. At several sites, UNMISS staff opened the gates and allowed in those seeking physical protection from the armed violence (Lilly, 2014). These sites came to be referred to as PoC sites.

Before moving on, a brief note is in order here regarding the laws and norms applicable to humanitarian activities in armed conflicts. To begin, international law such as IHL, international human rights law, and international criminal law will apply to international humanitarian actors, as will relevant domestic laws. Norms guiding the field of humanitarian practice are also heavily driven by the development of soft law (Lohne and Sandvik, 2017, p. 15). This includes global and context-specific guidelines, performance standards, codes of conduct, action plans, expert opinions, and handbooks (Lohne and Sandvik, 2017, p. 15). As the empirical findings explored below illuminate, the myriad rules and principles that govern the conduct of humanitarian actors do not always point in the same direction.

In order to facilitate the work of international humanitarian actors in the PoC sites in South Sudan, the UN Humanitarian Country Team in South Sudan approved limited use of military force protection and military assets by humanitarian actors in the sites (internal UN communication, 2016). Apart from this special arrangement, global guidance by the Inter-Agency Standing Committee (IASC) (2006) on the use of military and civil defence assets (MCDA) remains in force, along with South Sudan-specific guidance that reflects the global rules. A few pertinent rules from the South Sudan-specific guidance merit mention here. In line with global guidance on the use of military assets, the South Sudan Humanitarian-UNMISS guidelines (2013) stipulate: ‘As a general rule, to promote distinction between military and humanitarian actors, humanitarian actors should not use UNMISS assets or armed escorts.’ Humanitarian actors are to consider such use only as a ‘last resort’, and only in exceptional circumstances when the following criteria are met: the objective of the mission is humanitarian ‘and the mission clearly maintains its humanitarian and civilian character’; there is an urgent and immediate humanitarian need; there is no comparable humanitarian alternative; the use of the asset/escort is limited in time and scale, with a clear exit strategy; the use does not compromise the capacity of humanitarian actors to operate safely and effectively in the longer term (South Sudan Civil-Military Advisory Group, 2013).

The South Sudan guidance also states that in complex emergencies like South Sudan, ‘the flexibility to use military and civil defence assets (MCDA) is greatly constrained and the importance of distinction becomes paramount as outlined in international humanitarian law’

(South Sudan Humanitarian Civil-Military Coordination Guidelines, citing the IASC MCDA guidelines). Where the use of UNMISS assets or armed escorts could 'have a negative impact on the neutral perception of humanitarian workers', humanitarian agencies are expected to develop mitigating measures. With regard to the need to 'do no harm', the guidance acknowledges that military assets 'can provide unique advantages in terms of capability, availability, and timeliness'. It is stated, however, that 'the immediate positive effects must be carefully balanced with long-term negative effects' (South Sudan Civil-Military Advisory Group, 2013).

As the cited passages attest, these context-specific guidelines on military asset use are infused with explicit and implicit references to IHL. They also make frequent mention of the traditional operational principles that humanitarian actors strive to abide by: independence, impartiality, neutrality, and humanity. Leader describes these traditional principles evocatively as the 'long spoon' humanitarian actors employ to avoid getting eaten, or corrupted, by other actors (Leader, 1998). In the interest of focusing the discussion, only the final humanitarian principle cited above, humanity, will be juxtaposed with IHL's principle of distinction. This particular humanitarian principle has been selected for scrutiny because humanitarian actors routinely hold it up – implicitly or explicitly – against the principle of distinction when making decisions about the use of military assets.

7.4 Empirical Findings from South Sudan

This section of the discussion will distil the empirical findings from South Sudan, focusing specifically on how issues of distinction arise when humanitarian actors contemplate using military assets and resources. Unless otherwise noted, all references made are to original field research carried out on the ground in South Sudan.

The delicate nature of efforts to be 'distinct' from other actors is evident when it comes to the use of military assets by humanitarian actors in South Sudan. On the subject of the use of UNMISS assets, one humanitarian actor states, 'We are constantly challenged, negotiating, trying to explain to people why we do this.' Another submits that this is an area where humanitarian actors must strive to explain to people, including other members of the humanitarian community, why they cannot get so close to others. The ultimate concern, he argues, is 'we need trust, and to be distinct'. Trust, here, refers specifically to relationships with local war-affected populations.

There is an incident that is much discussed, in August 2015 in South Sudan, which involved a group of international humanitarian actors[2] flying with UNMISS to a site in Jonglei state where UNMISS was conducting a force patrol. At the same site, UNMISS civilian staff – specifically, human rights monitors – were also engaging with members of the local population. The decision to travel in an UNMISS helicopter without formal permission attracted the ire of the wider humanitarian community. One humanitarian actor explains, 'We, though, NGOs and UN, put a stop to it. [It] goes against the whole cluster system, collective needs assessments, if agencies break the rules and go "cowboy".'

While in this particular case, the humanitarian agency that travelled with UNMISS was not an unknown or peripheral humanitarian actor, many emphasise that it is the smaller humanitarian organisations that typically cause the most concern. The head of an international humanitarian NGO says, 'Every year we watch ICRC stand by itself. Oxfam, Mercy Corps, MSF will not use military assets or escorts. They might be even more principled than CARE, Save [the Children], Concern, Goal.' Apart from these respected organisations, he explains, there are concerns about the decision-making of the dozens of smaller humanitarian organisations operating in the vicinity.

In one humanitarian actor's view, it is likely out of ignorance that an organisation would board an UNMISS flight to deliver humanitarian assistance: 'They do not understand that by using these assets, it is detrimental.' Another humanitarian actor attributes such breaches to a lack of knowledge as well: 'It seems some humanitarians here did not know about the humanitarian principles – that they cannot just jump into a vehicle with a UN logo on it.' One humanitarian NGO actor notes that there might be formal agreement at the headquarters level regarding a certain position or arrangement, 'but what it boils down to is practical application. It's really [for the Heads of Mission] to make sure global best practices get filtered down to staff'. Another NGO actor suggests that headquarters staff of humanitarian agencies are failing in this respect: they 'commit a sin of not briefing staff before they go out', failing to train them in IHL and not requiring them to sign Codes of Conduct.

[2] The identity of these actors is withheld for reasons of confidentiality.

It is further intimated that headquarters staff might not themselves appreciate the importance of safeguarding humanitarian space – defined here simply as the room that humanitarian actors have to carry out their tasks unimpeded. Headquarters staff may subscribe to a short-term vision that aligns with short project cycles, as one humanitarian actor in South Sudan suggests, 'not in maintaining space in years to come'. Donor contracts potentially play an important role here. On the one hand, they might perpetuate such short-term thinking by structuring their funding of humanitarian projects in short cycles. On the other hand, they have the power to impose conditions on project funding and thus to create incentives that militate against using military assets. A UN humanitarian actor proposes, however, that both donors and headquarters staff ultimately play a less significant role than humanitarian actors who are deployed to the field. This individual states: 'To be frank, I believe that those in the field are at the coal-face and will work out appropriate arrangements regardless of overarching guidelines . . . so long as humanity remains the guiding light.'

Cutting against the belief that actors on the ground might not 'know better', it is also reported that one of the humanitarian actors who travelled on the aforementioned UNMISS flight contested the application of the civil–military guidelines in place in South Sudan. This particular actor allegedly protested that 'These are not *our* principles', taking the view that they belonged instead to the UN Office for the Coordination of Humanitarian Affairs (OCHA). Giving the benefit of the doubt, another humanitarian actor surmises that unsanctioned trips like this are not done 'out of malice, to get a leg over another agency' but rather out of a genuine wish to reach populations in need. In the opinion of another humanitarian actor, his colleagues who flout the need for civil–military separation simply 'have not calculated that distinction has been compromised, in order to access communities' located outside of the PoC sites in South Sudan.

It is also suggested that any gaps between headquarters and the field may be attributed to the personalities and proclivities of individual actors. One UNMISS peacekeeper proposes that the relationship dynamics between humanitarian actors and others are heavily based on personality. Confirming this, an UNMISS civilian staff states: 'Things are so personality based, what you get at HQ is not what you will see in implementation.' One humanitarian actor working for an international NGO adds that his organisation's relationship with UNMISS varies across different parts of South Sudan and across different parts of the UN mission. He had a 'very poor' relationship with the UNMISS state coordinator in one location, for example, because of a specific incident where one of his national staff got into trouble with the SPLA and UNMISS forces failed to respond in time. He has a 'good' relationship, however, with UNMISS elsewhere because of the particular individuals working there. His attitude towards these various UNMISS actors has concrete implications. For those UNMISS actors he gets along with and trusts, he tends to bring them with him to places and 'give coordinates of where we are going'.

At this juncture, it is important to contemplate which international actors humanitarians are striving to be distinct from in South Sudan. The point of interest here is where international humanitarian actors are drawing lines in their interactions with other international actors. One humanitarian actor in South Sudan proposes that when humanitarian actors are deciding whether to rely upon the resources of other international actors, the 'big thing' to consider is distinction. This individual proposes that while humanitarian actors inevitably need to 'link up' with various parties and stakeholders, they must also remain separate. For this humanitarian actor, the 'other international actors' that humanitarian actors need to keep a distance from are not limited to actors in military uniform: they include UNMISS civilian staff and even UN humanitarian actors such as the UN High Commissioner for Refugees (UNHCR). Significantly, these statements suggest the imposition of a dividing line between humanitarian actors and other *civilian* actors. While the empirical findings associated with the wider study are not discussed in the present chapter in detail, they establish that this is not an isolated or outlier perspective. On the contrary, intra-civilian tensions are something that humanitarian actors struggle with on a day-to-day basis. How these struggles implicate the principle of distinction will be considered below.

The discussion will now turn to the perspectives of other international actors in South Sudan regarding military asset use by humanitarian actors.[3] At the Bor PoC site in Jonglei state, an UNMISS civilian staff member contends that humanitarian actors have become 'too comfortable using UN assets and not all following the humanitarian principles'. Another UNMISS civilian staff member reports that humanitarian actors have gone too far in the other direction, insinuating that they are exaggerating the need for separation. Humanitarian actors have requested, for example, that her uniformed UNMISS colleagues refrain from

[3] All actors cited in this paragraph were interviewed not in South Sudan but while participating in a training exercise in Sweden in 2016.

participating in local patrols in certain areas. She relays that her military colleagues were incredulous, asking, 'We cannot be here because of a uniform?' Particularly in the early days of the mission, she explains, 'because we were not used to working so closely with humanitarians, our uniformed colleagues were unhappy and could not understand why [humanitarians] would not want them, but then would call whenever they heard a shooting'. From the vantage point of these UNMISS peacekeeping forces, humanitarian actors are equivocating and inconsistent in their appeals to distinction; this will be revisited below. Significantly, humanitarian entreaties for separation have also been interpreted as a personal insult to those left outside the boundary. As one UNMISS peacekeeper confides, 'We feel dismissed as arrogant.' Ultimately, he proposes, the fact is that humanitarian actors still need military actors – even if they do not like them.

One UNMISS peacekeeper describes some humanitarian actors as taking a hard line or 'fundamentalist' approach to their enforcement of the humanitarian principles. He attributes this to a concern for purity and refers to one international humanitarian actor known for strictly enforcing distinction as 'the Taliban guy'. And yet, as he notes, even this particular individual will still rely on UNMISS for evacuation. Having shared these personal misgivings as an individual, he adds that as a member of UNMISS he recognises that others may need to limit their reliance on the (military) resources offered by the UN Department of Peacekeeping Operations (DPKO). Emphasising that he understands it is his job to enforce this institutional outlook, he clarifies, 'We're fine with DPKO use being last resort.' In a similar vein, another UNMISS peacekeeper takes issue with humanitarian actors who behave as though proximity to UNMISS is 'like cursing the prophet'. For his part, he respects those humanitarian actors who bend the rules in order to reach war-affected populations. If a humanitarian actor wishes to travel with UNMISS to places in South Sudan where no one is providing services, he believes they should be supported to do so.

Another UNMISS peacekeeper who has tried to support humanitarian actors in this way says he has faced challenges. He recounts a story of an armed escort he helped to arrange for humanitarian actors in Pibor, a county in Boma State, South Sudan. His efforts were undermined when the humanitarian actors abruptly broke off from the convoy. As he recalls, 'They just changed their minds and left the area, just screwed off. I thought, "What's the point of being here". They are keen to go on their own, they moan about us, but then this happens.' An UNMISS

Relief, Reintegration, and Protection (RRP) official who liaises between humanitarian actors and UN peacekeeping forces voices surprise that humanitarian actors were happy to have UNMISS escort their convoys in peacetime, 'but in wartime they had a problem'. He is perplexed by the hesitation of humanitarian actors to work with him as an UNMISS RRP official because, in his view, '*We* are neutral. As RRP, we talk to both sides.' While he acknowledges that in peacetime UNMISS supported the 'baby government' of South Sudan, he is adamant that this ceased when the war broke out.

Returning now to the perspective of international humanitarian actors; their interpretation of 'last-resort' rules around military asset use in South Sudan varies widely. First, there are those who advocate for a flexible approach. As one such humanitarian actor emphasises, 'It's "last resort". It does not say "No"!' One humanitarian actor, who has repeatedly had his requests for humanitarian transport on a UN Humanitarian Air Services (UNHAS) helicopter denied, laments that this impeded his efforts to reach populations in need outside the PoC site. He proposes that these refusals 'took the weapons out of our hands, because we did not have any other option. We watch UNMISS go for missions here and there, but we cannot do it'. Other humanitarian actors maintain that a strict approach to last-resort policies inappropriately privileges the personal safety of humanitarian actors over the delivery of services to war-affected populations. One humanitarian actor contends, 'It's really costly, the risk management is stopping people from getting out to where the need is.' This individual laments that humanitarian actors are fixated on delivering services inside of the PoC sites where they have better access – 'it's a distortion'.

There are also those who urge their fellow humanitarians to adopt a stricter approach to last-resort rules. Critiquing the flexible approach, one humanitarian actor states: 'People say, "Oh, we use these assets because there's not enough donor money", [though this is] not actually an acceptable last-resort scenario according to the rules.' Another humanitarian actor faults those who use military assets for yielding to the temptation of short-term gains. From this individual's perspective, those humanitarians who view rigid principles and guidelines as disabling fail to understand that 'As space collapses we can leverage this to negotiate access, ensure safety and welfare of staff.' Another actor advises that international humanitarian actors should reflect on the reasoning behind appeals to distinction: 'Why is it important for me not to board an UNMISS helicopter, why should I use a non-military asset?' In his view, the central concern is that 'you become tainted'. Given that UNMISS has in the past allowed the SPLA to travel on its flights, he submits that any humanitarian actor who now travels with UNMISS – and even those who elect not to – will be compromised. This is because, '[p]eople will perceive us as part of UNMISS', which in this actor's opinion is code for supporting the SPLA. Of the relationship between humanitarian actors and the wider UN mission in South Sudan, he concludes, 'I know we are not ideal, I know there are many mistakes done, but we simply need to try to stay away.'

Some humanitarian actors remain adamant that, ultimately, distinction is something that can be jettisoned when it interferes with other pressing priorities. One international humanitarian actor draws attention to (what was then) active fighting in Upper Nile, South Sudan. This actor inquires, 'If you are wounded, do you care if our [international NGO] or a UN surgeon operates? Do you care who your food comes from, in a true emergency?' This individual goes on to say that 'Where there is an acute need, in an emergency, I think distinction is not something that matters. I think it matters more on a policy level, what will the rest of the world, the government here, the press, think.' From this perspective, competent military engagement in humanitarian assistance would be preferable to a humanitarian organisation doing it poorly for the sake of ensuring it is purely humanitarian. Another international humanitarian actor, highlighting the plight of war-affected populations in Southern Unity State, submits:

> For obvious reasons, I support distinction as much as possible. But I think it hits a threshold where the need to just get in and provide services and do something outweighs the distinction risks. That comes way, way, down the line, [when] you have tried everything else.

In a context where war-related violence is leading to many civilian deaths daily, he probes, 'So we are not going to bring food in because it would involve a military helicopter? Really?' Picking up this thread, a UN humanitarian actor contends: 'When you are between a rock and a hard place, you have to choose. There are pluses and minuses. Maybe I will lose on distinction, but I will win on something. . . . I would gain more than I would lose.' Another humanitarian actor confides he has discreetly taken a few trips outside of the PoC site where he works, together with UNMISS peacekeeping forces. He says that had he not gone on these journeys, 'I would not have been able to see anything.' He elaborates, 'I would think twice if bending the rules involved a bunch of agencies, but if

I, just myself, if I could see myself, touch the ground, then I can come back.' Another humanitarian actor is concerned that distinction is preventing humanitarian actors 'from even thinking about what could be possible – it's hampering *thinking* even before *doing*'. He offers the hypothetical of armed attacks on UN food distributions to local civilian populations in South Sudan. He proposes that the 'best scenario is to plunk in a bunch of peacekeepers, set a perimeter, do patrols', conceding that this would necessitate disregarding 'everything we know about distinction'.

Continuing with this line of thought, one humanitarian actor suggests that even where staff are able to cite the relevant guidelines 'chapter and verse', they tacitly understand that if they follow the proper process on the ground they will never get anything done. A UN humanitarian actor echoes this: 'What is written is good, the policy is really good. But when you are out, on the ground, if you follow every single word, you will not be able to do anything.' This individual suggests that 'In particular situations ... [you] want to react – you just have to bend the rules. I do what I believe is right, whether it's within or against the rules, I just follow my guts.'

Contemplating such misgivings about the rules on military asset use, one international humanitarian actor is sympathetic to the impulse but also troubled by the implications. This individual agrees that 'Yes, the humanitarian imperative is front and centre, getting to that place to provide assistance is paramount.' The problem, however, is that 'What is immediate, might not be best'. Another humanitarian actor ventures, 'I think it's an ethical dilemma. You do not care about distinction at that point in time, but then you think: do you want someone who is a non-mutual party doing that work?' Notably, this is the very same individual who asked rhetorically whether war-affected populations care where their food comes from (see above). This attests to the fact that struggles over distinction can play out at the most micro of levels: within one individual.

7.5 Implications for IHL

Having explored empirically how international humanitarian actors grapple with distinction in connection with military asset use in South Sudan, the discussion will now consider the significance of this operational reality for IHL's principle of distinction. At first glance, it might appear that the most pertinent concern is whether international humanitarian actors are complying with international law. Returning to the shell motif introduced above, one could investigate whether the practices of humanitarian actors track along with the boundaries of the civilian and combatant shells. While this focus on alignment with IHL might certainly generate useful findings, taking it as the starting point perpetuates the marked preference of international legal academics for pursuing compliance questions. This proclivity merits scrutiny, particularly with respect to dynamics that may consequently be obscured or overlooked.

To begin, in a 1993 speech Thomas Franck argued that international lawyers are today 'emancipated from the constraints of defensive ontology', freeing them up to engage in critical work about the law's content (Franck, 1995, p. 6). Although Franck included IHL scholars in this post-ontological era, doctrinal approaches continue to firmly dominate IHL scholarship (Lohne and Sandvik, 2017, p. 4); relatively few challenges have been mounted to IHL's treasured tenets and founding myths (Mégret, 2006, p. 266). One reason for this may be that scholars tend to turn to compliance as a response to breakdowns in IHL implementation. Noting widespread civilian suffering in contemporary warfare, for example, Kaldor argues that armed conflict can only be controlled if law is taken seriously (2003). If the civilian–combatant distinction is under strain then, on this view, what is needed is better IHL compliance.

The downside of this compliance focus, as Koskenniemi articulates, is that it 'silently assumes that the political question – what the objectives are – has already been solved' (2001, p. 485). Those who foreground compliance concerns will also tend to view war as a natural phenomenon. A drawback of this treatment of war as pre-legal is that it obscures IHL's constitutive role. Mégret pushes back against such conceptualisations, describing war instead as 'the relatively improbable artefact of a culturally contingent tradition of violence' (2006, p. 303). Problematically, the entities whose behaviour IHL seeks to regulate – such as the civilian and the combatant – are often treated as pre-legal as well. Kinsella challenges such tendencies in her genealogy of the principle of distinction (2011). She demonstrates that this principle is not premised upon the difference between the civilian and the combatant, so much as it produces this difference (Kinsella, 2011, p. 113).

A number of other obstacles potentially greet the scholar who attempts to untangle IHL from its enduring archetypes. Dampening nostalgia can be provocative, such as when Mégret describes Henri Dunant's experience at the Battle of Solferino as a 'footnote to colonial business as usual'

(2006, p. 273). In the context of the present discussion, the stakes can be quite high. One is, after all, contemplating who is to be protected in war, and (by implication) who is not. Finally, the methodology and methods that international law scholars typically employ may play a role. Baylis proposes that IHL scholars tend to ask 'whether' questions – such as whether a state complies with a given law – simply because these questions can actually be answered using traditional research methods (Baylis, 2010). This potentially neglects important nuances. As but one example, an actor's behaviour may align with international law even though the actor is completely unaware of the relevant legal rule (Dill, 2015, p. 10).

Moving on, a 'why' question that is ripe for exploration here is the following. Why is it that humanitarian actors would resort to the use of military assets at the risk of undermining their civilian image – and potentially their status in IHL? As noted above, international humanitarian actors themselves offer a number of reasons why this might be the case. One possibility is that it is done out of a malicious intent or a competitive instinct, so as to get a 'leg up' over other humanitarian actors – though this is rejected out of hand. Another proposal is that breaches stem from ignorance of the rules, as some humanitarian actors are poorly briefed and simply do not 'know better'. A further submission is that violations reflect an outright rejection or a lack of ownership of the relevant rules. This viewpoint is encapsulated in one humanitarian actor's insistence that 'these are not *our* principles'. In this particular instance, the international actor who is protesting the application of these rules to their conduct is reportedly of Western origin. It is noteworthy that, in separate interviews in South Sudan, national staff of international NGOs also questioned the application of international legal rules to their work. The potential lack of ownership of international rules by local humanitarian actors has been documented globally – most notably in the perceptions studies carried out by the NGO Médecins sans frontières (Abu-Sada, 2012).

It is also apparent from the commentary of international humanitarian actors that competing values are in play. Evidently, the resulting clash is one that various humanitarian actors elect to resolve in different ways. For the sake of analysis, the behavioural responses exhibited by humanitarian actors will be organised into two ideal types. The first ideal type captures those humanitarian actors who take a strict approach to distinction. These individuals typically take a long-term view and see practices that undermine distinction as counter-productive. This is exhibited by the humanitarian actor who suspects his humanitarian colleagues 'have not calculated that distinction has been compromised' in the name of service delivery in South Sudan. The second ideal type encapsulates humanitarian actors who interpret distinction flexibly and balance it with other goals they wish to pursue. This approach tends to be accompanied by a more immediate outlook and case-by-case decision-making. This is exemplified by the humanitarian actor who ventures, 'Where there is an acute need, in emergency, I think distinction is not something that matters.'

As mentioned earlier, for international humanitarian actors who deliver assistance in South Sudan, the competing principle that is most often juxtaposed with distinction is that of humanity. While IHL lawyers tend to think of the principle of humanity as the counterpoint to military necessity, it is worth noting that it means something very specific for the international humanitarian actors who deliver aid. Simply put, humanity requires one to address human suffering wherever it is found. This entails going to hard-to-reach places in order to deliver humanitarian services. In contrast, the principle of distinction – insofar as it calls for the clear separation of civilian and combatant spheres – may limit the ability of humanitarian actors to venture out. It functions in this way where it constrains reliance upon military assets and humanitarian actors have no other way to reach those in need.

Staying with the two ideal types introduced above, the discussion will now pivot to consider the perceptions of other international actors. UN peacekeepers in South Sudan express varying opinions. With respect to the first ideal type, there are those peacekeepers who respect the need humanitarian actors have to enforce the distinction, and those who accuse humanitarian actors of taking an unreasonably rigid approach. Individuals who adopt the latter view tend to speak favourably of the second ideal type, professing admiration for humanitarian actors who 'bend the rules' to reach populations in need. While this would seem to indicate an appreciation of the need for flexibility, the empirical findings suggest that military actors are in fact quite frustrated by what they experience as humanitarian equivocation. In particular, they are perplexed by humanitarian actors who vociferously insist on keeping their distance in the name of distinction but then do not hesitate to rely upon military actors for help. From the vantage point of these peacekeeping forces, humanitarian actors are trying to have it all: they are at once policing the civilian–combatant boundary and at the same time overstepping it when they deem necessary. Intriguingly, it is intimated that being shut out of certain spaces 'because of a uniform' would be easier to accept if it were consistently enforced.

It is noteworthy that UNMISS peacekeepers experience the tandem humanitarian practices of distancing and encroachment as prevarication. This highlights the importance of clarifying what distinction requires of different international actors in South Sudan. On this front, a notable feature of the complaints voiced by front-line UN peacekeepers is an omission: IHL is rarely marshalled. There is more to be said here, for example, about the legal status of UN peacekeeping forces. While these actors wear military uniforms and often carry weapons, they will generally be entitled to civilian protection under IHL (Leuven Manual, 2017, pp. 97–99). This is with the exception of instances in which the mission as a whole becomes a party to the conflict, or an individual peacekeeper directly participates in hostilities (Leuven Manual, 2017, pp. 97–99). The fact that peacekeeping forces are routinely consigned to the combatant shell as a matter of practice elides the complexity of their legal status. One might also highlight here the responsibilities IHL assigns to peacekeeping forces for maintaining the civilian character of certain spaces and for facilitating the delivery of humanitarian assistance under certain conditions. In South Sudan, UNMISS has been explicitly tasked with securing and expanding humanitarian space. Were IHL to be brought more firmly into the picture here, humanitarian actors who reach out to UNMISS in the wake of a shooting might be less open to charges of prevarication. Such calls would instead be framed as an invocation of UNMISS' official duties to protect humanitarian actors, along with all other civilians in South Sudan (UNMISS, 2013).

Matters are further complicated when one considers that international humanitarian actors also deploy distinction in their interactions with international actors whose civilian status is clearer than that of UN forces. These humanitarian practices may be seen as appealing to micro-distinctions within the civilian category. Given the ostensibly hard casing of the civilian shell, the instinct of the IHL lawyer may be to treat these practices as a violation of the principle of distinction – or perhaps as having no relevance for IHL at all. It is proposed that the urge to make normative pronouncements about these intra-civilian tensions must be resisted, or at the very least deferred. This is for the simple reason that it short-circuits attempts to understand what is actually going on.

Certainly, the invocation of distinction vis a vis other civilian actors might appear to be far removed from the codified IHL rule and from the targeting concerns it is linked to. The picture changes, however, when one entertains the notion that perceptions might have a serious role to play. As one example, some international humanitarian actors in South Sudan harbour a dubious impression of the civilian status of UNMISS civilian staff. They feel that such civilians are so closely integrated with UN peacekeeping forces that the former are perceived to be legitimate targets by local onlookers. They fear that associating with these civilian actors will create the impression that they, too, are affiliated with armed actors. An elephant in the room here is UNMISS' political character, which, it is acknowledged at mission level, 'can mean that some positions or activities are not considered neutral by all parties in the country' (UNMISS, 2013). Bearing this in mind, it is perhaps not surprising that humanitarian actors might stay away from members of the wider UN mission as a matter of everyday practice. It is also evident that perception concerns are in play when humanitarian actors call for separation from other *humanitarian* actors such as UNHCR. Certainly, there is a separate conversation that must be had here in connection with issues of branding, visibility for donors, and inter-agency turf battles. Bracketing that for the moment, what is of interest in the present discussion is the fact that some humanitarian (NGO) actors see UN humanitarian agencies as too close to the UN peacekeeping mission. This triggers the same concerns they articulate with regard to UNMISS civilian actors, leading them to invoke distinction in their interactions with these humanitarians as well. Elsewhere, I consider how these dynamics unfold in global civil–military training sites (Sutton, 2018).

Having urged against framing intra-civilian distinction practices as violations of IHL or dismissing them as extra-legal concerns, an attempt will be made here to elucidate their relationship to IHL's principle of distinction. It is proposed that such practices simultaneously attest to, and challenge, the power of this IHL rule in its traditional configuration. On the one hand, the appeal to distinction – in any form – draws on and perpetuates the force of the principle of distinction as a treasured IHL tenet. On the other hand, the transposing of the operative line to civilian–civilian relations destabilises the bright line binary civilian–combatant arrangement around which the IHL rule is organised.

It is submitted that in order to make sense of the operational reality of the principle of distinction, one must attend to the practices and perceptions of the actors who are expected to enact such rules. While international law scholars are increasingly attending to practices, the importance of perceptions is routinely overlooked. In thinking about how humanitarian actors produce distinction in their day-to-day operations, this chapter opens up space for reflecting upon law, practices, perceptions, and their interplay. It extends an invitation to IHL scholars to contemplate how individuals like the humanitarian actors considered here see the world, how they imagine the world sees them, and how these perceptions align with the actual viewpoints of others. The payoff of such an exploration, in the context of the present discussion, is a nuanced understanding of how the civilian figure promulgated by humanitarian actors is shaped.

Conclusion

This chapter has elucidated an approach through which legal scholars might begin to engage with the operational reality of IHL's principle of distinction in all of its evident complexities. With reference to original empirical material from South Sudan, it was demonstrated that humanitarian actors are grappling with issues of distinction and, moreover, that they are divided on how to conduct themselves when distinction clashes with other important ideals. This conundrum will no doubt be familiar to any practitioner who forms part of the crowded field of international actors responding to contemporary armed conflicts. At this juncture, however, there is a dearth of legal scholarship that squarely confronts the significance of these operational challenges for IHL, and vice versa. What is needed now is an in-depth examination of what it is that distinction demands of international actors in settings like South Sudan – as a matter of law and also in terms of practice and perception. While questions of IHL compliance may certainly comprise part of this investigation, they should not supplant a more granular exploration of how humanitarian actors engage with law in their everyday practices. The modest aim of this chapter has been to illustrate what such an investigation might look like, with reference to the conundrums posed by military asset use in South Sudan.

References

Abu-Sada, C., ed. (2012). *In the Eyes of Others: How People in Crises Perceive Humanitarian Aid*, New York: MSF-USA.

Alexander, A. (2007). The genesis of the civilian. *Leiden Journal of International Law* 20, 359–76.

Baylis, E. (2010). The transformative potential of rigorous empirical research. *American Society of International Law Annual Meeting*, vol. 104, 24–27 March, 2010.

Blanchard, L. P. (2016). Conflict in South Sudan and the challenges ahead. *Congressional Research Service*, September 2016, available online at https://fas.org/sgp/crs/row/R43344.pdf.

Corbin, J., and Strauss, A. (2008). *Basics of Qualitative Research: Techniques and Procedures for Developing Grounded Theory*, 3rd ed., Thousand Oaks, CA: SAGE Publications.

Desmond, M. (2014). Relational ethnography. *Theory and Society* 43, 547–79.

Dill, J. (2015). *Legitimate Targets? Social Construction, International Law and US Bombing*, Cambridge: Cambridge University Press.

van Engeland, A. (2011). *Civilian or Combatant? A Challenge for the 21st Century*, Oxford: Oxford University Press.

Eritrea-Ethiopia Claims Commission Partial Award, Western Front, Aerial Bombardment and Related Claims, Eritrea's Claims 1, 3, 5, 9-13, 14, 21, 25 and 26 (2005), 45 ILM 396, 525 (2006).

Escorihuela, A. L. (2011). Humanitarian law and human rights law: the politics of distinction. *Michigan State Journal of International Law* 19(2), 299–407.

FAQs: UN Humanitarian Civil-Military Coordination, Military Civil Defence Assets and the Use of Military Escorts in South Sudan, circulated internally in South Sudan, May 2016.

Fenton, W., and Loughna, S. (2013). The search for common ground: civil-military coordination and the protection of civilians in South Sudan. *Overseas Development Institute Humanitarian Policy Group*, Working Paper, December 2013.

Franck, T. (1995). *Fairness in International Law and Institutions*, Oxford: Oxford University Press.

Garbett, C. (2015). *The Concept of the Civilian: Legal Recognition, Adjudication and the Trials of International Criminal Justice*, New York: Routledge.

Inter-Agency Standing Committee (2006). *Guidelines on the Use of Military and Civil Defence Assets to Support United Nations Humanitarian Activities in Complex Emergencies*, Rev. 1, January 2006.

International Group of Experts (2017). *Leuven Manual on the International Law Applicable to Peace Operations*, Cambridge: Cambridge University Press.

Kaldor, M. (2003). Beyond militarism, arms races and arms control. In G. Lundestad et al., eds., *War and Peace in the 20th Century and Beyond: The Nobel Centennial Symposium*, available online at http://essays.ssrc.org/sept11/essays/kaldor.htm.

Kinsella, H. (2011). *The Image before the Weapon: A Critical History of the Distinction between Combatant and Civilian*, Ithaca, NY: Cornell University Press.

Koskenniemi, M. (2001). *The Gentle Civilizer of Nations: The Rise and Fall of International Law 1870–1960*, Cambridge: Cambridge University Press.

Leader, N. (1998). Proliferating principles; or how to sup with the devil without getting eaten. *Disasters* 22(4), 288–308.

Lilly, D. (2014). Protection of civilians sites: a new type of displacement settlement?. *Overseas Development Institute Humanitarian Policy Network*, September 2014.

Lohne, K., and Sandvik, K. B. (2017). Bringing law into the political sociology of humanitarianism. *Oslo Law Review* 4(1), 4–37.

Macionis, J., and Gerber, L. (2011). *Sociology*, 7th ed., Toronto: Pearson.

McDonald, A. (2004). The challenges to international humanitarian law and the principles of distinction and protection from the increased participation of civilians in hostilities. *Spotlight on Issues of Contemporary Concern in International Humanitarian Law and International Criminal Law*, Working Paper, University of Tehran Round Table, April 2004.

Mégret, F. (2006). From 'Savages' to 'Unlawful Combatants': A Postcolonial Look at International Humanitarian Law's 'Other'. In Ann Orford, ed., *International Law and Its Others*, Cambridge: Cambridge University Press.

Protocol Additional to the Geneva Conventions of 12 August 1949, *and Relating to the Protection of Victims of International Armed Conflicts*, 8 June 1977, 1125 UNTS 3, Can TS 1991 No. 1.

South Sudan Civil-Military Advisory Group, *Guidelines for the Coordination between Humanitarian Actors and the United Nations Mission in South Sudan (UNMISS)*, endorsed 6 December 2013.

Sutton, R. (2018). A hidden fault-line: how international actors engage with IHL's principle of distinction. In M. Deland et al., eds., *International Humanitarian Law and Justice: Historical and Sociological Perspectives*, New York: Routledge.

United Nations Security Council (2005). Resolution 1590, 2005.

United Nations Security Council (2011). Resolution 1996, 2011.

United Nations Security Council (2014). Resolution 2155, 2014.

8

Private Military and Security Companies and International Humanitarian Law

The Montreux Document

REBECCA SHAW

Introduction

The contemporary private military and security industry does not threaten the content or spirit of international humanitarian law (IHL). Despite its occasionally poor reputation and potentially contentious position within conflict zones, as well as in pre- and post-conflict situations, firms within the industry do not operate beyond the bounds of legal recourse. Nonetheless, concerns do remain as to the willingness and capacity of private military and security companies (PMSCs), their employees, and their employers, to behave in accordance with IHL. It is also uncertain if the international community is likely or able to hold these different sets of actors to account under IHL. While the ideals of IHL remain unchallenged by PMSCs, less clear are the operational realities, and enforcement with regard to the industry and its use. Indeed, as is discussed in other chapters in this volume, limitations in its application expose flaws in how the international community engages with IHL to address different types of behaviour and actors in conflict.

The tension between the clarity of the position of PMSCs within IHL and concerns about the capacity of the international community to effectively enforce and uphold IHL in practice has led to a series of international efforts to respond. These include attempts by the United Nations (UN), international organisations (IOs), and the industry itself to both reaffirm the legal responsibility of actors with regard to their engagement with PMSCs and to enhance the regulatory environment within which they operate.[1] One of these responses, the Montreux Document, which was drafted between 2006 and 2008, is an attempt by the International Committee of the Red Cross (ICRC) and the Swiss government to ease concerns about the behaviour and use of the private military and security industry, through a restatement of existing relevant international law and a formulation of a series of good practices designed to guide states in their interactions with PMSCs. Despite the promise of the Montreux Document, the reality is that little has changed. The Montreux Document, as a restatement of existing law, maintains states as the actors with primary responsibility and does not create new enforcement or accountability frameworks, leaving the regulatory environment unaffected.

In this chapter, I examine the private military and security industry and note PMSCs' position within international legal and regulatory frameworks. In light of IHL's lack of explicit engagement with the contemporary private military and security industry, I explore the creation of the Montreux Document as an effort to address and clarify the industry's position in law. Subsequently, I examine the Document's successes and failings in establishing a more coherent response to PMSCs. As noted in other chapters, the role of a range of actors in conflict raises concerns as to the gap between the ideals and 'letter' of IHL, and its operational application. While the Document marks a significant assertion of state responsibility with regard to their interactions with PMSCs, it also highlights international awareness of flaws, weaknesses, and potential gaps in IHL. Nonetheless, the Montreux Document does not provide new binding regulations; it therefore fails to appease concerns about the enforcement of IHL with regard to PMSCs and effectively stymies efforts to address the industry in a more robust and binding fashion.

8.1 The Contemporary Private Military and Security Industry

The private military and security industry active today is international and multi-faceted, encompassing small, specialised firms, and large multinational corporations. These PMSCs are not only deployed by states but are also employed by non-governmental organisations (NGOs), IOs, and even by other corporate actors such as resource extraction firms. The industry offers an expansive range of military- and security-adjacent

[1] For a detailed discussion of these various regulatory responses to PMSCs, see Shaw (2016).

tasks, including weapons and systems maintenance, intelligence gathering, and the provision of security guards. While the industry is relied upon in a range of non-conflict situations, for the purposes of this chapter and any examination of their position within IHL, the activities of PMSCs within conflict zones are most significant.

The private military and security industry as currently active is the most recent iteration of the private provision of force, an industry that has been present in various forms for millennia. Private and often extraterritorial, with financial or ostensibly suspicious motivations, mercenaries have never been fully accepted as a legitimate and honourable military and security resource (Percy, 2007a, 2007b), although private forces in a range of manifestations remained active. With the rise of the state in a recognisable modern form, states shifted away from private force, instead relying on armies comprised of citizen soldiers (Percy, 2007b, p. 90). Despite this civilianisation, some level of private force did remain active, either as units that were eventually integrated into state military apparatuses (Percy, 2007b, pp. 91–92) or in small, specialised bands of soldiers.

In the twentieth century, groups of private soldiers were particularly active in the wars of decolonisation. These forces were 'loosely organized and extremely colourful' (Percy, 2007b, p. 206). During the 1960s, 1970s, and 1980s, the presence of private soldiers was recorded in conflicts in Angola, Benin, the Congo, Yemen, the Comoros Islands, and the Seychelles, among others (Mockler, 1985).[2] It was in response to these Cold War mercenaries and their high-profile activities that the growth in anti-mercenary sentiment and normative prohibitions around mercenaries began to coalesce into international legal frameworks. Provisions banning mercenaries were included in the 1977 *Additional Protocol I* to the *Geneva Conventions* (art 47), and anti-mercenary conventions were ratified by the Organisation of African Unity (now under the auspices of the African Union) (*OAU Convention for the Elimination of Mercenarism in Africa*, 1977) and the UN (*International Convention against the Recruitment, Use, Financing and Training of Mercenaries*, 1989). Although these anti-mercenary frameworks were largely ineffective in a legal sense, they nonetheless shaped the growth of post-Cold War PMSCs and the international understanding of the industry.

[2] For a discussion of some of these private forces active in the twentieth century, see Seagrave (1981); Mockler (1985).

The end of the Cold War is generally accepted to be the point at which the modern private military and security industry began to take shape. Various political, material, and ideological changes in the international system[3] with the end of Cold War bipolarity sparked the rise of the first wave of companies specialising in the provision of private force. Unlike prior bands of explicitly mercenary actors, these private military companies (PMCs), like today's firms, were 'commercial enterprises . . . and registered businesses' emphasising 'private enterprise, efficiency and expertise' (Adams, 2002, p. 5; Singer, 2008, p. 45). Private military companies, including most famously Executive Outcomes (EO) and Sandline International, undertook a range of tasks, displaying significant military capabilities (Percy, 2007b, pp. 209–10; Singer, 2008). In the employ of the Sierra Leonean government, EO, for example, undertook an operation in 1995 in which it deployed helicopter gunships, 'other air and artillery assets' and 'stand-up battles' to defeat the Revolutionary United Front (RUF) (Singer, 2008, pp. 110–14). Despite their degree of commercial success in the immediate post-Cold War period, many PMCs were eventually disbanded. As a consequence of unfavourable publicity, attempts to develop domestic legal responses, and concerns about their international legality, many of the firms became unable to operate effectively (O'Brien, 2000, p. 59; Krahmann, 2012, p. 2). Contemporary PMSCs emerged from the wreckage of PMCs.[4]

The type of PMSCs operating today developed from international shifts following the end of the Cold War as well as the demise of PMCs. More crucial, however, the events of the wars in Afghanistan (2001–14) and Iraq (2003–11) caused the exponential expansion of the industry. In 2008, for example, during the United Kingdom's Operation Herrick in Afghanistan, the UK Ministry of Defence employed one contractor for every two personnel (Davies cited in House of Commons Hansard, 2008). In the same year, a US Congressional Budget Office (2008, p. 1) report noted that the United States employed one contractor in Iraq for every one member of its armed forces serving there. Private military and security companies do not always work for states, however, and many operate in the employ of NGOs and corporations (Vaux et al., 2002, pp. 15–16; Schreier and Caparini, 2005, p. 19;

[3] For a further discussion of these factors, see Avant (2004) and Singer (2008), among others.

[4] As they are not PMSCs, this chapter does not address the Wagner Group, or other mercenary forces and PMCs active in and following the 2022 Russian invasion of Ukraine.

Spearin, 2008, 2011). In their choice of employers and provision of particular services, many firms have been careful to maintain a more positive reputation than that which undermined PMCs, something that has shaped the international position of PMSCs. Similarly, their work for states such as the United States and United Kingdom has had an effect on the nature of the regulation developed around PMSCs.

In many ways, the PMSCs that arose from the wars in Iraq and Afghanistan are distinct from other forms of private force. Their less negative international reputation is reinforced by PMSCs' claim 'they do not engage in combat' (Percy, 2007b, p. 61), something that differentiates them not only from PMCs but also from other forms of private force, including the mercenaries banned under international legal frameworks. This distinction is also crucial for their position within IHL. While it is still the case that PMSCs undertake tasks where they 'carry and use weapons ... and fulfil essential military functions', they also have a broader scope, offering other 'functions for military support and military counselling' (Gómez del Prado, 2008, pp. 435–36). The provision of more auxiliary tasks has allowed the industry to not only expand its reach but also capitalise on the distance between the contemporary PMSCs and the illegal mercenaries to which they are often rhetorically linked. This distance coupled with the changes in the industry as a consequence of the wars in Iraq and Afghanistan has informed the regulatory approach taken by the international community.

8.2 The Private Military and Security Industry and International Humanitarian Law

As noted above, while mercenaries are explicitly addressed within the UN and AU conventions, PMSCs are not. Likewise, the anti-mercenary provisions in Article 47, *Additional Protocol I*, do not apply to PMSCs. Indeed, in a legal and regulatory sense, PMSCs are different to the extent that they cannot be considered to be mercenaries at all. Nonetheless, PMSCs are not beyond the reach of international law and the behaviour of PMSCs' employees and employers is encompassed under international humanitarian law. Nonetheless, concerns that existing approaches to PMSCs are insufficient with regard to upholding and enforcing IHL have informed new responses to the industry. PMSCs are interesting for the way that they illuminate a potential disconnect between ideals of IHL and its operational reality, and for how this has inspired the creation of new soft law frameworks.

As is explored in other chapters of this text, IHL is 'a set of rules that seek to limit the effects of armed conflict', shaping how wars are fought and protecting those involved (ICRC, 2017). International humanitarian law provides legal protections and responsibilities for all combatant and civilian actors in conflict. The distinction between combatants and civilians (or non-combatants), and the ensuing protection of civilians, is central to IHL, providing specific restrictions and protections. Within the *Geneva Conventions*, a civilian, in contrast to a combatant, is a person who is not a member of the armed forces of a party to the conflict, a member of a militia or volunteer corps, or a person who takes up arms to engage in the conflict without being part of a regular unit (*Additional Protocol I*, arts 43, 50). In addition to being legitimate military targets of attack, combatants are permitted to actively participate in hostilities. This so-called 'combatant's privilege' allows combatants to 'fight without fear of persecution' (de Nevers, 2009, p. 172). The distinction between combatant and civilian, de Nevers notes (2009, p. 172), does not only protect civilians and allow combatants to fight, it also serves to 'keep others out of combat'. Those who participate in combat without conforming to the category of 'combatant' are considered to be 'unprivileged belligerents', a status which alters their protection under IHL and may lead to their prosecution as criminals (de Nevers, 2009, p. 172). These definitions are particularly important for PMSCs, which insist they do not use violence in conflict.

It is on this civilian–combatant distinction that some concerns about PMSCs are grounded, arising from what is seen to be their possibly uncertain standing between these legal categories. Nonetheless, except in limited circumstances when they are integrated into state armed forces or directly accompany a military force (see Cameron, 2006, pp. 582–87; de Nevers, 2009, p. 177), both the companies and their employees fit within the category of 'civilians'. As civilians, PMSCs are 'protected from direct attacks in both non-international and international armed conflicts – as long as they do not fight' (Henckaerts and Doswald-Beck, 2005; Cameron, 2006, pp. 587–90; Gillard, 2006a, pp. 531–36; de Nevers, 2009, pp. 172–75). In the decade following the end of the Cold War, some private military firms, including EO as discussed, explicitly engaged in combat operations (Singer, 2008), jeopardising their civilian status, but the contemporary PMSCs in question in this chapter are not employed to use force offensively (Percy, 2007b, pp. 228–31). As de Nevers notes, if a PMSC is employed to protect civilians, the firm 'may lawfully defend themselves and those they are protecting without putting their civilian status at risk' (de Nevers, 2009, p. 179). In a case such as this, factors including the nature of the PMSCs' employment and their relationship to the conflict would influence understandings of their position within IHL. For instance, if the PMSC is employed to protect military personnel that are legitimate targets under IHL, attacks on the PMSC and its employees would not be illegal under IHL, and the use of force by PMSCs' employees in these circumstances would compel them to enter the conflict (Gillard, 2006a, p. 540; de Nevers, 2009, p. 180).[5] On occasion, contracts and circumstance lead PMSCs' employees to behave in a manner that undermines their status as civilians and threaten their associated protections (de Nevers, 2009, p. 171). The potential for incidents such as this to occur, and the corresponding international alarm and confusion, have informed efforts to clarify the relationship between PMSCs and international legal frameworks, including IHL.

Despite the rapid growth of the private military and security industry during the wars in Iraq and Afghanistan, and the complexity of the roles the firms undertake, the position of PMSCs and their employees and employers within IHL should not be too controversial. As noted, the private military and security industry does not challenge IHL: private military and security companies are not a threat to IHL, nor are they exempt from it. Nonetheless, the behaviour of the international community towards the industry suggests that this is not straightforward in practice and that new guidelines are necessary. This indicates the possible disconnect between the operational realities of the law and the clarity of the ideals that inform IHL.

8.3 An International Response to the Private Military and Security Industry

Private force has long been seen as a controversial means by which to obtain military or security services and skills. Despite the links, perceived or actual, between the contemporary private military and security industry and historical forms of private force, including mercenaries, the international approach to PMSCs has been markedly different: where contemporary PMSCs, as legitimate international corporate actors, are regulated, mercenaries are prohibited. Nonetheless, new regulatory

[5] De Nevers (2009, p. 180) notes that, from some perspectives, this participation in hostilities could be seen as self-defence; she also notes that others would suggest any civilian use of force in combat is unprivileged and illegal under IHL.

efforts to address PMSCs do build from the Cold War-era international legal responses to mercenaries.

International legal responses to mercenaries are ineffective. The UN Convention against mercenaries 'could never be used to control mercenaries, even if a state wished to do so' (Percy, 2007a, p. 375). Not only does the Convention fail to elaborate any sort of monitoring mechanism, it also applies a dysfunctional definition of 'mercenary' centred on allegiance, motivation, intent, and financial gain (Taljaard and International Herald Tribune, 2004; Scheimer, 2009, pp. 623–24). Of the UN Convention, Geoffrey Best (1983, p. 375) cited a 'learned friend', who suggested, 'any mercenary who cannot exclude himself from this definition deserves to be shot – and his lawyer with him!' The definitions applied fail to account for complexity in motivations, and their narrowness also discounts forces that are comprised of either nationals of a party to the conflict or are not explicitly contracted to be combatants. The Cold War-era anti-mercenary mechanisms are consequently 'so weak that [they are] virtually unusable' (Percy, 2007a, p. 368). Although the legal efforts to prohibit mercenaries and their use were not successful, their creation is indicative of the influence of the anti-mercenary norm.[6] These anti-mercenary provisions have also informed the growth of the contemporary private military and security industry and newer regulatory responses to PMSCs.

In light of the disparities between the mercenaries of the Cold War-era convention, and other manifestations of private force, the UN has looked to address changes in the use and behaviour of private force. The 'UN Special Rapporteur on the use of mercenaries as a means of impeding the exercise of the right of peoples to self-determination' role, established in 1987, was created to examine private force amid increasing concerns about the behaviour of different kinds of actors, particularly the 'characteristics and methods of mercenarism' (Commission on Human Rights, 1987; Office of the United Nations High Commissioner for Human Rights, 2017). Although the role did initially have an explicit focus on mercenary use and behaviour, this expanded to include newer forms of private force.

As the industry evolved in the early 2000s, the UN Working Group on the use of mercenaries as a means of violating human rights and

[6] For a further examination of the weakness of these international frameworks and their relationship to the anti-mercenary norm, see Percy (2007a).

impeding the exercise of the right of peoples to self-determination was created in 2005,[7] replacing the role of the Special Rapporteur. The Working Group's mandate was designed to address not only mercenaries but also the 'emergent threats' posed by PMSCs (Gómez del Prado, 2008, p. 3). As José Luis Gómez del Prado (2011, p. 160), a former member of the UN Working Group noted, many of the more recent manifestations of private force are excluded from the UN anti-mercenary convention's definition of 'mercenary'. Consequently, from 2009, the Working Group led the consultations and drafting process for a possible new regulatory, oversight, and monitoring mechanism for PMSCs and their use (Office of the United Nations High Commissioner for Human Rights, 2009). Elements of a possible international convention were circulated at the UN in 2010, during which time the Working Group noted that the industry 'remains fundamentally unregulated at the international level and often insufficiently regulated at the national level' (United Nations General Assembly, 2010, p. 4). The process of developing a new binding international response to PMSCs continues under the auspices of the Open-ended Intergovernmental Working Group[8].

The Open-ended Intergovernmental Working Group, which was created in 2010 (Office of the United Nations High Commissioner for Human Rights, 2010), was initially mandated to explore a possible 'legally binding instrument on the regulation, monitoring and oversight of the activities of private military and security companies, including their accountability' (Human Rights Council, 2010, p. 2). Negotiations under the Open-Ended Intergovernmental Working Group have thus far not resulted in a binding document but the UN's efforts to respond to the contemporary private military and security industry have acknowledged the existence of a regulatory problem around PMSCS and concerns about their position within current frameworks. Such perceptions of regulatory uncertainty informed the creation and approach of the Montreux Document.

[7] The Group's mandate tasked it with not only investigating mercenaries and mercenary use but also the changing nature of the industry. The Working Group thus examines PMSCs and was instrumental in preparing a draft international response to PMSCs.

[8] The Open-Ended Intergovernmental Working Group to consider the possibility of elaborating an international regulatory framework on the regulation, monitoring, and oversight of the activities of private military and security companies (IGWG). The IGWG's mandate is more narrowly focused than that of the Working Group. Rather than mercenarism and its impact, the IGWG looks to PMSCs and seeks to create a new international binding regulatory regime.

8.4 The Montreux Document

The Montreux Document, which was formally launched in 2008, forms part of a move to address concerns regarding the legal and regulatory frameworks in which the private military and security industry operates and is employed. The Document is underpinned by an effort to reaffirm the applicability of existing legal frameworks, including IHL, to states in their interactions with PMSCs. The result of a joint process between the ICRC and the Swiss government, the Document looks to provide PMSCs' home, territorial, and contracting states a restatement of their existing obligations under international law and presents a formulation of non-binding good practices for states in their relationships with PMSCs.

The Montreux Document looks to states and their different interactions with PMSCs, focusing on 'recalling State responsibility' with regard to their use of PMSCs (Swiss Confederation: FDFA and ICRC, 2008, p. 4). The Montreux Document's creators succeeded not only in arriving at a final Document but also in attracting state involvement. As of 2023, the Montreux Document has been signed by fifty-eight states and three international organisations[9] (Swiss Confederation: Federal Department of Foreign Affairs, 2016), demonstrating the reach of the Document's approach to PMSCs. In terms of explicit state engagement, the Document is therefore the 'most widely supported international instrument specifically concerning private security companies' (Ralby, 2015, p. 16). Indeed, Leander (2012, p. 108) suggests the Document is 'the most important interstate initiative pertaining to the use of force by commercial actors taken [since the 1989 UN Convention on mercenaries]'. This success may be as a consequence of the process' approach to the industry and its use. In contrast to the efforts of the UN Working Group and Intergovernmental Working Group, the Document process has not sought to develop new binding regulation. Rather, the Montreux

[9] State participants of the Montreux Document are Afghanistan, Albania, Angola, Australia, Austria, Belgium, Bosnia and Herzegovina, Bulgaria, Canada, Chile, China, Costa Rica, Croatia, Cyprus, Czech Republic, Denmark, Ecuador, Estonia, Finland, France, Georgia, Germany, Greece, Hungary, Iceland, Italy, Iraq, Ireland, Japan, Jordan, Kuwait, Liechtenstein, Lithuania, Luxembourg, Former Yugoslav Republic of Macedonia, Madagascar, Monaco, Netherlands, New Zealand, Norway, Poland, Portugal, Qatar, Sierra Leone, Slovenia, South Africa, Spain, Sweden, Switzerland, Uganda, United Kingdom, Ukraine, United States of America, and Uruguay.

The participating international organisations are the EU, the Organization for Security and Co-operation in Europe (OSCE), and NATO.

Document suggests existing frameworks are sufficient, something that may undermine the UN's attempts to create a binding framework.

The initial January 2006 Montreux drafting workshop was significant in part for being the 'first time governmental experts were brought together to discuss issues relating to PMCs/PSCs and respect for international humanitarian law and human rights' (Serger, 2006, p. 3). The Montreux drafting and consultation process between 2006 and 2008 engaged civil society actors and industry stakeholders. The process also involved not only large contracting states like the United States and United Kingdom but also states where the industry was particularly active, such as Afghanistan. The final Montreux Document was launched in September 2008 and finalised in November of that year.[10]

Following the Document's launch, the process shifted to its promotion and application (Swiss Confederation: FDFA and ICRC, 2008, p. 31). Regional consultations were held to 'promote and disseminate the Montreux Document' (Beerli, 2013), leading to the Montreux +5 process. Designed to ensure the Document's ongoing influence five years after its launch, Montreux +5 illuminated some of the perceived flaws and strengths of the Document, notably with regard to its implementation. According to a Geneva Centre for the Democratic Control of Armed Forces (DCAF) report released as part of Montreux +5, issues with the Document's implementation arose from a range of sources, including determining appropriate state and PMSC functions; the challenges of applying domestic legal frameworks to PMSCs that operate transnationally; and problems with both '[m]onitoring compliance' and addressing the '[g]aps in legal accountability and judicial liability' (Buckland and Burdzy, 2013, pp. 17–47). The report identified future directions for the Montreux process, including further engagement with PMSCs, the development of example contracts and laws, and a focus on training (Buckland and Burdzy, 2013, pp. 49–51).

Building on this and other similar reports, the Montreux +5 conference was held in December 2013; the Chair's Conclusions from the conference noted the Document is possibly 'both nothing new and all new at the same time!' (Avant, 2000 cited in FDFA, 2013, p. 1). In addition to concerns raised in the report noted above, the conference highlighted the Montreux Document's achievements in clarifying the specific legal obligations of states with regard to their engagement with

[10] For a thorough engagement with the drafting and development of the Montreux Document, see Cockayne (2009).

PMSCs active in conflict and noted the wider importance of the Document (Spoerri cited in ICRC, 2013). The Document was applauded for having successfully undermined '[t]he argument that these companies operate in a legal void' (Spoerri cited in ICRC, 2013), something seemingly achieved through a mere restatement of existing law. Despite these acknowledged successes, concerns remained as to the usefulness of the Document. The Montreux +5 conference found agreement on 'the need for greater efforts to ensure [the Document's] implementation, for personnel in the industry to undergo further training and for the industry to be made more accountable' with a focus beyond merely conflict situations (ICRC, 2013). As a result of concerns about oversight and accountability, the participating states and IOs at the conference agreed to 'step up their efforts' to hold PMSCs accountable for their actions (ICRC, 2013). Like the Document itself, however, the agreement was neither binding nor tied to a clear action plan.

The Montreux +5 conference revealed both aspirations for longer-term progress and concerns as to whether the Document's creation had accomplished any real change. At the conference, Document participants agreed to create the Montreux Document Forum (MDF), which is 'intended to strengthen the dialogue among participating states and international organisations' (Geneva Centre for the Democratic Control of Armed Forces, 2017).[11] The MDF was formally established in December 2014 (MDF, 2015), and it seeks to further 'the implementation of the Montreux Document', encourage state support, and act as a space 'to share good practices and discuss challenges regarding the regulation of PMSCs' (ICRC, 2014). Thus, although the Document was strictly finalised in 2008, those engaged with the process continue to further develop non-binding efforts, such as the MDF, to enhance state engagement with PMSCs within existing legal frameworks, including IHL.

8.5 The Montreux Document, PMSCs, and IHL

The Montreux Document, as noted above, was not an attempt to develop new binding regulation around states' interactions with PMSCs. It is also not the case that PMSCs, and the states that interact with them, require amendments to be made because they are somehow exempt from IHL.

[11] The Geneva Centre for the Democratic Control of Armed Forces (now the Geneva Centre for Security Sector Governance) hosts the Secretariat for the Montreux Document Forum.

The Document is founded on the assumption that existing international law is sufficient. What is curious, therefore, is the role and purpose of the Montreux Document with regard to IHL. The very creation of the Document emerged from societal perceptions that PMSCs and states were operating, or could operate, outside of the full reach of law. As discussed in other chapters of this volume, in some instances, there appears to be a disconnect between the ideals and realities of IHL, something seemingly manifest in the case of PMSCs. In light of this, the Document's insistence on international legal frameworks being adequate, and its reiteration of these principles, suggest that the issues that exist with PMSCs are not necessarily with the content of IHL, but rather with its application, enforcement, influence, and relevance.

At a drafting workshop, early in the Document process, Gillard (2006b, p. 1), then an ICRC legal advisor, characterised the ICRC's Montreux efforts as an attempt to dispel concerns that PMSCs, and the states they engage with, operate within a legal vacuum. Indeed, the Document's creation was a response to the potentially misguided discussion around PMSCs that 'systematically underestimate[d] the level of national and international regulation and the possibility of strengthening existing controls' (Krahmann, 2006, p. 1). From such a perspective, rather than a need to respond to PMSCs and address whatever 'gap' they occupy within international law, the law should be sufficient. The best response to PMSCs would therefore be to enforce and uphold current frameworks, rather than attempting the lengthy process of creating new international binding instruments. This legitimises the Montreux Document's efforts to enhance current legal frameworks, potentially at the expense of the UN's work towards a new convention.

The Montreux Document is nonetheless based on concerns about the position of PMSCs within international legal frameworks, regardless of whether or not those frameworks themselves are sufficient or are sufficiently upheld. Indeed, the ICRC itself noted that the Document was created because '[s]o far, PMSCs have largely been left without oversight by States and no specific international regulations are in place for them' (cited in Swiss Confederation: FDFA and ICRC, 2008, p. 38). The Montreux Document is the result of recognition by states and others that there is a need for a new response to the failure, or perceived failure, to adequately address PMSCs within legal frameworks.

In participating in the Montreux Document, states acknowledge the necessity of a renewed engagement with PMSCs, and for a coalescing and restatement of the states' own current legal obligations within the

Document. In the Document's approach, PMSCs are to be regulated rather than prohibited, noting the industry's distinction from mercenaries. Initial discussions during the creation of the Montreux Document addressed the widespread concerns that, owing to their fundamental differences, and the flaws in the existing frameworks, 'international law on mercenaries is largely inapplicable to the relatively new phenomenon of PMSCs' (Swiss Confederation: FDFA and ICRC, 2008, p. 38). The Document's foreword located its development as part of the response to the post-Cold War upheavals in the industry, which fundamentally altered the nature of private force. The size of the contemporary industry, coupled with the range of tasks they undertake, make PMSCs a 'wholly new phenomenon' (Seger and Spoerri cited in Swiss Confederation: FDFA and ICRC, 2008, p. 5). This framing of PMSCs as different to both PMCs and mercenaries underpins the importance of the Montreux Document as a new international approach to a new phenomenon. This approach also legitimises the Montreux Document's non-binding, state-centric nature, as PMSCs are conceptualised as a corporate phenomenon requiring regulation rather than prohibition. Nonetheless, the level of concern around the relevance of IHL, and of international law more broadly, led the Document's authors to affirm that PMSCs are not above legal consequences, and 'certain well-established rules and principles do clearly apply' (Swiss Confederation: FDFA and ICRC, 2008, p. 38). The Montreux Document thus promotes 'respect for international humanitarian law and human rights law whenever … [PMSCs] are present in armed conflicts' (ICRC, 2011).

Owing to the Document's approach to PMSCs as both non-mercenary actors and legitimate international corporate actors, the Document maintained a neutral position on PMSCs and the potential ethical quandaries of their use. '[W]ithout rejecting or welcoming the use of PMSCs' the Document does not constitute 'a bar for States who want to outlaw PMSCs' (Swiss Confederation: FDFA and ICRC, 2008, p. 41). Rather, the Swiss government noted the Document's importance as 'the first document of international significance to define how international law applies to the activities of private military companies' (Federal Department of Foreign Affairs, 2016). The Montreux process successfully debunked 'the prevailing misconception' that PMSCs are beyond the reach of international law (Swiss Confederation: FDFA and ICRC, 2008, p. 5). During the Document endorsement meeting in November 2008, several states 'hailed the Document as a step forward, and as a robust reaffirmation by diverse states of the applicability of human rights and IHL to PMSCs operating during situations of armed conflict' (Cockayne, 2009, p. 425). The aims of the Document are thus clear. The need for the Document's creation, however, is grounded on the failings, concerns, and, uncertainties in the existing system, something the Document, while reiterating the concerns, does little to actually advance.

The Montreux Document was designed to be an 'instrument that compiled all the pertinent legal obligations relevant to PMSCs' (Swiss Confederation: FDFA and ICRC, 2008, p. 41). More significantly, it was hoped the Document would act as a catalyst to encourage actors to engage with, and uphold, these obligations. While the legal coverage appeared to be 'normatively comprehensive', Droege (2006, p. 5) raised concerns that this legal regime 'is not implemented in practice'. The 2006 workshop noted that although the existing international and domestic legal frameworks already encompass much of their activity, there nonetheless remain challenges in 'ensur[ing] respect of the relevant international humanitarian law and human rights standards by all relevant actors as a matter of practice' (Serger, 2006, p. 1; see also Droege, 2006, p. 5). While the legal framework is robust, therefore, some uncertainty persists with regard to the relevance and enforcement of these rules.

The Document emerged as a response to wider uncertainty, whether warranted or not, about the legality of states' engagement with PMSCs and the importance of accountability and enforcement. At a November 2006 drafting workshop, participants noted the crucial regulatory responsibility of states, and the state duty to uphold human rights law and IHL (FDFA: Directorate of International Law, 2007, p. 3). The final Document 'reminds States of their obligations and offers them guidance on how PMSCs should sensibly be dealt with' (Swiss Confederation: FDFA and ICRC, 2008, p. 40), it 'does not affect existing obligations of States under customary international law or under international agreements to which they are parties' (Swiss Confederation: FDFA and ICRC, 2008, p. 9; UN, 2008, p. 5). The process recalled that final responsibility remains with states, and declined to attempt to create new regulations, which, in theory, allows states' behaviour to remain unchanged.

Beyond the legal framework, the Document is notable for the creation of a list of seventy-three 'Good Practices relating to Private Military and Security Companies', which sets the Montreux Document above a mere restatement of existing legal pronouncements to instead make a broader commentary on the use of the industry (Swiss Confederation: FDFA and ICRC, 2008, pp. 16–17; UN, 2008, pp. 12–26). The good practices are state-accepted guidelines that effectively form a voluntary code of conduct for states in their different types of engagement with PMSCs. The 'good practices' guide states as they 'ensur[e] respect for international humanitarian law and human rights law and otherwise promot[e] responsible conduct in their relationships with PMSCs operating in areas of armed conflict' (UN, 2008, p. 12).

The good practices, like the rest of the Document, place the responsibility for action, change, and good behaviour on states. The good practices are voluntary and seek to assist states rather than establish new binding responsibilities (Swiss Confederation: FDFA and ICRC, 2008, p. 17). The Document affirms, for example, that states should create their own mechanisms to 'ensure transparency and supervision in the selection and contracting of PMSCs' (Swiss Confederation: FDFA and ICRC, 2008, p. 16; UN, 2008, p. 13). Although they are non-binding, their initial acceptance by states confers a degree of legitimacy onto the good practices. If the good practices, and the Montreux Document as a whole, are to have further influence, however, this will depend on how states move forward, if they are willing and able to implement the proposals, and if this is translated into longer-term behavioural changes.

Conclusion

International humanitarian law binds contemporary PMSCs and the states with which they engage and the position of PMSCs' employees as civilians under IHL permits them certain legal protections in conflict. The changes to the private military and security industry with the wars in Iraq and Afghanistan not only increased the size and scope of the industry but also led to an uptick in concerns that the industry was somehow operating beyond the reach of international law, or that it constituted a threat to the nature of IHL as it exists. Despite these concerns, PMSCs and their employers do not exist in a state of lawlessness, nor do they challenge the foundations of IHL. Nonetheless, there are issues with regard to the applicability and enforcement of the ideals of IHL to the realities of states' engagement with PMSCs in times of conflict. As a consequence, regulatory efforts designed to reaffirm the applicability of IHL and other legal frameworks to PMSCs have emerged.

One of these responses, the Montreux Document, arose as a direct challenge to the uncertainties around states' use of PMSCs and their corresponding legal responsibilities. The Document instead asserts the applicability of law to states in their home, territorial, and contracting relationships with PMSCs. The existence of the Document demonstrates both international concerns with regard to the position of PMSCs within international legal frameworks, and the desire of states to respond to this uncertainty. The weaknesses of the Document, however, as well as the failures of states to engage with the UN process to create a new convention, demonstrate a lack of interest on the part of the international community to do take substantive or binding action with regard to new regulation of PMSCs.

The non-binding, voluntary approach taken in the Montreux process encouraged state participation and underpins the Document's successes. The Montreux Document relies on existing IHL and on states to uphold it. While the acceptance of the Document by states grants the Document legitimacy and reinforces states' acceptance of the current laws, the Document does little to ensure a change in state practice. The approach of the Montreux Document has not only failed to guarantee a behavioural shift on the part of states, it has also allowed states to justify disengagement with potentially binding international efforts to address PMSCs. The Montreux Document, therefore, while encouraging states to uphold and enforce IHL, stymies further attempts to improve international oversight of PMSCs and their use.

References

Adams, T. K. (2002). Private military companies: Mercenaries for the Twenty-first Century. *Small Wars & Insurgencies* 13(2), 54–67.

Avant, D. D. (2000). From mercenary to citizen armies: Explaining change in the practice of war. *International Organization* 54(1), 41–72.

(2004). Mercenaries. *Foreign Policy* 143, 20.

Beerli, C. (2013). Private military/security companies: Rules should be implemented. Montreux: International Committee of the Red Cross.

Best, G. (1983). *Humanity in Warfare: The Modern History of the International Law of Armed Conflicts*. London: Routledge.

Buckland, B. S., and Burdzy, A. M. (2013). *Progress and Opportunities, Five Years On: Challenges and Recommendations for Montreux Document Endorsing States*. Geneva: DCAF.

Cameron, L. (2006). Private military companies: Their status under international humanitarian law and its impact on their regulation. *International Review of the Red Cross* 88(863), 573–98.

Cockayne, J. (2009). Regulating private military companies: The content, negotiation, weaknesses and promise of the Montreux Document. *Journal of Conflict and Security Law* 13(3), 401–28.

Commission on Human Rights (1987). E/CN.4/RES/1987/16, The use of mercenaries as a means of impeding the exercise of the right of peoples to self-determination. New York: United Nations.

Congressional Budget Office (2008). Contractors' support of U.S. operations in Iraq. Washington, DC: Congress of the United States.

De Nevers, R. (2009). Private security contractors and the laws of war. *Security Dialogue* 40(2), 169–90.

Droege, C. (2006). Private military and security companies and human rights: A rough sketch of the legal framework. Workshop of Governmental Experts and Industry Representatives on Private Military/Security Companies Zurich: Swiss Confederation – Federal Department of Foreign Affairs: Directorate of International Law.

Federal Department of Foreign Affairs (2013). *Montreux + 5 Conference: Chairs' Conclusions – Geneva*, 13 December 2013. Geneva: Swiss Confederation.

Federal Department of Foreign Affairs (2016). *The Montreux Document*. Bern: Swiss Confederation.

Federal Department of Foreign Affairs: Directorate of International Law (2007). *Expert Meeting of Governmental and Other Experts on Private Military and Security Companies*, 13–14 November 2006, Montreux, Switzerland – Chair's Summary. Montreux: Swiss Confederation.

Geneva Centre for the Democratic Control of Armed Forces (2017). The Montreux Document. Geneva: DCAF.

Gillard, E. (2006a). Business goes to war: Private military/security companies and international humanitarian law. *International Review of the Red Cross* 38 (863), 525–72.

Gillard, E. (2006b). Private military/security companies: The status of their staff and their obligations under International Humanitarian Law and the responsibilities of states in relation to their operations. Workshop of Governmental Experts and Industry Representatives on Private Military/Security Companies Zurich: Swiss Confederation – Federal Department of Foreign Affairs: Directorate of International Law.

Gómez del Prado, J. L. (2008). *Private Military and Security Companies and Challenges to the UN Working Group on the Use of Mercenaries*. Madison, WI: Privatization of Security and Human Rights in the Americas.

(2011). Impact on human rights of a new non-state actor: Private military and security companies. *The Brown Journal of World Affairs* 18 (1), 151–69.

Henckaerts, J., and Doswald-Beck, L. (2005). *Customary International Humanitarian Law, Volume 1: Rules.* Cambridge: Cambridge University Press for the International Committee of the Red Cross.

House of Commons Hansard (2008). 'Iraq: Peacekeeping Operations'. Written Answers, Vol. 483, Session 2007–2008, 26 November 2008, Column 1552 W. London: Government of the United Kingdom.

Human Rights Council (2010). A/HRC/RES/15/26. Resolution adopted by the Human Rights Council. 15/26: Open-ended intergovernmental working group to consider the possibility of elaborating an international regulatory framework on the regulation, monitoring and oversight of the activities of private military and security companies. Geneva: United Nations General Assembly.

International Committee of the Red Cross (2011). The Montreux Document on private military and security companies. Geneva: ICRC.

International Committee of the Red Cross (2013). News Release – Switzerland: Conference highlights efforts to regulate private security companies. Geneva: ICRC.

International Committee of the Red Cross (2014). Private military and security companies: Implementation of Montreux Document. Geneva: ICRC.

International Committee of the Red Cross (2017). 'War and Law'. Geneva: International Committee of the Red Cross. Available at www.icrc.org/en/war-and-law.

Krahmann, E. (2006). Regional organizations: What role for the EU? Workshop of Governmental Experts and Industry Representatives on Private Military/Security Companies Zurich: Swiss Confederation – Federal Department of Foreign Affairs: Directorate of International Law.

Krahmann, E. (2012). From 'mercenaries' to 'private security contractors': The (re) construction of armed security providers in international legal discourses. *Millennium – Journal of International Studies* 40(2), 343–63.

Leander, A. (2012). What do codes of conduct do? Hybrid constitutionalization and militarization in military markets. *Global Constitutionalism* 1(1), 91–119.

Mockler, A. (1985). *The New Mercenaries: History of the Hired Soldier from the Congo to the Seychelles.* London: Sidgwick & Jackson.

Montreux Document Forum (2015). Montreux Document Forum: The Forum. Geneva: Geneva Centre for the Democratic Control of Armed Forces.

O'Brien, K. (2000). PMCs, myths and mercenaries: The debate on private military companies. *The RUSI Journal* 145(1), 59–64.

Office of the United Nations High Commissioner for Human Rights (2009). Mercenaries: UN experts focus on new international Convention. Geneva: United Nations.

Office of the United Nations High Commissioner for Human Rights (2010). Human Rights Council establishes Working Group on activities of Private Security Companies, renews mandate on Sudan and Somalia. Geneva: United Nations Human Rights.

Office of the United Nations High Commissioner for Human Rights (2017). Special Rapporteur on use of mercenaries as a means of impeding the exercise of the right of peoples to self-determination. Geneva: United Nations Human Rights.

Organisation of African Unity (1977). OAU Convention for the Elimination of Mercenarism in Africa, CM/817 (XXIX) Annex II Rev.1. Libreville: Organisation of African Unity.

Percy, S. V. (2007a). Mercenaries: strong norm, weak law. *International Organization* 61(2), 367–97.

Percy, S. V. (2007b). *Mercenaries: The History of a Norm in International Relations*. Oxford: Oxford University Press.

Ralby, I. (2015). Accountability for armed contractors. *Fletcher Security Review* 2 (1), 15–20.

Scheimer, M. (2009). Separating private military companies from illegal mercenaries in international law: Proposing an international Convention for legitimate military and security support that reflects customary international law. *American University International Law Review* 24, 609–46.

Schreier, F., and Caparini, M. (2005). *Privatising Security: Law, Practice and Governance of Private Military and Security Companies*, Occasional Paper No. 6. Geneva: Geneva Centre for the Democratic Control of Armed Forces.

Seagrave, S. (1981). *Soldiers of Fortune*. Alexandria, VA: Time-Life Books.

Serger, P. (2006). *Workshop of Governmental Experts and Industry Representatives on Private Military/Security Companies: Summary of the Chair*. Zurich: Swiss Confederation – Federal Department of Foreign Affairs: Directorate of International Law.

Shaw, R. (2016). Redefining private force: The private military and security industry and the construction of a new normative environment. PhD thesis, School of Political Science and International Studies, The University of Queensland.

Singer, P. W. (2008). *Corporate Warriors: The Rise of the Privatized Military Industry*, Updated ed. Ithaca, NY: Cornell University Press.

Spearin, C. (2008). Private, armed and humanitarian? States, NGOs, international private security companies and shifting humanitarianism. *Security Dialogue* 39(4), 363–82.

(2011). UN Peacekeeping and the international private military and security industry. *International Peacekeeping* 18(2), 196–209.

Swiss Confederation: FDFA (2016). Participating states of the Montreux Document. Bern.

Swiss Confederation: FDFA and International Committee of the Red Cross (2008). The Montreux Document: On pertinent international legal obligations and good practices for States related to operations of private military and security companies during armed conflict. Montreux: International Committee of the Red Cross.

Taljaard, R., and International Herald Tribune (2004). Private military companies: The danger of latter-day mercenaries. New York: New York Times.

United Nations (2008). A/63/467/-S/2008/636 Letter dated 2 October 2008 from the Permanent Representative of Switzerland to the United Nations addressed to the Secretary General & Annex to the letter: Montreux Document on pertinent international legal obligations of private military and security companies during armed conflict. New York: United Nations.

United Nations General Assembly (1989). A/RES/44/34. International Convention against the Recruitment, Use, Financing and Training of Mercenaries. New York: United Nations.

United Nations General Assembly (2010). A/65/325. Use of mercenaries as a means of violating human rights and impeding the exercise of the right of peoples to self-determination: Note by the Secretary-General. New York: United Nations.

Vaux, T., Seiple, C., Nakano, G., and Van Brabant, K. (2002). *Humanitarian Action and Private Security Companies: Opening the Debate.* London: International Alert.

9

Protecting Warfighters from Superfluous Injury and Unnecessary Suffering

RAIN LIIVOJA

> Let us never forget that our enemies are men. Though reduced to the disagreeable necessity of prosecuting our right by force of arms, let us not divest ourselves of that charity which connects us with all mankind. ... Let our valour preserve itself from every stain of cruelty, and the lustre of victory will not be tarnished by inhuman and brutal actions.
>
> (Vattel, 1834, p. 362)

Introduction

Who do the laws of war protect? 'Civilians' would probably be the most common answer. Undeniably, the contemporary law of armed conflict places an emphasis on the protection of civilians – both from direct attack and from the effects of hostilities more broadly. This focus requires little by way of explanation or justification: since the turn of the twentieth century, civilians have constituted the vast majority of victims of armed conflicts.[1]

Yet this preoccupation with civilians has hardly been a constant feature of the law. In fact, the 1949 *Geneva Convention IV* was the first multilateral treaty to be specifically devoted to the wartime protection of civilians. Moreover, it was only designed to safeguard a subgroup of civilians – namely those who find themselves in the hands of the enemy (*Convention (IV) relative to the Protection of Civilian Persons in Time of War*, art. 4). It was not until the adoption of the 1977 *Additional Protocols* that this regime was supplemented with a codification of rules for the protection of the civilian population at large.

[1] For a careful analysis of the shifting military-to-civilian death ratio, see Epps (2013, pp. 319–29).

Until World War II, the law of armed conflict focused on the protection of combatants who had been placed *hors de combat* – taken out of active hostilities through incapacitation or capture (Best, 1980, pp. 59–60). Thus, in the late nineteenth century – thanks in no small amount to the efforts of Henri Dunant and Florence Nightingale – the arch-victim of armed conflict was the wounded combatant. This explains the succession of treaties on the protection of the wounded, sick, and shipwrecked, starting with the 1864 *Geneva Convention*,[2] and paving the way for the adoption of the 1949 *Geneva Conventions I* and *II*. In the first half of the twentieth century, however, the quintessential victim of an armed conflict was the prisoner of war. Hence, the detailed treaty on the treatment of prisoners of war concluded in 1929 (*Convention Relative to the Treatment of Prisoners of War*) and its successor, the 1949 *Geneva Convention III*.

During all this time, however, the law also sought to limit violence that could be done to those directly participating in hostilities. These rules on the conduct of hostilities came to prohibit or restrict the use of certain instruments or tactics of warfare. These rules can be found in the 1899 and 1907 *Hague Regulations*, the 1977 *Additional Protocol I*, and a handful of weapon-specific treaties. Some of these rules aim to maintain a certain degree of civility between the warring parties by prohibiting deceptive misuses of uniforms and insignia, in particular various protective emblems, such as the red cross (*Hague Regulations*, art 23(f); *Additional Protocol I*, arts 37–39). Other rules seek to prohibit the use of means of warfare, weapons, and projectiles, which may be seen as unjustifiably barbarous (*Hague Regulations*, art 23(a), (e); *Additional Protocol I*, art 35).

The most fundamental of the rules in this latter group has been captured in Article 35(2) of *Additional Protocol I* in the following language: 'It is prohibited to employ weapons, projectiles and material and methods of warfare of a nature to cause superfluous injury or unnecessary suffering.' The fierce agreement about the foundational nature of this rule is only matched by the disagreement as to its precise meaning and efficacy. For one, it has occasionally been suggested that this

[2] See also *Hague Convention (III) for the Adaptation to Maritime Warfare of the Principles of the Geneva Convention of 22 August 1864* (1899); *Geneva Convention for the Amelioration of the Condition of the Wounded and Sick in Armies in the Field* (1906); *Hague Convention (X) for the Adaptation to Maritime War of the Principles of the Geneva Convention* (1907); *Convention for the Amelioration of the Condition of the Wounded and Sick in Armies in the Field* (1929).

'unnecessary suffering rule' also, or even primarily, protects civilians.[3] This is a misconception. The rule is solely concerned with the protection of combatants (*Nuclear Weapons Advisory Opinion*, 1996: Shahabuddeen J., p. 403; Higgins J., p. 585). Civilians are, in the context of the conduct of hostilities, protected by the principle of distinction (which prohibits the launching of attacks against them) and the principle of proportionality (which sets limits on collateral damage). Whether an attack launched against a civilian uses a particularly gruesome weapon is irrelevant because the attack is prohibited irrespective of the means used (*Nuclear Weapons Advisory Opinion*, 1996: Higgins J., p. 585, para. 12). The exclusive focus of the unnecessary suffering rule on the well-being of combatants arguably makes it 'exceptional' in the fabric of the law of armed conflict (Casey-Maslen and Haines, 2018, p. 208).

This paper considers the origins of the rule, and how key aspects of the rule are interpreted. It will then turn to one of the more contentious issues – namely whether the rule is only concerned with the inherent properties of particular weapons or whether it also deals with the use of weapons.

9.1 Genesis

The unnecessary suffering rule originates, in a form recognisable to the contemporary observer, in the mid-nineteenth century. It emerged as a result of advances in military technology. In the 1860s, several armed forces developed and adopted bullets that would explode on impact or immediately thereafter. Such bullets were first developed for use against hard targets (materiél) and later against soft targets (combatants) (Tate, DiMaio and Davis, 1981, pp. 636–37; Kalshoven, 2013, p. 35). This troubled Russia, which in 1868 convened a conference to consider regulating such bullets. Russia's motives remain the source of some contention: the ostensible reasons were humanitarian in that the bullets in question caused gruesome injuries (Jevglevskaja, 2015). However, Frits Kalshoven (2013, p. 35) suggested that '[f]ear for the morale of own armed forces probably was at the root of the initiative', and others have

[3] See, for example, India (1978), p. 284, para. 5: talking about prohibiting weapons 'in order to avoid unnecessary suffering to civilians and combatants'; Bill for a Depleted Uranium Munitions Study Act 2005: proposing that Congress find that 'it would be a violation of [Additional Protocol I] to cause superfluous injury or unnecessary suffering to civilians'.

claimed that the bullets were 'an unreliable and already obsolete weapon at the time' (af Jochnick and Normand, 1994, pp. 66–67).

In any event, the conference adopted a treaty that prohibited the wartime use of 'any projectile of less weight than four hundred grammes, which is explosive, or is charged with fulminating or inflammable substances' ('*St Petersburg Declaration*'). The weight limit was arbitrary but intended to draw a line between two categories of projectiles: rifle bullets, which remained well below the weight limit, and artillery shells, which were much heavier (Kalshoven, 1985, p. 207; Granat, 1993, p. 153). The idea was to ban explosive rifle bullets as anti-personnel projectiles. Hans Blix (1988, p. 139) put the rationale of the prohibition as follows:

> [I]f explosive or inflammable projectiles were to be effective against objects such as buildings, they would have to weigh more than 400 grammes. If they weighed less they would be effective only against human beings but would then cause injury in excess of what was necessary to disable and thereby 'uselessly aggravate' suffering.

The 400-gram weight limit has since become obsolete (UK Ministry of Defence, 2004, para. 6.10.2; Danish Ministry of Defence, 2016, p. 351). Lightweight explosive projectiles of the sort covered by the *St Petersburg Declaration* were widely used by all sides against aircraft in World War II (Spaight, 1947, p. 213). Consequently, the express prohibition contained in the Declaration has arguably lost its legal effect (Blix, 1988, p. 139) and has transformed into a prohibition of explosive anti-personnel rounds. Indeed, multiple contemporary military manuals proscribe the use of explosive bullets specifically designed for an anti-personnel use.[4] Furthermore, the United States did not become a party to the *St Petersburg Declaration* and does not consider its stipulations to form part of customary international law (US Department of Defense, 2016, p. 347, para. 6.5.4.3). In the view of the United States, exploding anti-personnel rounds are prohibited only if they conflict with the unnecessary suffering rule (US Department of Defense, 2016, p. 346, para. 6.5.4.3).

Whatever the current scope and significance of the prohibition contained in the *St Petersburg Declaration*, that is not the instrument's main

[4] See, for example, UK Ministry of Defence (2004, para. 6.10); Danish Ministry of Defence (2016, p. 351); New Zealand Defence Force (2017, paras. 7.6.1 and 7.6.2); but see Australian Defence Force (2006, para. 4.10) (faithfully referring to the 400-gram limit); German Federal Ministry of Defence (2013, para. 438) (focusing on anti-personnel use if the weight is considerably under 400 grams).

contribution to the law of armed conflict. The rationale for the prohibition, as it appears in the preamble of the Declaration, has far broader significance (de Preux, 1987, p. 401; see also Crawford, 2019, pp. 544–66). The *Declaration*'s preamble states, in relevant part, that the only legitimate object of hostilities is to 'weaken the military forces of the enemy'; that, to this end, it is 'sufficient to disable the greatest possible number of men'; and, crucially, that 'this object would be exceeded by the employment of arms which uselessly aggravate the sufferings of disabled men, or render their death inevitable'. All of this is premised on the idea that 'the progress of civilization should have the effect of alleviating as much as possible the calamities of war'. In short, the drafters of the *St Petersburg Declaration* thought it uncivilised – perhaps barbarous – to use weapons that would inflict on combatants harm unjustified by military exigence.

Even though, as noted, the United States did not sign the *Declaration*, similar sentiments prevailed there at the time. In 1863, President Abraham Lincoln approved instructions for the Union Forces concerning the laws and customs of war (US War Department, 1863). The document has become commonly known as the Lieber Code, after its principal drafter, Francis Lieber. While the Code decried many practices of warfare as barbarous (US War Department, 1863, arts. 24, 27, 56, 148), it set very few hard limits to what could be done in war. Instead, much of the code revolved around the notion of military necessity. John Fabian Witt argues that, under the Code, '[v]irtually any use of force was permissible if required by military necessity' and that '[i]n Lieber's hands, military necessity was both a broad limit on war's violence and a robust license to destroy' (Witt, 2012, p. 234). But a restriction on suffering almost inexorably derived from the idea of military necessity. Indeed, the Code expressly stipulated that '[m]ilitary necessity does not admit of cruelty – that is, the infliction of suffering for the sake of suffering' (US War Department, 1863, art. 16). As the epigraph to this chapter testifies, Emer de Vattel's thinking some hundred years earlier was very much along the same lines. While Lieber had little time for the detailed rules Vattel had developed – which he thought inappropriately sought to disconnect the conduct of warfare from the military ends pursued (Witt, 2012, pp. 182, 218) – Lieber and Vattel ultimately agreed on a military necessity restriction on the suffering of combatants.

The reasoning behind the *St Petersburg Declaration* subsequently morphed into a freestanding rule prohibiting the use of weapons causing superfluous injury or unnecessary suffering (*cf* de Preux, 1987, p. 402, para. 1415). This rule made its first appearance in the 1874 *Brussels Declaration* (art. 13(e)), a document that was intended to become a treaty but never entered into force. The same rule was then included essentially verbatim and without much discussion in the *Hague Regulations* (art. 23 (e)), attached to the 1899 and 1907 *Hague Conventions on Land Warfare*, and subsequently reiterated in the 1977 *Additional Protocol I* in the form cited earlier. Breaches of the rule were expressly criminalised under the 1998 *Rome Statute of the International Criminal Court* (art. 8(2)(b)(xx)). There is broad agreement that some version of the unnecessary suffering rule forms part of customary international law and thus binds states that are not party to the *Hague Conventions* or *Additional Protocol I* (*US et al. v. Göring et al.*, 1946, pp. 253–54; Haines, 2001, pp. 263–64; ICRC, 2005, rule 70; Turns, 2006, p. 211). There is also no doubt that the unnecessary suffering rule applies equally in international and non-international armed conflicts (International Institute of Humanitarian Law, 1990, para. A(3); International Institute of Humanitarian Law, 2006, rule 1.2.3; Boothby, 2016, p. 67).

The development of the rule has been plagued by linguistic difficulties, which has led to conceptual uncertainties and interpretive ambiguities. French is the only authentic language of the *Brussels Declaration* and both iterations of the *Hague Regulations*. With admirable consistency, these instruments sought to prohibit the use of arms, projectiles, or material '*propres à causer des maux superflus*'.[5] This was translated into English in several ways. The translation of the *Brussels Declaration* (art. 13(e)) referred to the use of arms 'which may cause unnecessary suffering'. The translation of the *1899 Hague Regulations* (art. 23(e)) used the phrase 'of a nature to cause superfluous injury'. One version of the translation of the 1907 *Regulations* (art. 23(e)) used the words 'of such a nature as to cause unnecessary pain'[6] and several others 'calculated to cause unnecessary suffering'.[7]

Additional Protocol I employs the phrase 'of a nature to cause superfluous injury or unnecessary suffering' ('*de nature à causer des maux superflus*'). Blix (1988, p. 138) hoped that this would 'straighten out some

[5] The 1880 Oxford Manual, a non-legally binding document drafted by the International Law Institute, is something of an aberration. It seeks to prohibit (art. 9(a)), the use of arms, projectiles, and material '*propres à causer des souffrances superflues ou à aggraver les blessures*' ('of a nature to cause superfluous suffering, or to aggravate wounds').

[6] 1907 Hague Regulations, 2 AJIL Supp. 90.

[7] 1907 Hague Regulations, Cd 5030, 36 Stat. 2277, 1 Bevans 631.

interpretive tangles' that resulted from the inconsistent English translation of the *Hague Regulations*. These hopes have not been fulfilled entirely, as a number of states (notably the United States) remain unbound by *Additional Protocol I* and refer to customary international law and the *Hague Regulations* as a codification of custom.

9.2 Elements

To examine the meaning of the unnecessary suffering rule, it is best to address its elements separately: the type of harm contemplated (injury and suffering), the threshold that the harm must reach in order to attract the prohibition (superfluity or unnecessariness), and the question of what leads to the harm (either calculation or the nature of the weapon).

9.2.1 'Injury' and 'Suffering'

The French word '*maux*', which can be found in all formulations of the unnecessary suffering rule, has been translated into English as both injury and suffering. These two words have, however, different meanings:

> 'Injury' describes identifiable wounds or other physical harm to limbs, organs, senses or other parts of the body, including through burns. ... In contrast, 'suffering' denotes primarily pain, but also extends to comprehend severe psychological distress.
>
> (Casey-Maslen and Haines, 2018, p. 211)

At the same time, '*maux*' is a broad notion that can cover both 'injury' and 'suffering' in the senses just mentioned (de Preux, 1987, p. 408, para. 1429; Dörmann, Doswald-Beck and Kolb, 2003, p. 303, fn. 20).

Suffering has considerable individual variation and is difficult if not downright impossible to quantify or assess objectively (Blix, 1988, p. 138; Scott, 1989, pp. 274, 277–78). This led a group of medical experts to propose during the drafting of *Additional Protocol I* that focusing on the wound or injury offered a better way of defining the effects of a weapon and that the term 'injury' should therefore be substituted for 'suffering' in legal discussions (ICRC, 1976, p. 140; Scott, 1989, p. 277). Many legal experts argued, however, that the more subjective concept of suffering 'had come to be accepted in its own right' and that it would be 'unthinkable ... to remove the subjective element contained in the word "suffering" from the body of international law' (ICRC, 1974, p. 8, para. 21). As one commentator has aptly noted, 'in seeking to protect humanity, it is "suffering", and not just injury, that one is trying to reduce' (Granat, 1993, p. 161).

To avoid doubt as to the accuracy of a broad conception of '*maux*', *Additional Protocol I* refers to both injury and suffering, as do a number of weapon-specific treaties (Blix, 1988, p. 138). There is broad consensus that the unnecessary suffering rule covers both objective injury and subjective suffering (de Preux, 1987, p. 407, para. 1426; Boothby, 2016, pp. 58–59; Dinstein, 2016, p. 74, para. 195). Sandesh Sivakumaran (2012, p. 388) further notes that '[t]oday, with greater understanding of psychiatric injury, this too should be covered'. This does not seem controversial. But he also goes on to say that 'psychological harm would not suffice' (Sivakumaran, 2012, p. 388). On this point, however, Christopher Greenwood (1998, p. 196) argues more persuasively that 'the concept of "injury" or "suffering" includes the totality of a victim's injury, and . . . a distinction between physical and psychological injuries would be artificial, as well as having no basis in past practice concerning weaponry'.

Finally, one commentator has argued that the term '*maux*' 'may be applied to damage caused to physical objects', specifically 'material physical objectives' (Meyrowitz, 1994, pp. 105, 110). This reading, though it might be textually plausible, is inconsistent with the drafting history of all the legal instruments containing the unnecessary suffering rule. The concern has invariably been for human suffering. I have not been able to find any support in the practice of states, academic writings, or judicial practice for the proposition that the superfluous injury rule deals with excessive damage to physical objects.

9.2.2 'Superfluous' and 'Unnecessary'

Injury and suffering can be inflicted by any weapon. The unnecessary suffering rule therefore cannot be seen as prohibiting all weapons causing injury or suffering. Only weapons causing injury and suffering beyond a certain threshold are captured by the rule. But difficulties arise from how that threshold is established.

Despite the well-intentioned attempt of the International Committee of the Red Cross (ICRC) to establish a common threshold for all weapons with reference to the kind of suffering and injury they cause (see Coupland, 1999), the law does not set an absolute or abstract bar to injury or suffering. There is broad agreement that a weapon is not unlawful simply because it is highly destructive, or because it causes severe injury, great suffering, or many casualties (*Nuclear Weapons*, 1996: Higgins J., pp. 586–87, para. 17; Greenwood, 1998, p. 184; Boothby, 2016, p. 63; US Department of Defense, 2016, pp. 359–60, para. 6.6.3; New Zealand Defence Force, 2017, para. 7.2.8). From a textual perspective, the notions 'unnecessary' and 'superfluous' are both 'comparative, not absolute, concepts' (Boothby, 2016, p. 62). The use of the word 'superfluous' in particular suggests that injury or suffering must be excessive in relation to something.

As the International Court of Justice succinctly put it in *Nuclear Weapons* (1996, p. 35, para. 78), superfluous injury and unnecessary suffering refer to 'a harm greater than that unavoidable to achieve legitimate military objectives'. The unnecessary suffering rule therefore requires 'some sort of equation between' (ICRC, 1974, p. 9, para. 24), or the weighing up (de Preux, 1987, p. 408, para. 1248), or balancing of (*Nuclear Weapons*, 1996: Shahabuddeen J., p. 402; Higgins J., p. 586; Parks, 1997, p. 18; Greenwood, 1998, p. 195; Casey-Maslen and Haines, 2018, pp. 211–12), the humanitarian and military effects or consequences of the use of the weapon.

The humanitarian considerations encompass the effect of the weapon on the combatant in battle, in other words, the injury or suffering caused by the weapons in the sense discussed earlier. The degree of injury and suffering would be assessed on the basis of such factors as mortality rates, the painfulness or severity of wounds, and the ease with which they may be treated, and the incidence of permanent damage or disfigurement (ICRC, 1974, p. 8, para. 23; Bothe, Partsch and Solf, 1982, para. 2.3.3; Blix, 1988, p. 138).

The military considerations have been variously described as covering the 'military task' (UK Ministry of Defence, 2004, para. 6.2.1) that the weapon is required to perform or the 'military advantage' (*Nuclear Weapons*, 1996: Shahabuddeen J., p. 402; Greenwood, 1998, p. 195; Casey-Maslen and Haines, 2018, pp. 211–12) sought to be achieved by its use. It has occasionally been suggested that rendering an adversary *hors de combat* would be the appropriate military advantage against which injury should be assessed (ICRC, 1974, p. 9, para. 25; de Preux, 1987, p. 403, para. 1417). However, the purpose of many weapons is not (only) to incapacitate personnel but to destroy military objects. The better view therefore seems to be that the element of military necessity in the choice of weapons also includes 'the destruction or neutralization of enemy matériel, restriction of movement, interdiction of lines of communication, weakening of resources and . . . enhancement of the security of friendly forces' (ICRC, 1974, p. 9, para. 25; Sivakumaran, 2012, p. 388; US Department of Defense, 2016, pp. 360–61, para. 6.6.3.1).

For the weapon to be unlawful under the unnecessary suffering rule, there must be some mismatch or imbalance between the humanitarian and military considerations. The law plainly tolerates a greater degree of injury and suffering when it comes to weapons that yield a greater military advantage (Greenwood, 1997, p. 446). As the District Court of Tokyo conceded in *Shimoda v. Japan* (1963, p. 634) when considering the use of nuclear weapons against Hiroshima and Nagasaki, 'the use of a certain weapon, great as its inhuman result may be, need not be prohibited by international law if it has a great military effect'.

The precise test or formulation for the imbalance has been articulated in different ways, even though there does not seem to be any substantive disagreement between these approaches. Some have restated the test as one of excessiveness. So, for example, Judge Shahabuddeen explained in *Nuclear Weapons* (1996, p. 402) that 'suffering is superfluous or unnecessary if it is materially in excess of the degree of suffering which is justified by the military advantage sought to be achieved'.[8] Others have focused on what is militarily required or what falls within military necessity. For example, the UK manual (UK Ministry of Defence, 2004, para. 6.2) speaks of 'injury or suffering greater than that required for the [weapon's] military purpose'.[9]

Most commonly, however, the superfluous injury test is expressed in terms of the injury or suffering caused being 'disproportionate' in relation to the military advantage anticipated (Spaight, 1911, p. 75; Fenrick, 1990, p. 500; UK Ministry of Defence, 2004, para. 6.2.1). Several military manuals and many commentators go on to further tighten this test of proportionality. They say that a weapon breaches the unnecessary suffering rule where the disproportion between humanitarian and military considerations is 'clear' or 'manifest' (Solf, 2013, p. 226, para. 2.3.3; US Department of Defense, 2016, p. 362, para. 6.6.3; Danish Ministry of Defence, 2016, p. 339; Boothby and von Heinegg, 2018, p. 165).

The notion of proportionality can create some confusion in this context because this concept is most commonly used in the law of armed conflict when considering whether incidental harms to civilians (in other

[8] cf. Greenwood (1997, p. 446); Australian Defence Force (2006), para. 2.7.

[9] cf. Australian Defence Force (2006), para. 2.7; German Federal Ministry of Defence (2013), para. 402; New Zealand Defence Force (2017), para. 7.2.9.

words, 'collateral damage') caused by an attack is excessive in relation to the military advantage anticipated.[10] Waldemar Solf (2013, p. 225, para. 2.3.1) went as far as suggesting that the unnecessary suffering rule is 'another way of stating the rule of proportionality defined in the context of the protection of the civilian population'.[11] That must be a misunderstanding: the unnecessary suffering rule that protects combatants and the proportionality rule that protects civilians are two entirely different norms (Meyrowitz, 1994, p. 109; Dinstein, 2016, p. 75, para. 198), even though both involve the weighing of humanitarian and military considerations.

Henri Meyrowitz (1994, p. 110) argued that the unnecessary suffering rule 'absolutely prohibits any recourse to [a] means or method' that is of a nature to cause superfluous injury or unnecessary suffering and 'hence excludes any evaluation of the proportional relationship between the suffering, injury or damage that would be caused if it were used and "the concrete and direct military advantage" that might be "anticipated"'. This view is correct only in so far as a weapon prohibited by the unnecessary suffering rule cannot be used even if it were to offer a concrete and direct military advantage under the circumstances. In other words, once the balancing of humanitarian and military considerations has led to the weapon being banned, this ban cannot be overcome by relying on some specific circumstances prevailing at the time of the attack. But none of these concerns explain why proportionality between the humanitarian and military consequences, as applied to the weapon in the abstract, would be inappropriate in the application of the unnecessary suffering rule.

Sivakumaran (2012, p. 389) has also expressed doubts about references to proportionality but for an altogether different reason. He suggests that the balance between humanitarian and military considerations 'can be upset' without the injury or suffering being disproportionate. In other words, he implies that something less than disproportionate injury or suffering could contradict the rule. While this is conceptually a cogent argument, it is not borne out by state practice. If anything, statements of States referring to 'clear' or 'manifest' disproportion suggest that an imbalance lower than an outright disproportion would not suffice to render a weapon unlawful.

[10] Even though *Additional Protocol I*, art. 51(5)(b), does not use the term 'proportionality'.
[11] Referring specifically to *Additional Protocol I*, arts. 51(5)(b) and 57(2)(a)(iii).

9.2.3 'Calculated' or 'of a Nature'

In order for a weapon to be prohibited under the unnecessary suffering rule, it is not sufficient that the weapon is capable of causing superfluous injury or unnecessary suffering. All weapons can be misused somehow, and many weapons can be misused in a manner that results in superfluous injury or unnecessary suffering to a particular person under particular circumstances. The potential for misuse cannot itself lead to a weapon being prohibited, as this would lead to the prohibition of all weapons.

The circumstances under which the weapon causing superfluous injury or unnecessary suffering contravenes the rule give rise to some controversy. Part of the disagreement can be traced back to the linguistic issues mentioned earlier. Depending on which (inauthentic) English translation of the *Hague Regulations* one consults, the original unnecessary suffering rule addresses weapons 'calculated' or 'of a nature' to cause superfluous injury or unnecessary suffering. The difference between the two approaches is that where a weapon is 'calculated' to cause certain kinds of injury, the critical factor appears to be the intention of the designer, whereas the 'of a nature' standard makes the test more dependent on the actual effects of the weapon (Dinniss and Kleffner, 2016, p. 440). In other words, the 'of a nature' test is more objective than the 'calculated' test (Blix, 1988, p. 138; Roberts and Guelff, 2000, p. 77; Dinstein, 2016, p. 74, para. 195).

The view prevails in the United States that 'calculated' is the appropriate test. Notably, this formulation was adopted in 1956 US Army *Manual on Land Warfare* (para. 34). Several US commentators then considered this phrase to be a more accurate translation of the French original (Baxter, 1977, p. 43) and a clearer expression of the intent of governments (Parks, 2005, p. 87, fn. 123). These sentiments were further reflected in the US submissions in the *Nuclear Weapons* proceedings before the International Court of Justice (ICJ) (10 November 1995), and more recently endorsed and adopted in the 2016 US *Law of War Manual* (2016, p. 358, para. 6.6.1). The latter manual helpfully explains the meaning of 'calculated' by suggesting that the rule 'prohibits weapons that are *designed to* increase the injury or suffering of the persons attacked beyond that justified by military necessity' (US Department of Defense, 2016, p. 359, para. 6.6.2, emphasis added).

The US view is distinctly a minority one. It has been rejected by most commentators, who have argued that 'calculated' is a mistranslation of the original French phrase and that the intent of the designer is irrelevant for assessing the lawfulness of the weapon (ICRC, 1974, p. 8, para. 22; Blix, 1988, p. 138; Granat, 1993, p. 162; Dörmann, Doswald-Beck and Kolb, 2003, p. 303, fn. 21; Casey-Maslen and Haines, 2018, pp. 201–11). In the lead-up to the adoption of *Additional Protocol I*, the competing interpretations were considered. During the Lucerne conference, several experts took the view that 'to the extent that the English text might be construed as more restrictive than the French, the latter should prevail' (ICRC, 1974, p. 8, para. 22). Also, '[t]he Conference certainly considered that the expression "calculated to cause" ... was not appropriate' (de Preux, 1987, pp. 406–7, para. 1426). As already noted, *Additional Protocol I* resolved the matter by referring in the authentic English text to weapons, projectiles and material and methods of warfare 'of a nature to cause superfluous injury or unnecessary suffering' and updating the French text to '*de nature à causer des maux superflus*'. It is therefore hardly surprising that the 'of a nature' test has been widely adopted in the military manuals of states that are party to *Additional Protocol I*.[12]

However, the United States is not a party to *Additional Protocol I*, so the content of the rule in customary law does matter. In this respect, it is significant that the *Convention on Certain Conventional Weapons*, to which the United States is a party, speaks in its preamble of 'the principle that prohibits ... weapons ... of a nature to cause superfluous injury or unnecessary suffering'. Thus, the 'of a nature' standard has been adopted outside the context of *Additional Protocol I*, lending support to its customary status.

The broad agreement that 'of a nature' is the appropriate standard does not entirely resolve the problem at hand. What exactly does it mean for a weapon to have a particular 'nature'? There appear to be two approaches to answering this question.[13] According to one, a weapon is 'of a nature' to cause superfluous injury or unnecessary suffering if it inevitably or invariably causes such suffering or injury (ICRC, 1974, pp. 7–11; Boothby, 2016, p. 58; Boothby and von Heinegg, 2018, p. 165). Thus, a weapon that is at least capable of being used without causing superfluous injury or unnecessary suffering remains unaffected by the rule and is lawful. The other approach looks at whether the normal, intended or expected use causes such injury or suffering (Boothby, 2016, p. 62; Dinniss, 2018, pp. 239–40). A weapon is

[12] See, for example, Danish Ministry of Defence (2016, p. 70); German Federal Ministry of Defence (2013, para. 401); New Zealand Defence Force (2017, para. 7.3.2(a)).

[13] These were already identifiable in ICRC (1974, pp. 9–10, para. 28).

prohibited when, if used as envisaged, it causes superfluous injury or unnecessary suffering, even though there may be (remote) instances where that is not the case. Which of these approaches enjoys general support remains difficult to tell, particularly as some commentators rely on both (Boothby, 2016, chap. 5).

9.3 Application

If a weapon is of a nature to cause superfluous injury or unnecessary suffering, its use in armed conflict is prohibited by Article 35(2) of *Additional Protocol I* and customary international law. The prohibition applies in all circumstances and irrespective of the way in which the weapon is used. Importantly, if one accepts that it is the normal, intended, or expected use that provides the benchmark for assessing superfluous injury or unnecessary suffering, this means that the weapon is prohibited even in exceptional circumstances where superfluous injury or unnecessary suffering could be avoided. In other words, assuming the correctness of the normal use test, no hypothetical use scenario is capable of rendering an otherwise unlawful weapon into a lawful one.

Consider, for example, the 7.62 × 51 mm NATO round, which is one of the most commonly used ammunition for sniper rifles, available from a number of manufacturers. A Danish study from the early 1990s suggested that the European version of these rounds had the tendency to fragment in the human body (Knudsen and Theilade, 1993). The authors of the study were concerned that these rounds would not comply with the 1899 *Hague Declaration*, which prohibits bullets that 'easily flatten' in the human body (Knudsen and Theilade, 1993, pp. 66–67). This concern was not fully justified, considering that the flattening of a bullet – in particular the 'mushrooming' typical of hollow point bullets – is quite distinct from fragmentation. However, the authors' concern could be plausibly recast as doubts about compliance with the unnecessary suffering rule. This is particularly so, given that versions of the same round were available at the time from other manufacturers that did not fragment on normal use (Knudsen et al., 1995). If, on the available ballistic evidence and considering the purpose of the rounds, the fragmentation caused superfluous injury or unnecessary suffering, that particular round would have been unlawful even if the risk of fragmentation could have been reduced, say, at great distances.

What is much less clear is whether the unnecessary suffering rule only prohibits the use of certain categories of weapons, or whether it also restricts the use of otherwise lawful weapons. In other words, the question is whether the rule restricts the use of a weapon that does not normally cause superfluous injury or unnecessary suffering but is used in a way or under circumstances where superfluous injury or unnecessary suffering is intended or at least anticipated.

One school of thought remains sceptical of attempts to relax the design-dependent focus of the rule. Also, several military manuals treat the unnecessary suffering rule purely in the context of weapons. Boothby (2016, p. 68) is critical of the suggestion, contained in the ICRC's customary international humanitarian law study, that the customary rule is capable of prohibiting weapons 'if used in certain or all contexts'. His approach seems to be based on the idea that the unnecessary suffering rule is specifically a rule of 'weapons law', rather than of the law of armed conflict more broadly. This view is in turn premised on the notion that 'weapons law' constitutes a discrete body of international law and that its principles are distinct from those of the law of armed conflict as a whole. This line of reasoning is problematic, considering how the general law of armed conflict principles concerning weaponry have been integrated into law of armed conflict instruments.

Consider further the example of the 7.62 × 51 mm NATO round. Non-fragmenting, non-exploding, and non-flattening versions of that round are legally unobjectionable and have been authorised for use, consistently with international law, in many armed forces. Imagine, however, those rounds being used by a particularly sadistic sniper, who develops the habit of targeting the adversary's genitalia with a view to maximising pain and inflicting adverse psychological effects that can result from genital trauma (see e.g. Frappell-Cooke, Wink and Wood, 2013). A strong argument could be made that such actions cause superfluous injury or unnecessary suffering but that this would not result from the nature of the projectile but rather its use.

Superfluous injury rule appears to be the only rule of the law of armed conflict that could conceivably prohibit the conduct of hostilities in a manner just described against combatants or other persons taking a direct part in hostilities. (As mentioned earlier, any targeting of civilians or other protected persons would be prohibited outright, so the means and effect of targeting would have no significance.) There are two ways in which the use of a weapon, in addition to the design of the weapon, could be captured by the unnecessary suffering rule.

For one, the rule itself appears to have evolved specifically to cover particular uses. In the *Brussels Declaration* and the *Hague Regulations*, the rule was plainly concerned with 'arms, projectiles and material'. *Additional Protocol I* adds 'methods'. Even on the most conservative reading, the term 'methods' incorporates ways in which weapons are used.[14] Thus, using a lawful weapon in a manner that is 'of a nature' to cause superfluous injury or unnecessary suffering is prohibited under *Additional Protocol I*. This reading can be confirmed by reference to military manuals of states party to *Additional Protocol I*. For example, the New Zealand manual (2017, para. 7.3.1) stipulates that members of the New Zealand Defence Force are not to 'use any weapon or munition in a method other than as they have been trained with the intention of causing superfluous injury or unnecessary suffering'.

The other way, potentially also open under customary law, would involve reading the unnecessary suffering rule as a prohibition on the (intentional) infliction of superfluous injury or unnecessary suffering rather than merely the prohibition on the use of superfluously injurious weapons. Significantly, in *Nuclear Weapons* (1996, para. 78), the ICJ identified the prohibition to 'cause unnecessary suffering to combatants' as one of the 'cardinal principles' of the law of armed conflict. In a similar vein, the Danish manual (2016, p. 338) refers to the 'prohibition on superfluous injury or unnecessary suffering'.

Either way, several commentators agree that using a lawful weapon to cause superfluous injury is prohibited. For example, Sir Christopher Greenwood (1998, p. 194) has argued that:

> where a particular weapon has a legitimate use but is also capable of being used in a way which will, in the circumstances, cause unnecessary suffering . . ., the principle prohibits the latter use (or method of warfare) even though it does not give rise to an outright ban on the weapon itself.

In a similar vein, Steven Haines (2001, pp. 264–65) has noted:

> There are many weapons that are lawful in relation to their normal anticipated use but which are open to alternative uses that are capable of producing superfluous injury and unnecessary suffering. . . . If, by using a weapon in a particular way, one knows that superfluous injury or unnecessary suffering will result, that use would breach the norm.

Greenwood (1998, p. 199) even suggested that 'the unnecessary suffering principle has generally been more important in prohibiting particular

[14] For a discussion of the different understandings of 'methods', see, for example, Liivoja and Chircop (2018, pp. 181–83).

uses of weapons (i.e., methods of warfare) than the weapons themselves'. This rings true, given that there is relatively little agreement about which weapons may have been completely outlawed by the operation of the unnecessary suffering rule.

The application of the rule to the manner in which weapons are used has additional significance in circumstances where the capacity of warfighters to sustain injury or to suffer has been altered by means of biomedical interventions. Such interventions could be of two kinds. On the one hand, there are so-called left-of-bang interventions that are designed to make warfighters more resilient and to reduce morbidity and mortality in case of trauma (Eisenstein et al., 2016). For example, tranexamic acid could be administered ahead of high-risk operations to prevent excessive blood loss in the event the warfighter sustains a traumatic injury (Eisenstein et al., 2016). Such interventions could therefore reduce the humanitarian harm that goes into the superfluous injury and unnecessary suffering calculus. On the other hand, interventions could be designed to increase human capacity in some respect beyond what is normal in the human population. Such interventions might inadvertently increase injury and suffering. For example, a hypothetical intervention to improve hearing might render warfighters more susceptible to suffering if sonic weapons are used by the adversary.

Taking such factors into consideration only when it comes to assessing the nature of the weapon would lead to consequences that are problematic from a policy perspective. For example, a higher calibre projectile, or one with an increased yawing effect, might be required to render an enhanced warfighter *hors de combat*. If that becomes the intended normal use of the projectile, then whether the weapon is of a nature to cause superfluous injury or unnecessary suffering would have to be assessed in light of that use. If the weapon passes that test, its use would also become lawful against adversary warfighters who are known not to be enhanced and thus likely to suffer excessively from the use of the projectile. Conversely, a sonic weapon that is deemed to be lawful when used against unenhanced troops as their normal use could lawfully be used against a hearing enhanced adversary even where it is known that superfluous injury would result.

Therefore, a better reading of the rule would indeed consider the uses of weapons. The use of a weapon with the knowledge that it would cause superfluous injury or unnecessary suffering in the circumstances ought to be regarded as prohibited by the rule.

Conclusion

The unnecessary suffering rule is a key norm of the law of armed conflict. It has the important role of providing a modicum of protection to able-bodied warfighters who are otherwise not high on the protection agenda of the law of armed conflict. Despite the long history of the rule – or perhaps because of the complexity of that history – one encounters a number of interpretive difficulties when applying the rule. Additional challenges arise as a result of left-of-bang interventions or human enhancement, which can disrupt the balance between humanitarian and military considerations that weapons must maintain. Some of those challenges can be overcome by applying the rule not only to weapons in the abstract but to specific uses of weapons.

More generally, the unnecessary suffering rule provides a vivid example of the challenges inherent in funnelling broad ideas of military necessity and sentiments of humanity into technical legal language. The purpose of the rule is obvious: it seeks to introduce a degree of civility into the choice of means and methods of warfare and to restrict the use of particularly barbarous weapons. But the result is not terribly precise. Antonio Cassese (1975, pp. 15, 35) described the unnecessary suffering rule as one of 'the most unclear and controversial rules of warfare[,] . . . to a great extent couched in such vague and uncertain terms as to be barren of practical results'. Others have also questioned the efficacy of the rule on the same basis (see e.g. de Preux, 1987, p. 404, para. 1415). But the vagueness of the rule can also be seen as a virtue. The rule complements the sometimes highly detailed weapon-specific regulation, which is constantly at the risk of being overtaken by technological developments. If nothing else, the unnecessary suffering rule forces states and warfighters to turn their minds to the degree of injury that can legitimately be inflicted upon the individual enemy fighter. In short, the rule forces one to see the adversary as a human being capable of great suffering, and not just an instrument of war.

References

Australian Defence Force (2006). *Australian Defence Doctrine Publication (ADDP) 06.4: Law of Armed Conflict.*

Baxter, R. R. (1977). Conventional weapons under legal prohibitions. *International Security* 1, 42–61.

Best, G. (1980). *Humanity in Warfare: The Modern History of the International Law of Armed Conflicts*, New York: Columbia University Press.

Bill for a Depleted Uranium Munitions Study Act 2005, HR 2410 (109th Congress).

Blix, H. (1988). Means and methods of combat. In UNESCO and Henri Dunant Institute, eds., *International Dimensions of Humanitarian Law*, Dordrecht: Martinus Nijhoff.

Boothby, W. H. (2016). *Weapons and the Law of Armed Conflict*, 2nd ed, Oxford: Oxford University Press.

Boothby, W. H., and von Heinegg, W. H. (2018). *The Law of War: A Detailed Assessment of the US Department of Defense Law of War Manual*, Cambridge: Cambridge University Press.

Bothe, M., Partsch, K. J., and Solf, W. A. (1982). *New Rules for Victims of Armed Conflicts: Commentary on the Two 1977 Protocols Additional to the Geneva Conventions of 1949*, Leiden: Nijhoff.

Casey-Maslen, S., and Haines, S. (2018). *Hague Law Interpreted: The Conduct of Hostilities under the Law of Armed Conflict*, Oxford: Hart.

Cassese, A. (1975). Weapons causing unnecessary suffering: are they prohibited? *Rivista di Diritto Internazionale* 48, 12–42.

Convention (I) for the Amelioration of the Condition of the Wounded and Sick in Armed Forces in the Field, Geneva, 12 August 1949 (entered into force 21 October 1950) 75 UNTS 31 (*Geneva Convention I).*

Convention (II) for the Amelioration of the Condition of Wounded, Sick and Shipwrecked Members of Armed Forces at Sea, Geneva, 12 August 1949 (entered into force 21 October 1950) 75 UNTS 85 (*Geneva Convention II).*

Convention (III) relative to the Treatment of Prisoners of War, Geneva, 12 August 1949 (entered into force 21 October 1950) 75 UNTS 135 (*Geneva Convention III).*

Convention (IV) relative to the Protection of Civilian Persons in Time of War, Geneva, 12 August 1949 (entered into force 21 October 1950) 75 UNTS 287 (*Geneva Convention IV*).

Convention (II) with respect to the Laws and Customs of War on Land, The Hague, 29 July 1899 (entered into force 4 September 1900, 189 CTS 429, Annex: Regulations concerning the Laws and Customs of War on Land (*Hague Convention II* and *1899 Hague Regulations*).

Convention (III) for the Adaptation to Maritime Warfare of the Principles of the Geneva Convention of 22 August 1864, The Hague, 29 July 1899 (entered into force 4 September 1900) 187 CTS 443 (*Hague Convention III).*

Convention (IV) regarding the Laws and Customs of War on Land, The Hague, 18 October 1907 (entered into force 26 January 1910) 205 CTS 277, Annex: Regulations concerning the Laws and Customs of War on Land (*Hague Convention IV* and *1907 Hague Regulations*).

Convention (X) for the Adaptation to Maritime War of the Principles of the Geneva Convention, The Hague, 18 October 1907 (entered into force 26 January 1910) 205 CTS 359 (*1907 Hague Convention X).*

Convention for the Amelioration of the Condition of the Wounded and Sick in Armies in the Field, Geneva, 27 July 1929 (entered into force 19 June 1931) 118 LNTS 303.

Convention Relative to the Treatment of Prisoners of War, Geneva, 27 July 1929 (entered into force 19 June 1931) 118 LNTS 343.

Coupland, R. M. (1999). The SIrUS Project: Towards a determination of which weapons cause 'superfluous injury or unnecessary suffering'. In H. Durham and T. McCormack, eds., *The Changing Face of Conflict and the Efficacy of International Humanitarian Law*, The Hague: Kluwer.

Crawford, E. (2019). The enduring legacy of the St Petersburg Declaration: Distinction, military necessity, and the prohibition of causing unnecessary suffering and superfluous injury in IHL. *Journal of the History of International Law* 20, 544–66.

Danish Ministry of Defence (2016). *Military Manual on International Law Relevant to Danish Armed Forces in International Operations.*

Declaration Renouncing the Use, in Time of War, of Explosive Projectiles under 400 Grammes Weight, 11 December 1868, in force upon signature, 138 CTS 297, 1 AJIL Supp. 95 ('*St Petersburg Declaration*').

Dinniss, H. A. H. (2018). Legal aspects of human enhancement technologies. In W. H. Boothby, ed., *New Technologies and the Law in War and Peace*, Cambridge: Cambridge University Press.

Dinniss, H. A. H., and Kleffner, J. K. (2016). Soldier 2.0: Military human enhancement and international law. *International Law Studies* 92, 432–82.

Dinstein, Y. (2016). *The Conduct of Hostilities under the Law of International Armed Conflict*, 3rd ed., Cambridge: Cambridge University Press.

Dörmann, K., Doswald-Beck, L., and Kolb, R. (2003). *Elements of War Crimes under the Rome Statute of the International Criminal Court: Sources and Commentary*, Cambridge: Cambridge University Press.

Eisenstein, N. M., Naumann, D. N., Bowley, D. M., and Midwinter, M. J. (2016). Pretrauma interventions in force health protection: Introducing the 'left of bang' paradigm. *Journal of Special Operations Medicine* 16, 59–63.

Epps, V. (2013). Civilian casualties in modern warfare: The death of the collateral damage rule. *Georgia Journal of International & Comparative Law* 41, 307–55.

Fenrick, W. J. (1990). The Conventional Weapons Convention: A modest but useful treaty. *International Review of the Red Cross* 30, 498–509.

Frappell-Cooke, W., Wink, P., and Wood, A. (2013). The psychological challenge of genital injury. *Journal of the Royal Army Medical Corps* 159, 52–56.

Geneva Convention for the Amelioration of the Condition of the Wounded in Armies in the Field, 22 August 1864, in force 22 June 1865, 129 CTS 361.

Geneva Convention for the Amelioration of the Condition of the Wounded and Sick in Armies in the Field, 6 July 1906, in force 9 August 1907, 202 CTS 144.

German Federal Ministry of Defence (2013). *Joint Service Regulation (ZDv) 15/2: Law of Armed Conflict – Manual.*

Granat, M. G. (1993). Modern small-arms ammunition in international law. *Netherlands International Law Review* 40, 149–68.

Greenwood, C. (1997). Current issues in the law of armed conflict: Weapons, targets and international criminal liability. *Singapore Journal of International & Comparative Law* 1, 441–67.

(1998). The law of weaponry at the start of the new millennium. In M. N. Schmitt and L. C. Green, eds., *The Law of Armed Conflict: Into the Next Millennium*, Newport, RI: US Naval War College.

Hague Declaration (IV, 3) respecting the Prohibition of the Use of Expanding Bullets, 29 July 1899 (entered into force 4 September 1900) 187 CTS 459.

Haines, S. (2001). Weapons, means and methods of warfare. In E. Wilmshurst and S. Breau, eds., *Perspectives on the ICRC Study on Customary International Humanitarian Law*. Cambridge: Cambridge University Press.

India (1978). Statement at the Diplomatic Conference on the Reaffirmation and Development of International Humanitarian Law Applicable in Armed Conflicts, *Official Records of the Diplomatic Conference on the Reaffirmation and Development of International Humanitarian Law Applicable in Armed Conflicts*, Geneva (1974–1977). Federal Political Department of Switzerland, vol. XVI, CDDH/IV/SR.28, 20 May 1976.

International Committee of the Red Cross (1974). Lucerne Conference Report.

International Committee of the Red Cross (1976). Statement concerning Unnecessary Suffering presented by the Informal Working Group of Medical Experts. In ICRC, *Conference of Government Experts on the Use of Certain Conventional Weapons (Second Session – Lugano, 28.1–26.2.1976): Report.*

International Committee of the Red Cross (2005). Customary International Humanitarian Law Database, Rule 70 (online), https://ihl-databases.icrc.org/customary-ihl/eng/docs/v1_rul_rule70.

International Institute of Humanitarian Law (1990). *Declaration on the Rules of International Humanitarian Law Governing the Conduct of Hostilities in Non-international Armed Conflicts.*

International Institute of Humanitarian Law (2006). *The Manual on the Law of Non-International Armed Conflict, with Commentary.*

Jevglevskaja, N. (2015). St Petersburg, 1868: First international agreement prohibiting the use of certain weapons. In F. Klose, M. Palen, J. Paulmann and

A. Thompson, eds., *Online Atlas on the History of Humanitarianism and Human Rights*, https://hhr-atlas.ieg-mainz.de/.

af Jochnick, C., and Normand, R. (1994). The legitimation of violence: A critical history of the laws of war. *Harvard International Law Journal* 34, 49–95.

Kalshoven, F. (1985) Arms, armaments and international law. *Recueil des Cours* 191, 183–342.

(2013). The history of international humanitarian law treaty-making. In R. Liivoja and T. McCormack, eds., *Routledge Handbook of the Law of Armed Conflict*, Abingdon: Routledge.

Knudsen, P. J. T., and Theilade, P. (1993). Terminal ballistics of the 7.62 mm NATO bullet autopsy findings. *International Journal of Legal Medicine* 106, 61–67.

Knudsen, P. J. T., Vigsnæs, J. S., Rasmussen, R., and Nissen, P. S. (1995). Terminal ballistics of 7.62 mm NATO bullets: Experiments in ordnance gelatin. *International Journal of Legal Medicine* 108, 62–67.

Legality of the Threat or Use of Nuclear Weapons (Advisory Opinion) [1996] ICJ Reports 226.

Legality of the Threat or Use of Nuclear Weapons. Public sitting held on Friday 10 November 1995, at 10 a.m., p. 72.

Liivoja, R., and Chircop, L. (2018). Are enhanced warfighters weapons, means, or methods of warfare?. *International Law Studies* 94, 161–85.

Meyrowitz, H. (1994). The principle of superfluous injury or unnecessary suffering: From the Declaration of St. Petersburg of 1868 to Additional Protocol I of 1977. *International Review of the Red Cross* 34, 98–122.

New Zealand Defence Force (2017). *DM 69: Manual of Armed Forces Law – Volume 4: Law of Armed Conflict*, 2nd ed., Amdt. 1.

Parks, W. H. (1997). Joint service combat shotgun program. *Army Lawyer*, 10, 16–24.

Parks, W. H. (2005). Conventional weapons and weapons review. *Yearbook of International Humanitarian Law* 8, 55–142.

de Preux, J. (1987). Protocol I – Article 35 – Basic rules. In Y. Sandoz, C. Swinarski and B. Zimmermann, eds., *Commentary on the Additional Protocols to the Geneva Conventions*, Geneva: ICRC & Nijhoff.

Project of an International Declaration concerning the Laws and Customs of War, Brussels, 27 August 1874, not in force. In *Actes de la Conférence de Bruxelles, Hayez*, 1874. p. 297 (‘*Brussels Declaration*’).

Protocol Additional (I) to the Geneva Conventions of 12 August 1949, and Relating to the Protection of Victims of International Armed Conflicts, Geneva, 8 June 1977, in force 7 December 1978, 1125 UNTS 3 (*Additional Protocol I*).

Protocol Additional (II) to the Geneva Conventions of 12 August 1949, and Relating to the Protection of Victims of Non-International Armed Conflicts,

Geneva, 8 June 1977, in force 7 December 1978, 1125 UNTS 609 (*Additional Protocol II*).

Roberts, A. and Guelff, R., eds. (2000). *Documents on the Laws of War*, 3rd ed., Oxford: Oxford University Press.

Scott, R. (1989). Unnecessary suffering? A medical view. In M. A. Meyer, ed., *Armed Conflict and the New Law*, London: British Institute of International and Comparative Law.

Shimoda v. Japan (1963) 32 ILR 626 at 634.

Sivakumaran, S. (2012). *The Law of Non-International Armed Conflict*, Oxford: Oxford University Press.

Solf, W. A. (2013). Protocol I – Article 35 – Basic Rules. In *New Rules for Victims of Armed Conflicts: Commentary on the Two 1977 Protocols Additional to the Geneva Convention of 1949*. Leiden: Nijhoff.

Spaight, J. M. (1911). *War Rights on Land*, London: Macmillan.

(1947). *Air Power and War Rights*, 3rd ed., London: Longmans, Green & Co.

Statute of the International Criminal Court, Rome, 17 July 1998, in force 1 July 2002, 2187 UNTS 90.

Tate, L. G., DiMaio, V. J. M., and Davis, J. H. (1981). Rebirth of exploding ammunition: A report of six human fatalities. *Journal of Forensic Sciences* 26, 636–44.

Turns, D. (2006). Weapons in the ICRC study on customary international humanitarian law. *Journal of Conflict & Security Law* 11, 201–37.

UK Ministry of Defence (2004). *Joint Service Publication (JSP) 383: The Joint Service Manual of the Law of Armed Conflict*, Shrivenham: Ministry of Defence.

US Department of the Army (1956). *Field Manual (FM) 27-10: The Law of Land Warfare*, Washington, DC: Department of the Army.

US Department of Defense (2016). *Law of War Manual*, Washington, DC: Department of Defense.

US et al. v. Göring et al. (1946) 1 TMWC 171.

US War Department (1863). General Orders No. 100 Instructions for the Government of Armies of the United States in the Field, 24 April 1863.

de Vattel, E. (1834). *The Law of Nations*, London: Sweet, Stevens & Sons; Maxwell.

Witt, J. F. (2012). *Lincoln's Code: The Laws of War in American History*, New York: Free Press.

10

Blurring the Lines

How Are Female Child Soldiers Protected by the Laws of War?

ROSEMARY GREY

Introduction

Over the course of centuries, the protections afforded to people under the laws of war have changed significantly, and the lines between those who are and are *not* entitled to these protections have been redrawn. In Emer deVattel's time, one's protections hinged on their status as 'civilised', as Killingsworth and McCormack's introduction to this book explains. That status no longer holds meaning in international humanitarian law (IHL), but the basic idea that people's protections hinge on certain legal statuses remains. For example, much depends on one's status as a civilian, a combatant, a prisoner of war, a soldier who is *hors de combat*, a woman, a child, to name a few.[1] Yet what happens when reality tramples on these neat boundaries – when people spill into multiple categories, or fall between the cracks? What legal protections do they enjoy in theory, and what do these protections actually offer in practice?

This chapter explores those questions in relation to young women and girls who, over the course of a single conflict, may occupy the roles of a child, a civilian, a combatant, a killer, a victim of sexual violence, and/or a mother. The difficulty of categorising these young women was highlighted by Radhika Coomaraswamy, United Nations (UN) Special Representative on Children and Armed Conflict, in the first trial at the International Criminal Court (ICC). As she observed, children who are recruited into armed groups:

[1] These categories are used in the 1949 *Geneva Conventions* and their 1977 *Additional Protocols*, among other places.

> [A]re forced to play multiple roles. They will play a role where they will be combatants one minute. They may be, especially girls, sex slaves another minute . . . but those who are sex slaves will also at some point do some military work. So I think [we have] the blurring of these lines.'
>
> (*Prosecutor v Lubanga*, 7 January 2010, p. 30)

These young recruits can be described as 'child soldiers', although that term is somewhat loaded. It tends to conjure up stereotypical images of a small boy struggling under the weight of an assault rifle rather than a fierce young woman with a child of her own on the way.[2] An example of such imagery can be found in the International Committee of the Red Cross' 1987 commentary on the *Additional Protocols* to the *Geneva Conventions*, which states that the prohibition on the use of child soldiers was prompted by 'the harrowing spectacle of boys, who have barely left childhood behind them, brandishing rifles and machine-guns and ready to shoot indiscriminately at anything that moves' (Sandoz, Swinarski and Zimmerman, 1987, para. 3183). Yet such imagery is no longer representative, if it ever was. In contemporary conflicts, girls account for a high proportion of under-age soldiers, with studies estimating that of the 250,000–300,000 child soldiers worldwide, up to 40 per cent are female.[3]

By focusing on female 'child soldiers', this chapter dovetails with a much broader literature on the protections afforded to women under the laws of war. A great deal has been written on this topic, with feminist scholars in the 1990s lamenting the silences around women's experiences of sexual violence in IHL (e.g. Askin, 1997; Bedont and Hall-Martinez, 1999; Copelon, 2000, pp. 217–40; Durham and Gurd, 2005), and more recent works arguing that IHL and international criminal law are now *overly* preoccupied with wartime rape, at the cost of addressing the other ways that war affects women's lives (e.g. Engle, 2005, pp. 778–816; Gardam, 2013, pp. 217–31). But rather than exploring the protections that IHL offers to 'women in war' as a homogenous group, in this chapter I will focus on *one* young woman in *one* conflict, the so-called Second Congo War. My decision to focus on this particular individual is inspired by an emerging body of feminist scholarship which challenges the tendency to speak about women as a group, and instead calls for greater

[2] For a critical perspective on inaccurate stereotypes of child soldiers as infantile, hapless, and male, see Denov (2010); Drumbl (2012).

[3] These estimates take 'child soldiers' to mean children under the age of eighteen, in line with the 2000 Optional Protocol to the Convention on the Rights of the Child on the involvement of children in armed conflicts. See: United Nations (2015); Bensouda (2012).

attention to the 'multiplicity and specificity of women's experiences' in times of war and genocide (e.g. Rashid, 2019, p. 3).

The young woman in question, who I will refer to using her in-court pseudonym 'P-0883', was one of thousands of people from the Democratic Republic of Congo (DRC) whose lives were upended by the so-called Second Congo War. She was also one of seventy-one prosecution witnesses to testify at trial in the ICC's *Ntaganda* case. The chapter commences with a brief overview of that case, before looking more closely at P-0883's particular evidence. Next, I explain the groundbreaking legal findings in this case that enabled the ICC to prosecute crimes committed against P-0883 and other 'child soldiers' who were subjected to similar offences. I will end with some more critical reflections about whether, and in what ways, the laws of war protected this particular individual.

10.1 The *Ntaganda* Case at a Glance

The DRC became an ICC member-state (in legal terms, a 'State Party') in April 2002. In July 2003, the Court's first Prosecutor, Luis Moreno-Ocampo, began 'closely analysing' the situation in the DRC's Ituri region (ICC, 2004). Two months later, the Prosecutor announced that he was ready to seek authorisation from the pre-trial judges to open an investigation into the DRC but that a referral and active support from the DRC would 'assist his work' (this referral and support would enable the Prosecutor to open the investigation without seeking judicial approval and would be crucial to accessing evidence and gaining custody of suspects as well). In March 2004, the DRC made the referral, and the Prosecutor opened the investigation on 23 June 2004 (ICC, 2004).

Prosecutor Moreno-Ocampo and his successor, Prosecutor Fatou Bensouda, would eventually bring six cases from the DRC, which is more than any other situation before the ICC to date.[4] All six cases concern crimes allegedly committed by irregular armed forces; there are no ICC cases yet on the public record concerning allegations against the DRC armed forces (e.g. Human Rights Watch, 2013). The *Ntaganda* case is one of these six ICC cases from the DRC. It concerns crimes committed during the so-called Second Congo War, which involved a series of conflicts throughout the DRC from 1998 to 2003. The impact of this

[4] These six cases were the *Lubanga, Ntaganda, Katanga, Ngudjolo Chui, Mbarushimana*, and *Mudacumura* cases.

conflict has been devastating. It has produced the largest civilian death toll of any conflict since World War II and gave rise to widespread sexual violence as well (Human Rights Watch, 2004). Since then, hostilities have continued intermittently, with the result that the impact of war drags on for countless women, men, and children in this country (e.g. Tsongo, 2022).

The accused in the *Ntaganda* case, Bosco Ntaganda, was the commander of a militia called the *Forces patriotiques pour la libération du Congo* (FPLC), the military wing of the *Union des patriotes congolais* (UPC) movement. The FPLC's membership came primarily from the Hema ethnic group, and their adversaries were mainly from the Lendu group.[5] Importantly, the *Ntaganda* case was not the ICC's first case concerning the FPLC. This group was also the focus of the Court's first case, the *Lubanga* case, as detailed below. However, whereas the *Lubanga* case was concerned only with the FPLC's recruitment and use of child soldiers, the *Ntaganda* case contained a much broader suite of charges. Specifically, Bosco Ntaganda was charged with war crimes relating to the use of child soldiers (namely, conscripting or enlisting children under the age of fifteen into an armed group, and using those children to participate actively in hostilities), along with war crimes and crimes against humanity relating to murder, sexual violence, forced displacement, attacks on civilian population, and destruction of property by FPLC forces (*Prosecutor v Ntaganda*, 16 February 2015).

The war crimes charges included specific counts for acts of rape and sexual slavery committed by FPLC commanders against child soldiers within the group (*Prosecutor v Ntaganda*, 16 February 2015, counts 6 and 9). This was a novel approach, that had not been tested in the ICC or any other international criminal tribunal before.[6] In July 2018, after a three-year trial, an ICC trial chamber convicted Ntaganda on all charges, including those relating to the sexual abuse of so-called 'child soldiers'

[5] For details on the UPC and FPLC's formation, objectives, and connection to ethnic groups in the DRC, see: *Ntaganda* trial judgment, 8 July 2018, paras. 285–315.

[6] In the Special Court for Sierra Leone's case against former Liberian President Charles Taylor, there was evidence pertaining to a girl who (similar to P-0883 in the *Ntaganda* case) was recruited by an armed group when she was under the age of fifteen and was sexually assaulted by a member of that group. However, this evidence was folded into the general charges of sexual slavery as a crime against humanity and outrages on personal dignity as a war crime; there was no separate charge for the war crimes of rape and sexual slavery against child soldiers by members of their own armed group, as there was in the *Ntaganda* case. See *Prosecutor v Taylor*, 30 May 2012, paras. 1179, 1206(vii), 1207 and 1451–56.

(*Ntaganda* trial judgment, 8 July 2018). That conviction was upheld by the ICC Appeals Chamber in March 2021 (*Ntaganda* appeal judgment, 30 March 2021). This was the first successful prosecution for sexual violence crimes in the history of the ICC.[7]

10.2 P-0883's War

At the outset, it must be acknowledged that courtrooms are not an ideal setting for presenting any individual's account of a war. When a person appears as a witness for one of the parties to a criminal trial (as P-0883 did), he or she has little ability to control their own narrative. As Julie Mertus (2004, p. 113) observes, '[b]y design, the legal process does not permit witnesses to tell their own coherent narrative; it chops their stories into digestible parts, selects a handful of parts and sorts and refines them to create a new narrative'. For example, a witness does not choose where in time their story begins, what events it should encompass, or which experiences to focus on. Rather, the calling party will steer the witness towards details relevant to the proof of their case, and in cross-examination the opposing party will press the witness on particular details, with a view to exposing vagueness, contradictions, or implausibility in their testimony.

This process of testing the evidence is supervised by the judges, to ensure it does not become disrespectful or distressing. In the ICC, for example, judges are obligated to take measures to respect the safety, dignity, and well-being of victims and witnesses, particularly if their evidence relates to sexual violence (e.g. *Rome Statute*, 1988, art. 68(1)). Yet even in the most sensitive courtroom, the witness does not control the story. They are there to inform the Court about specific aspects of the Prosecution or Defence case, not to recount their whole experience of war, which may include acts of resistance or even perpetrating violence, as well as being the victim of a crime. These factors limit a witness' ability to *tell* their story, and the use of witness protection measures, while necessary for the witness' safety and well-being, further constrain our ability to *hear* it.

[7] In 2016, in the *Bemba* case, DRC politician Jean-Pierre Bemba Gombo was convicted by the ICC for murder, rape, and pillage committed by troops under his command in the Central African Republic. However, he was acquitted on appeal in 2018, returning the ICC Office of the Prosecutor's number of successful prosecutions for sexual violence to zero.

In relation to P-0883, for instance, the judges ensured that the public could not see her face, and they concealed her voice using voice-distortion technology. In addition, her testimony took place mostly in private sessions, meaning it was inaudible to court-watchers and redacted from the publicly available transcript. As a result, only fragments of P-0883's testimony can be gleaned from the court records – namely, those parts repeated by the prosecution or judges in public documents. Still, these fragments offer a sense of what she experienced as a young woman in one of most brutal conflicts in the past century.

According to her evidence, P-0883 was abducted by an armed group on her way home from school when she was roughly twelve years old. (Her evidence was inconsistent as to whether her abductors belonged to the FPLC, or whether she was abducted by a different group who later handed her over to the FPLC) (*Ntaganda* trial judgment, 8 July 2018, paras. 174–88; *Ntaganda* sentencing judgment, 7 November 2019, para. 126, fn. 345). She further testified to being brought to an FPLC training camp, where she remained for several months and learned to use weapons and developed other military skills (*Ntaganda*, 7 November 2018, para. 709; *Ntaganda* trial judgment, 8 July 2018, paras. 174–88, 362, 1120). The trainees were not free to leave this camp, according to P-0883. In her words, the soldiers 'followed behind at all times. They would try to see if we were trying to flee. Everywhere where we were, they were behind us with weapons' (*Ntaganda*, 30 November 2016, p. 25). P-0883 recalled going on night patrols with other FPLC soldiers, carrying weapons and ammunition for adult soldiers, and being sent into battle where she was injured (*Ntaganda*, 7 November 2018, paras. 654, 665, 709).

P-0883 further testified that while at the camp, she was repeatedly raped by male FPLC soldiers. As she said, these men raped the female recruits 'whenever they wanted' and threatened to shoot them if they refused (*Ntaganda* trial judgment, 8 July 2018, paras. 407, 409, 974–78; *Ntaganda*, 7 November 2018, para. 709). As a result of this sexual violence, P-0883 contracted a sexually transmitted disease and also became pregnant while still a teenager herself (*Ntaganda* trial judgment, 8 July 2018, para. 409; *Ntaganda*, 7 November 2018, para. 709; *Ntaganda*, sentencing judgment, 7 November 2019, para. 111). She returned to her village after being treated for her battle injury, where she gave birth to the child and learned that both of her parents were dead (*Ntaganda* trial judgment, 8 July 2018, para. 174). In her remarks to the trial judges, P-0883's grief about this violence was profound. As well as describing her ongoing physical and psychological injuries, she focused on her lost opportunity for education, stating:

> My life is still massively affected by [my time in the FPLC]. I stopped my studies, I did not study anymore. These days, what can somebody do if they have not got any studies? My life was ruined. My life was ruined. I caught illnesses, diseases. This violence that I suffered makes me suffer enormously. It's very difficult, very difficult for me.
>
> (*Ntaganda* sentencing judgment, 7 November 2019, para. 184)

All three trial judges found P-0883's evidence of sexual violence to be reliable. They did not rely on her evidence about the circumstances of her abduction, due to the inconsistencies in that evidence (*Ntaganda* trial judgment, 8 July 2018, paras. 180–85). Nonetheless, they accepted her evidence that she was under fifteen when she was abducted, about her experiences in the FPLC training camp, and the sexual violence she experienced (*Ntaganda* trial judgment, 8 July 2018, paras. 186–88). In reaching this conclusion, the trial judges noted that P-0883 'provided clear accounts which were rich in detail' and 'mainly testified about what she had personally experienced, and refrained from general comments or approximations' (*Ntaganda* trial judgment, 8 July 2018, para. 175). Responding to the Defence's claim that P-0883 had fabricated her accounts of sexual violence, the trial judges stated: 'delayed reporting of rape is a comprehensible consequence of the victims' experience, especially in conflict areas' (*Ntaganda* trial judgment, 8 July 2018, para. 187). This assessment of P-0883's evidence was challenged by the Defence on appeal, but without success: the Appeals Chamber found no error in the Trial Chamber's approach (*Ntaganda* appeal judgment, 30 March 2021, paras. 803–13, 842–44). Thus, her evidence of sexual violence and experience of military training was accepted by three trial judges and five appeal judges, which is a very strong indication of its credibility.

10.3 P-0883's Protections under the Laws of War

A young woman (or girl) in P-0883's position is entitled to numerous protections under IHL, due to the particular categories that she occupies. One of these categories is as a 'child', which in this context means a person aged fifteen or under. Under IHL, both states and irregular armed groups (such as the FPLC) are forbidden from conscripting or enlisting children of this age into their ranks, or using those children to participate actively in hostilities (*Additional Protocol I*, 1977, art. 77(1)–(3);

Additional Protocol II, 1977, art. 4(3)(a)–(d); *Convention on the Rights of the Child*, 1989, art. 38). In fact, the acts of recruiting and using child soldiers are not only forbidden; they are also war crimes for which individuals can be prosecuted and punished by the ICC. These war crimes are explicitly listed in the treaty that established the ICC (*Rome Statute*, arts. 8(2)(b)(xxvi), 8(2)(e)(vii)) and were charged in the *Ntaganda* case. Thus, when the FPLC recruited P-0883 and trained her in military skills, as she testified that they did, this was a clear violation of IHL and a war crime under the *Rome Statute* (*Ntaganda* trial judgment, 8 July 2018, paras. 977, 1120–24). In 2018, the Court convicted Ntaganda of this war crime (among other things), and P-0883's testimony was one of the pieces of evidence that the judges relied upon (*Ntaganda* trial judgment, 8 July 2018, paras. 347, 362). In this sense, her status as a 'child' (under the age of fifteen) at the time of her recruitment by the FPLC provided legal protections under IHL and international criminal law.

What about the prolonged sexual violence that P-0883 described? Was that also prohibited under the laws of war? Did the fact that the alleged sexual violence occurred *within an armed group*, meaning that the putative victim and perpetrator were both part of the FPLC, preclude this sexual violence from being classified as a war crime? At the heart of this debate is the question that runs throughout this book: just who is protected by the laws of war? And do certain people fall through the cracks? For context, we should note that this important question about whether IHL prohibits sexual violence *within* an armed group was sidestepped in the ICC's first case concerning the FPLC: the *Lubanga* case.

The accused in that case, Thomas Lubanga Dyilo, was the president of the UPC and commander-in-chief of its military wing, the FPLC. As early as 2004 and 2005, there were reports that soldiers under Lubanga's command were committing sexual crimes against civilians in the DRCs' Ituri region, and against child soldiers within the FLPC's own ranks (e.g. Amnesty International, 2004, p. 13; Human Rights Watch, 2005, pp. 19–21).[8] Nonetheless, when Prosecutor Moreno-Ocampo applied for a warrant to arrest Lubanga in January 2006, and when he sought confirmation of charges against Lubanga in August 2006, sexual violence was not part of the Prosecution's case. The charges were limited to the war crimes of conscripting or enlisting children under the age of fifteen into an armed group or using them to participate actively in

[8] See also UN Organization Mission in the Democratic Republic of the Congo (2004, paras. 1–2, 24, 37, 80, 153).

hostilities. Moreover, the Prosecution made *no suggestion* that these charges included the sexual assault of child soldiers by other members of the FPLC (see *Situation in the Democratic Republic of Congo*, 10 February 2006; *Prosecutor v Lubanga*, 28 August 2006).

The absence of sexual violence charges in the *Lubanga* case was greeted with concern by many court-watchers (e.g. Hayes, 2013, pp. 7, 16). For example, Women's Initiatives for Gender Justice (2006), a Hague-based NGO with local partners in the DRC, sought leave to file an *amicus curiae* brief in the *Lubanga* case. It indicated that the *amicus curiae* brief, if accepted, would request that the pre-trial judges decide if the Prosecutor abused his discretion by deciding to charge Lubanga only with the recruitment and use of 'child soldiers' when there had been reports of widespread rape and murder by forces under Lubanga's control (*Lubanga*, 7 September 2006). However, this initiative did not succeed: the pre-trial judges denied leave on the basis that the proposed *amicus curie* brief raised issues beyond the scope of the charges, and therefore had 'no link' to the case (*Lubanga*, 26 September 2006, p. 3). In January 2007, the Pre-Trial Chamber confirmed the charges brought by the Prosecutor against Lubanga. Thus, the charges, as confirmed, did not include any allegations of sexual crimes (*Lubanga*, 7 February 2007).

The reasons for this gap in the charges have been examined at length elsewhere. It appears that, in the face of significant time pressures (there was a general pressure on the ICC's first Prosecutor to start cases, and particular pressure to secure custody of Lubanga before the DRC authorities released him from detention), Prosecutor Moreno-Ocampo de-prioritised accountability for sexual crimes in favour of a timely arrest and trial (Glassborrow, 2008).[9] Another contributing factor seems to be that, during the ICC's early years, when the *Lubanga* case began, there was some uncertainty within the ICC Office of the Prosecutor as to whether sexual crimes could legally be charged as war crimes when the victim and perpetrator were members of the same fighting force. As one OTP interviewee stated when interviewed by the author in 2017, 'the feeling at the time' was that sexual violence within an armed group was not a war crime because 'if you look at it from a classical point of view, war crimes are crimes that you commit against the Other', that is, against persons and property associated with the opposing side (Grey, 2019, p. 253).

[9] See also analysis in Grey (2019, pp. 250–54).

Although Lubanga was sent to trial without any charges of sexual violence, the issue of sexual violence continued to loom over the case. For instance, in the leadup to the trial, the Trial Chamber accepted an *amicus curiae* brief from the UN Special Representative for Children and Armed Conflict, Radhika Coomaraswamy. The brief explained that 'when the Special Representative spoke to girl combatants in the eastern Democratic Republic of Congo, they spoke of being fighters one minute, a "wife" or "sex slave" the next, and domestic aides and food providers at another time' (*Lubanga*, 18 March 2008, para. 22). In light of these experiences, Coomaraswamy urged the Trial Chamber to interpret the war crime of 'using children to participate actively in hostilities' to include activities performed primarily by female children, including being used for sex (*Lubanga*, 18 March 2008, paras. 24–26).

The concerns raised about the charges in the *Lubanga* case, including the interventions by Women's Initiatives for Gender Justice and by the UN Special Representative, seem to have had an effect on the Prosecution's strategy at trial. That strategy was revealed on 26 January 2009, when the trial began. Within the first minutes of his opening address, Prosecutor Moreno-Ocampo referred to sexual violence against girl soldiers in the FPLC, stating: 'in the [FPLC] camps child soldiers were exposed to the sexual violence perpetrated by Thomas Lubanga's men in unspeakable ways.' Echoing the Coomaraswamy's brief, he continued: 'Girl soldiers, some aged 12 years, were used as cooks and fighters, cleaners and spies, scouts and sexual slaves. One minute they will carry a gun, the next minute they will serve meals to the commanders, the next minute the commanders will rape them' (*Lubanga*, 26 January 2009, pp. 11–12).

As the *Lubanga* trial progressed, the Prosecution led evidence to support these allegations of sexual violence within the FPLC, including by calling eight men and one woman who were allegedly former FPLC child soldiers (Grey, 2019, p. 135). The victims' legal representatives urged the Trial Chamber to change the legal characterisation of this evidence in accordance with the Regulations of the Court (reg. 55), so as to add charges for sexual violence. However, the Appeals Chamber ruled that it was too late to make this change, because adding charges of sexual violence would not simply be a re-characterisation of facts already within the scope of the case; rather, it would *exceed* the facts and circumstances confirmed by the Pre-Trial Chamber. That is, Prosecution's failure to lead evidence of sexual violence against child soldiers before the charges were confirmed meant that this sexual violence could not be brought into the case at trial.

Nonetheless, in its closing brief, the Prosecution attempted to justify the belated evidence of sexual violence in the *Lubanga* case. It urged the Trial Chamber to interpret the crime of 'using children to participate actively in hostilities' in a way that would include the use of girls as bodyguards, sexual slaves, cooks, and fighters (*Lubanga*, 1 June 2011, paras. 227–34). One could see, during the closing argument in the *Lubanga* trial, that this argument did not sit easily with the judges. On the second-last day of the trial, Judge Elizabeth Odio Benito asked the Prosecution to clarify how the allegations of sexual violence fit into its case, seeing as these allegations had not been discussed at the pre-trial stage (*Lubanga*, 25 August 2011, pp. 53–54). In response, Prosecutor Moreno-Ocampo argued that the war crimes of conscripting children under the age of fifteen and using them to participate actively in hostilities included using them for sexual purposes (*Lubanga*, 25 August 2011, pp. 54–55). However, he did not address Judge Odio Benito's 'timing' question, namely how the trial judges could properly assess the evidence of sexual violence that was led at trial, given that the Prosecution had not mentioned this evidence back in 2006, when seeking confirmation of the charges in the *Lubanga* case.

That 'timing' question proved to be determinative. In 2012, the trial judges convicted Lubanga of the war crimes of conscripting, enlisting, and using child soldiers but declined to determine Lubanga's accountability for sexual violence because this fell beyond the scope of the case (*Lubanga*, 12 April 2012, paras. 629–31). While a crushing disappointment for the victims and survivors, this was the only fair outcome, given that the Prosecutor had not charged Lubanga with sexual violence in substance or in form.

In *Lubanga*, the majority of the Trial Chamber left unanswered the question of whether *in principle* (i.e. if charged at the correct time), sexual violence perpetrated against child soldiers by members of their own armed group can amount to a war crime under the *Rome Statute*. Judge Odio Benito addressed that question in a separate opinion, finding that as a matter of law, the use of child soldiers for sexual purposes could fall within the scope of the war crime of using children to participate actively in hostilities (*Lubanga*, Odio Benito J, 12 April 2012, paras. 15–21).[10]

[10] Note: Her Honour did not suggest that Lubanga's conviction should include sexual crimes, given that these crimes were not part of the charges as presented by the Prosecutor prior to trial.

However, this was a dissenting opinion; it did not affect the outcome of the case.

Against that backdrop, it was a relief to see that in the *Ntaganda* case, the Prosecution made it a priority to obtain an affirmative answer to that question. This endeavour was made possible by ICC Prosecutor Fatou Bensouda, who, with expert advice from her staff and her Special Advisor on International Humanitarian Law (appointed in 2010), took the bold step of prosecuting the sexual abuse of child soldiers within the FPLC using the war crimes of rape and sexual slavery. For those unfamiliar with IHL, it may be helpful to explain why these charges were controversial back in 2014, when the charges in the *Ntaganda* case were laid.

There was no question that the rapes reported by P-0883 and other children in the FPLC were egregious, and no question that rape is generally a grave breach of IHL and a war crime. The question was whether these same legal principles apply where the victim is not in the power of the 'adverse party' (such as when a civilian is sexually assaulted by a member of an invading army, or when a captured combatant is sexually assaulted by enemy forces) but is in the same fighting force as the perpetrator (such as when a commander rapes a child soldier within their own armed group). Ntaganda's defence team insisted that IHL did not apply in such cases. In its view, 'crimes committed by members of armed forces on members of the same armed force do not come within the jurisdiction of international humanitarian law nor within international criminal law' (*Ntaganda*, 13 February 2014, p. 27). In essence, the Defence was arguing that the victims of sexual violence must be associated with an 'adverse party' (as opposed to being part of the perpetrator's own group), in order for that sexual violence to be prosecuted as a war crime under the *Rome Statute*.

In the *Ntaganda* case, the Prosecution systematically dismantled this claim by the Defence. This required presenting a detailed examination of IHL to show that the *Rome Statute*'s war crimes of rape and sexual slavery are indeed applicable to sexual violence *within* an armed group. Analysing customary international law, as well as the 1949 *Geneva Conventions* and their 1977 *Additional Protocols*, the Prosecution argued that the IHL protections whose reach is limited to persons in the power of the adverse party are the *exception*, not the rule (*Ntaganda*, 21 February 2017, para. 60; see also paras. 61–63). Such exceptions include the 'grave breach' protections in the third and fourth *Geneva Conventions* (relating to prisoners of war and civilians, respectively), because these protections apply only to persons who have 'fallen into the power of the enemy' or who are 'in the hands' of a party 'of which they are not nationals' (*Ntaganda*, 21 February 2017, para. 64). But outside of these kinds of exceptional provisions, the Prosecution argued, IHL offers a broad protection against inhumane treatment to *any person* in the power of another, be they friend or foe. For instance, wilfully killing a wounded comrade, or wilfully failing to take all reasonable measures to search for and collect shipwrecked sailors of any affiliation are violations of IHL and also war crimes (*Ntaganda*, 21 February 2017, para. 63). Likewise, the war crimes of rape and sexual slavery, as listed in Articles 8(2)(b)(xxii) and 8(2)(e)(vi) of the *Rome Statute*, are based on IHL's broad protection against inhumane treatment to *any person* in the power of another.

For those reasons, the Prosecution argued that the general 'adverse party' requirement for war crimes, which the Defence claimed to be part of IHL, was a 'phantom requirement' without legal basis (*Ntaganda*, 21 February 2017, para. 5). The ICC's Appeals Chamber, the highest bench within the Court, agreed with the Prosecution. In a unanimous decision delivered in June 2017, the Appeals Chamber held that rape and sexual slavery within an armed group *is* a violation of IHL and a war crime under the *Rome Statute*, even if the victim and perpetrator belong to the same armed force as one another, so long as the sexual violence is causally linked to the armed conflict; in legal terms, there must be a 'nexus' between the sexual violence and the state of war (*Ntaganda* appeal judgment on counts 6 and 9, 15 June 2017). This 2017 decision by the Appeals Chamber raised the ire of some influential commentators. Kevin Jon Heller (2017), now the ICC Prosecutor's Special Advisor on 'International Criminal Law Discourse', argued that the decision was not simply 'unprecedented', it was 'simply incorrect', and 'it risks de-legitimising both the Court and the law of war crimes itself'. Such heated responses were perhaps unsurprising, given the lack of precedent in prosecuting sexual crimes committed *within* an armed group. And yet, as the Prosecution's and the Appeals Chamber's reasoning made clear, the lack of precedent did not mean that prosecutions of this nature were legally impossible. To the contrary, this analysis showed that the *Rome Statute* allows for the prosecution of rape and other sexual crimes committed by members of an armed group against other members of that group in both international and non-international armed conflicts; there is no 'adverse party' requirement for these war crimes.

In 2018, the trial judges convicted Ntaganda of the war crimes of rape and sexual slavery in relation to P-0883 and two other girls who had been recruited by the FPLC. The Trial Chamber accepted that these three girls had been subjected to sexual acts by their commanders, and that these sexual acts were committed through force or coercion, in circumstances where the victims were effectively enslaved (*Ntaganda* trial judgment, 8 July 2018, paras. 975–82). As to the 'nexus' requirement, the Trial Chamber was satisfied that these sexual crimes were sufficiently linked to the armed conflict in Ituri: the victims were in the power of the FPLC because of that group's recruitment campaign, which was aimed at building its military strength in this conflict (*Ntaganda* trial judgment, 8 July 2018, paras. 983–86). The Trial Chamber held that Ntaganda bore responsibility for these rapes due to his position of authority in the FPLC and his acceptance that, in the course of implementing the group's plan to drive all Lendu people out of the localities targeted during their military campaigns, these crimes would occur as a virtual certainty (*Ntaganda* trial judgment, 8 July 2018, para. 811). It also found that he personally subjected his own female bodyguards to rape, although those particular rapes were not charged in the case (*Ntaganda* trial judgment, 8 July 2018, para. 1196).

Ntaganda appealed against that conviction but without success. In its 2021 appeal judgment, the Appeals Chamber found no error in the Trial Chamber's findings that P-0083 and other female 'child soldiers' were subjected to sexual violence within the FPLC (*Ntaganda* appeal judgment, 30 March 2021, paras. 803–13, 842–44). Nor did the Appeal Chamber fault the Trial Chamber's conclusion that this sexual violence was linked to the armed conflict, or that Bosco Ntaganda was responsible for these sexual crimes.[11] As a result, Ntaganda was held criminally responsible for the sexual crimes committed against child soldiers within the FPLC, an outcome that to the disappointment of many, was not accomplished in the *Lubanga* case.

It is also notable to observe that, in the *Ntaganda* case, P-0883's experience of being made forcibly pregnant was not the subject of a separate charge. In a later case, the *Ongwen* case, the Prosecution would bring separate charges of 'forced pregnancy' as a war crime and crime against humanity under the *Rome Statute*, in respect of victims who, having been raped by a commander of an armed group, were then detained by that commander with the intent of continuing to subject them to rape, enslavement, and other *Rome Statute* crimes (see Grey, 2017). But in the *Ntaganda* case, the Prosecution did not bring charges of this nature in relation to P-0083, suggesting that although this was a

[11] The Defence did not challenge the Trial Chamber's analysis that the nexus requirement had been met, hence the issue was not litigated on appeal.

landmark case for sexual violence against child soldiers, there may be scope to build on this milestone by bringing a fuller range of charges in future cases where 'child soldiers' are not only raped but also become pregnant, as a result of sexual violence within an armed group.

Concluding Reflections

The above analysis shows that, at least in theory, the laws of war protected P-0883 in multiple ways. These laws prohibited her recruitment by the FPLC, as well as the subsequent sexual abuse that she endured while in that group. These outcomes illustrate Judith Gardam's (2013) argument that IHL 'is a powerful and effective regime *if* you can fit into one of its categories' (emphasis added). The *Ntaganda* case is a step forward in this respect, because it established that victims of sexual violence who were previously thought to fall outside of IHL's categories are indeed protected even within their own group. Importantly, the Appeals Chamber's reasoning in the *Ntaganda* case was not restricted to 'child soldiers' in the sense of persons under the age of fifteen; rather the decision indicated that sexual violence against *any individual* within an armed group by another member of that armed group could be prosecuted in the ICC as a war crime, provided that the 'nexus element' for war crimes was satisfied (*Ntaganda* appeal judgment on counts 6 and 9, 15 June 2017).

But what does that mean to a twelve-year-old girl in the DRC who is abducted by an armed group? Did these laws *actually* protect her from repeated rape, and being sent into battle where she was injured and could have been killed? It seems clear that when the conflict was unfolding, these legal protections were aspirational only. If anyone can be said to have protected P-0883, it was P-0883 herself. By engaging in survival sex, following orders, and enduring unimaginable hardship, this young woman outlived the war. Here we have, in one person's experience, a sobering reminder that the protections offered by IHL are not self-executing; they are aspirational standards in this sense. When violations of IHL are prosecuted as war crimes, this can go some way towards restoring the dignity of the victims and may contribute to the deterrence of similar crimes in future. But so long as war continues, so too will war crimes. Until then, IHL and international criminal law may at least provide normative guidance on how to protect humanity in war, and some accountability when the agreed-upon legal standards are breached.

References

Amnesty International. (2004). Democratic Republic of Congo: Mass rape – time for remedies, 25 October 2004.

Askin, K. (1997). *War Crimes against Women: Prosecution in International War Crimes Tribunals*, The Hague: Martinus Nijhoff.

Bedont, B., and Hall-Martinez, K. (1999). Ending impunity for gender crimes under the International Criminal Court. *Brown Journal of World Affairs* 6 (1), 65–85.

Bensouda, F. (2012). The incidence of the Female Child Soldier and the International Criminal Court. Speech delivered on 4 June 2012 at the Eng Aja Eze Foundation, New York.

Convention on the Rights of the Child, adopted 20 November 1989 (entered into force 2 September 1990).

Copelon, R. (2000). Gender crimes as war crimes: Integrating crimes against women into international criminal law. *McGill Law Journal* 46, 217–40.

Denov, M. (2010). *Child Soldiers: Sierra Leone's Revolutionary United Front*, Cambridge: Cambridge University Press.

Drumbl, M. (2012). *Reimagining Child Soldiers in International Law and Policy*, Oxford: Oxford University Press.

Durham, H., and Gurd, T., eds. (2005). *Listening to the Silences: Women and War*, The Hague: Martinus Nijhoff.

Engle, K. (2005). Feminism and its (dis)contents: Criminalizing wartime rape in Bosnia and Herzegovina. *American Journal of International Law* 99(4), 778–816.

Gardam, J. (2013). A new frontline for feminism and international humanitarian law. In V. E. Munro and M. Davies, eds., *The Ashgate Research Companion to Feminist Legal Theory*, London: Ashgate.

Glassborrow, K. (2008). ICC investigative strategy under fire. *Institute for War and Peace Reporting*, 27 October 2008.

Grey, R. (2017). The ICC's first 'forced pregnancy' case in historical perspective. *Journal of International Criminal Justice* 15(5), 905–30

(2019). *Prosecuting Sexual and Gender-Based Crimes at the International Criminal Court: Practice, Progress and Potential*, Cambridge: Cambridge University Press.

Hayes, N. (2013). Sisyphus wept: Prosecuting sexual violence at the International Criminal Court. In W. Schabas, Y. McDermott and N. Hayes, eds., *The Ashgate Research Companion to International Criminal Law*, London: Ashgate.

Heller, K. J. (2017). ICC Appeals Chamber says a war crime does not have to violate IHL. *Opinio Juris*, 15 June 2017.

Human Rights Watch (2004). World Report 2004.

Human Rights Watch (2005). The prosecution of sexual violence in the Congo War, 7 March 2005.

Human Rights Watch (2013). DR Congo: War Crimes by M23, Congolese Army, 5 February 2013.

International Criminal Court (2004). Press Release: The Office of the Prosecutor of the International Criminal Court opens its first investigation, 23 June 2004.

Mertus, J. (2004). Shouting from the bottom of the well. *International Feminist Journal of Politics* 6(1), 110–28.

Prosecutor v Lubanga, Document Containing the Charges, ICC-01/04-01/06-356-Anx2, Pre-Trial Chamber I, 28 August 2006.

Prosecutor v Lubanga, Request Submitted pursuant to Rule 103 (1) of the Rules of Procedure and Evidence for Leave to Participate as Amicus Curiae in the Article 61, ICC-01/04-01/06-403, Pre-Trial Chamber I, 7 September 2006.

Prosecutor v Lubanga, Decision on Request pursuant to Rule 103 (1) of the Statute, ICC-01/04-01/06-480, Pre-Trial Chamber I, 26 September 2006.

Prosecutor v Lubanga, Decision on the confirmation of charges, ICC-01/04-01/06-803-tEN, Pre-Trial Chamber I, 7 February 2007.

Prosecutor v Lubanga, Submission of the Observations of the Special Representative of the Secretary General of the United Nations for Children and Armed Conflict pursuant to Rule 103 of the Rules of Procedure and Evidence, ICC-01/04-01/06-1229, Trial Chamber I, 18 March 2008.

Prosecutor v Lubanga, Transcript, ICC-01/04-01/06-T-107-ENG, Trial Chamber I, 26 January 2009.

Prosecutor v Lubanga, Transcript, ICC-01/04-01/06-T-223-ENG, Trial Chamber I, 7 January 2010.

Prosecutor v Lubanga, Prosecution's Closing Brief, ICC-01/04-01/06-2748-Red, Trial Chamber I, 1 June 2011.

Prosecutor v Lubanga, Transcript, ICC-01/04-01/06-T-356-ENG, Trial Chamber I, 25 August 2011.

Prosecutor v Lubanga, Judgment, ICC-01/04-01/06-2842, Trial Chamber I, 12 April 2012.

Prosecutor v Lubanga, Separate and Dissenting Opinion of Judge Odio Benito, ICC-01/04-01/06-2842, Trial Chamber I, 12 April 2012.

Prosecutor v Ntaganda, Transcript, ICC-01/04-02/06-T-10-Red-ENG, Pre-Trial Chamber II, 13 February 2014.

Prosecutor v Ntaganda, Updated Document Containing the Charges, ICC-01/04-02/06-458-AnxA, Pre-Trial Chamber II, 16 February 2015.

Prosecutor v Ntaganda, Transcript, ICC-01/04-02/06-T-168-Red-ENG, Trial Chamber VI, 30 November 2016.

Prosecutor v Ntaganda, Corrected version of 'Prosecution's Response to Ntaganda's "Appeal from the Second Decision on the Defence's Challenge to the Jurisdiction of the Court in respect of Counts 6 and 9'", ICC-01/04-02/06-1794-Corr, Appeals Chamber, 21 February 2017.

Prosecutor v Ntaganda, Judgment on the appeal of Mr Ntaganda against the 'Second decision on the Defence's challenge to the jurisdiction of the Court in respect of Counts 6 and 9', ICC-01/04-02/06-1962, Appeals Chamber, 15 June 2017.

Prosecutor v Ntaganda, Judgment, ICC-01/04-02/06-2359, Trial Chamber VI, 8 July 2018.

Prosecutor v Ntaganda, Prosecution's final closing brief, ICC-01/04-02/06-2277-Anx1-Corr-Red, 7 November 2018.

Prosecutor v Ntaganda, Sentencing Judgment, ICC-01/04-02/06-2442, Trial Chamber VI, 7 November 2019.

Prosecutor v Ntaganda, Appeal Judgment, ICC-01/04-02/06-2666-Red, Appeal Chamber, 30 March 2021.

Prosecutor v Taylor, Judgment, SCSL-03-01-T, Trial Chamber, 30 May 2012.

Protocol Additional to the Geneva Conventions of 12 August 1949, and relating to the Protection of Victims of International Armed Conflicts ('Additional Protocol I'), 8 June 1977.

Protocol Additional to the Geneva Conventions of 12 August 1949, and relating to the Protection of Victims of Non-International Armed Conflicts ('Additional Protocol II'), 8 June 1977.

Rashid, A. (2019). *Gender, Nationalism, and Genocide in Bangladesh*, London: Taylor & Francis.

Rome Statute to the International Criminal Court, Opened for signature 17 July 1988, 2187 UNTS 90 (entered into force 1 July 2002).

Sandoz, Y., Swinarski, C., and Zimmerman, B., eds. (1987). *Commentary on the Additional Protocols*, Geneva: ICRC.

Situation in the Democratic Republic of Congo, Decision on the Prosecutor's Application for Warrants of Arrest, Article 58, ICC-01/04-02/06-20-Anx2, Pre-Trial Chamber I, 10 February 2006.

Tsongo, E. (2022). What is the latest conflict in the DR Congo about? *Al Jazeera*, 21 June 2022.

United Nations (2015). 4 out of 10 child soldiers are girls. 12 February 2015 (online), www.un.org/youthenvoy/2015/02/4-10-child-soldiers-girls/#:~:text=Children%20are%20increasingly%20vulnerable%20as,cent%20of%20them%20are%20girls.

UN Organization Mission in the Democratic Republic of the Congo (2004). Special report on the events in Ituri, January 2002–December 2003. UN DOC. s/2004/573, 16 July 2004.

Women's Initiatives for Gender Justice (2006). Letter to ICC Prosecutor, available at: www.iccwomen.org/documents/Prosecutor_Letter_August_2006_Redacted.pdf.

11

A Step Back to Take a Step Forward

The Future of Justice in Conflict

MARK KERSTEN

Introduction

The International Criminal Court (ICC) is the first international tribunal that regularly intervenes in ongoing and active conflicts. For many of its most fervent proponents, the ICC signals that there can be 'no peace without justice'.[1] For the ICC's champions, no longer should peace be negotiated without consideration of the need to hold perpetrators of mass atrocities to account. In the words of former ICC Prosecutor Luis Moreno-Ocampo, 'negotiators have to learn how to adjust to the reality. The court is a reality' (see Allen, 2009). The 'civility' of international criminal justice can not only curb the violent excesses of war; for its advocates, the liberal cosmopolitan norms that underpin international criminal justice can now be brought to bear on the 'barbarity' of ongoing war and atrocity.

The ICC's creation indeed represents something of a game changer in the relationship between conflict resolution and peace-making, on the one hand, and the pursuit of accountability for mass atrocities, on the other. 'The ICC is the archetypal ex ante tribunal', write Mahnoush H. Arsanjani and W. Michael Reisman (2005, p. 385). It is a Court 'established before an international security problem has been resolved or even manifested itself ... established in the midst of the conflict in which the alleged crimes occurred' (Arsanjani and Reisman, 2005). No longer must wars end for international criminal justice to be pursued. On the contrary, in its first two decades of operations, the ICC has readily intervened in ongoing and active conflicts – and it is widely expected, and

[1] Indeed, this slogan has inspired the name of an NGO, *No Peace Without Justice*. See: www.npwj.org.

called upon, to do so. The majority of situations into which the institution has opened official investigations have been active conflicts. But the ICC's forays into situations of ongoing hostilities have not been kind to perceptions of the Court's role in contributing to peace and effecting in-conflict justice, nor to its efficacy in achieving its brand of retributive justice.

Since its first intervention into the conflict between the government of Uganda and the Lord's Resistance Army (LRA), the ICC has been regularly criticised for undermining peace. This is true even in cases where evidence of such contentions is weak or simply speculative as well as in situations where the Court has not been able to intervene, like Syria (see Larcom, Sarr and Willems, 2013). For example, former US Secretary of State Hillary Clinton stated in 2012 that pursuing war crimes charges against Syrian President Bashar al-Assad would 'complicate a resolution of a difficult, complex situation because it limits options to persuade leaders perhaps to step down from power', while then-Swedish Foreign Minister Carl Bildt said doing so 'would put Assad in a head lock and make him less flexible, because we'd be telling him, "your only option is to fight to the death"' (see Spencer, 2012; Dworkin, 2013).

At the same time as it is pilloried for its alleged effects on peace, the ICC has also been criticised for its inability to apprehend targeted suspects involved in the commission of mass atrocities in the active conflicts in which it intervenes. In its two decades, only 21 suspects whose alleged crimes were linked to a violent political conflict have faced judges at the ICC. As a result, the perceptions of the Court's impacts on peace, as well as justice and accountability, have suffered.

Twenty years after it became a functioning international organisation and court, there are subtle signs that the ICC is increasingly reluctant to target individuals engaged in ongoing and active wars. Such is the social learning of an institution whose reputation has been hampered by its record in situations of active warfare.

This chapter illustrates how perceptions of the ICC have been undermined by its forays into active conflicts, how this appears to have led to a newfound reluctance to seek arrest warrants for active belligerents, and what the Court can do to both ameliorate views of its impacts on peace as well as build stronger cases against alleged perpetrators who are simultaneously active combatants. The chapter proceeds as follows. Section 11.2 provides an overview of the so-called 'peace versus justice' debate and the perceived and real costs of the ICC's interventions into ongoing wars. It then describes the apparent reluctance of ICC prosecutors to target individuals actively engaged in political violence. Despite these shortcomings and reputational costs, the Court cannot be expected to discontinue its practice of intervening in ongoing and active conflicts. Section 11.3 thus delves into how the ICC could move forward without repeating past behaviour and replicating its shortcomings. First, this section argues that the Court and its proponents must learn from the (mixed) empirical record of its interventions, temper expectations, and take the critical observations and concerns of diplomats, states, and researchers more seriously. Second, the section explores the possibility of the Court outsourcing real-time, in-conflict evidence collection to private, non-profit non-governmental organisations. The chapter ends with some concluding reflections on the future of justice in conflict.

11.1 The International Criminal Court and the 'Peace versus Justice' Debate

11.1.1 Overview of the Peace–Justice Debate

While the argument over the relationship between peace and justice dates farther back than the negotiations of the ICC's Statute in Rome (see Kersten, 2016a, pp. 3–4), the entrance of the ICC onto the global stage has inflamed the so-called 'peace versus justice' debate. This is in large part because, among international criminal courts, the ICC is unique; unlike the ad hoc tribunals and hybrid courts, established to deal with justice *after* the end of hostilities, the Court was established to intervene in active theatres of war around the globe and as they emerged.[2]

The ICC's design is unique. First, the ICC is a *permanent* institution. Unlike its hybrid and ad hoc predecessors, the Court was created to be able to respond to emerging mass atrocities rather than deal with crimes committed during specific and time-bound conflicts. Second, the ICC's forward-looking temporal jurisdiction is limitless. Once it has jurisdiction over a territory and a preliminary examination determines that crimes under the Rome Statute have been perpetrated, are sufficiently grave, and are not being genuinely investigated and/or prosecuted by

[2] The International Criminal Tribunal for the Former Yugoslavia did investigate crimes in ongoing conflicts in the Balkans and, indeed, did so years after its establishment, in Kosovo. However, it was restricted to the area of the former Yugoslavia. Additionally, the Special Criminal Court, a hybrid tribunal that is in the processes of being set up in the Central African Republic, is also likely to investigate crimes perpetrated in the context of ongoing hostilities there.

national authorities, there is no conflict dynamic or level of hostilities that prohibits the ICC from opening an investigation or issuing arrest warrants for active combatants. The chief Prosecutor may, of course, exercise their discretion and, at least theoretically, exercise another criterion, the 'interests of justice', in order to delay an intervention or the issuance of arrest warrants.[3] However, this seems a remote possibility and 'interests of justice' have never been invoked to date, and it remains a mystery precisely what they – the 'interests of justice' – constitute.

Third, the ICC is widely expected to, and in some cases pressured to, intervene in active wars. No sooner does a violent political conflict erupt than speculation arises as to whether and how the ICC may become involved. This has been evident in the cases of political violence in Myanmar, Palestine, Syria, and Burundi (see Amnesty International, 2013; Human Rights Watch, 2016; Hunt, 2017; United Nations News Centre, 2017). The Court is, in a sense, viewed as a 'first responder' to conflicts characterised by human rights violations and mass atrocities. Finally, as a result of all of the above factors, the ICC has an institutional interest in intervening in ongoing conflicts. If it cannot fulfil its design or the expectations of it as an institution that responds to actively unfolding international crimes, then the Court's reputation will inevitably suffer. Insofar as it can be treated as an institutional agent (Barnett and Finnemore, 2004, p. 23; see also Bosco, 2014, p. 17), the ICC wants to be seen as an effective force in the most potent crises affecting global politics. Nowhere is this clearer than when situations are referred to it by the United Nations (UN) Security Council (see below).

Thus, while it is true that concerns regarding the effects of prosecuting perpetrators of international crimes on peace, order, and stability precede the creation of the ICC, the Court's emergence as an international institution has elevated, or perhaps better, *exacerbated*, the real and perceived tensions between peace and justice.

In its simplest terms, the peace–justice debate represents a division between those who believe that there is 'no peace without justice' and those who insist that there can be 'no justice without peace'. For proponents of in-conflict justice, judicial interventions can help to marginalise actual perpetrators (see e.g. Wippman, 2006, p. 120), deter potential perpetrators (see e.g. Minow, 1998, p. 11; see also Lie, Binningsbø and

[3] Some scholars have written that it is precisely the 'interests of justice' which could be invoked by the Prosecutor as a means to defer an investigation or prosecution in favour of fragile peace processes (see e.g. Roht-Arriaza, 2000, p. 81).

Gates, 2006, p. 7; Cronin-Furman, 2013), and act as a positive force in bringing warring parties to the negotiation table (see e.g. Bensouda, 2013). Justice is not only an integral part of a full and sustainable peace, but peace should be achieved *through* justice. For example, according to former ICC chief Prosecutor Fatou Bensouda (2013),

> The debate about peace versus justice or peace over justice is a patently false choice. Peace and justice are two sides of the same coin. The road to peace should be seen as running via justice, and thus peace and justice can be pursued simultaneously.

For sceptics of such benevolent effects, international criminal justice pursued prior to the termination of hostilities risks undermining attempts at conflict resolution by dissuading real and potential targets of judicial sanction from engaging in peace processes. Justice, they insist, must wait for peace or, as Snyder and Vinjamuri (2003/2004, p. 6) exclaim: 'Justice does not lead; it follows.' For some critics, '"no peace without justice" is not a peacemaking slogan, but a call to war' (Weissman, 2010). Peace must thus be prioritised over accountability. As Julie Flint and Alex de Waal (2009) wrote in response to the issuance of an ICC arrest warrant for Sudanese President Omar al-Bashir over his alleged responsibility for atrocities in Darfur:

> International justice is a virtuous enterprise, but not risk-free. Sudanese people are already paying a high price for the abandonment of the diplomatic approach that has yielded such benefits over the last four years. . . . There will be no justice in Sudan without peace. When peace and justice clash, as they do in Sudan today, peace must prevail.

The argument has also been put forward that justice and peace must be carefully sequenced so as not to disrupt conflict resolution and/or post-conflict settlements (see e.g. Refugee Law Project, 2005; Vinjamuri, 2015, pp. 20–23). This position has often been proposed as a middle-ground solution to the peace–justice debate. As Leslie Vinjamuri (2015, p. 29) writes, '[C]ontrary to the mantra that justice delayed is justice denied, the most promising way to promote justice may be to postpone it.' However, what sequencing as a state-based political policy would look like in practice remains unclear, as do details of how sequencing would work as a premeditated policy employed in a post-conflict state (see Kersten, 2011). Indeed, informing senior-level perpetrators that they may be prosecuted but only later in time would seem to give such actors the incentive to retain the capacity to inflict violence so as to be able to push any future prosecution further down the line.

Others propose that the solution to the dichotomy of the peace–justice debate is to approach the matter more 'holistically' and thus to conceive of justice beyond its punitive, retributive version (International Center for Transitional Justice, 2009; see also Olsen, Payne and Reiter, 2010, pp. 24–25). For one scholar, for example, 'the way forward ... is to explore whether and how the ICC can contribute to peace as part of a comprehensive and holistic justice strategy' (Clark, 2011, p. 545). Such observers thus introduce mechanisms of restorative and transitional justice, including truth commissions, traditional or alternative forms of justice, reparations, as means to move beyond the peace–justice debate. While undoubtedly compelling and useful, this approach focuses more on the relationship between trial justice and other forms of justice, and thus does little to increase understanding of the effects of international criminal justice itself on conflict resolution and peace-making. Nor is it clear that an approach that mixes various transitional justice mechanisms would minimise or altogether avoid any possible deleterious effects of ICC interventions. Moreover, proposals for alternatives to criminal prosecution by state actors engaged in conflict should be met by a healthy dose of scepticism. Such alternatives may be proposed not because of any principled dedication to transitional justice mechanisms that may be less likely to disrupt peace but precisely because such mechanisms will preclude criminal liability for state-level perpetrators.[4] None of this is to suggest that a holistic approach to transitional justice is misguided; on the contrary, there is clearly no 'one-size' justice that 'fits all', and continued attention should be brought to bear on how various justice mechanisms can be enacted in a complementary fashion. But the effects of international criminal justice on peace are unlikely to be clarified by muddying the waters and adding additional interpretations of justice to the mix.

More recently, scholars have put forward more modest assessments and acknowledged that claims concerning the empirical effects of the ICC on the situations in which it intervenes remain specious – and certainly insufficient as a means of ascertaining whether such interventions are either 'good' or 'bad' for conflict and post-conflict states (see

[4] For example, as Priscilla B. Hayner (2011, p. 14) writes, unlike trials 'the proposal for a truth commission has generally not upset peace negotiations, and it has been common for both rebel and government negotiators to agree with relative ease to such a proposal'. However, she adds, 'they may be looking for a weak inquiry, or one that they hope to control'.

Wegner, 2015; Kersten, 2016b; see also Thoms, Ron and Paris, 2010). There is no obvious resolution to the debate. On the contrary, empirical evidence suggests that the Court's effects are often mixed and ambiguous (see Kersten, 2016b). For example, a growing consensus suggests that ICC's intervention in northern Uganda was among the factors that encouraged the LRA to engage in peace negotiations with the Government of Uganda between 2006 and 2008, yet may also have dissuaded senior LRA officials from agreeing to a comprehensive peace agreement (see Wegner, 2012, p. 11). At the same time, it is clear that the impacts of the ICC are often blown out of proportion. Little heed is paid to the types of actors that are targeted by the Court and how this might determine the ICC's effects (Kersten, 2017). The preference of many observers is to simply recycle the popular tropes of the peace–justice debate. For example, when an arrest warrant was issued for Libya's Colonel Gaddafi, commentators feared this would leave him with little incentive but to reject a negotiated settlement to the civil war and 'ensure that he will stay in Libya to the bitter end and go down fighting' (International Crisis Group, 2011). There is, however, no evidence that has been produced that suggests that the ICC had a significant effect on Gaddafi's strategic decision-making during the war or his interest in a negotiated settlement with the Libyan opposition and rebel groups (see Kersten, 2016a, pp. 135–42). As explored further below, more sober reflections regarding the ICC's impact on peace and conflict processes are needed and, it appears, are increasingly accepted beyond the small cabal of researchers focused on the Court's empirical record as well as key figures at the ICC itself. For example, in her remarks on the impacts of the Court on justice on peace, ICC President Silvia Fernández de Gurmendi (2015) observed that 'there is no real answer to this'. The ICC's effects remain more murky than clear and require more, and deeper, research and analysis.

Despite the growing maturity of the field of international criminal justice, it is fair to say that calls for the Court to intervene in ongoing conflicts are invariably met with a recitation of the original tropes of the peace–justice debate. Perhaps in part due to the continued uncertainty over the effects of the Court's interventions, it is repeatedly proclaimed the ICC's involvement will either deliver peace or risk undermining it and fuelling conflict. Such dichotomous framing is, at times, also invoked by senior-level government officials and diplomats (see e.g. Mbeki and Mamdani, 2014), including some who could potentially find themselves the target of investigation (see e.g. Kiir and Machar, 2016). Such machinations have come at a significant cost to the ICC.

11.1.2 The Cost of Justice in Conflict

The International Criminal Court's pursuit of justice in conflict has not reinforced its reputation as a positive contributor to conflict resolution. While empirical research into the matter has not been conducted, it seems unlikely that anyone who initially feared that the ICC had negative effects on peace would not believe, let alone assert, the opposite. Moreover, concerns over its impacts may undermine its attempts to achieve universal jurisdiction. In explaining its (subsequently revoked) notice of withdrawal from the ICC, the government of South Africa explicitly noted its concerns regarding what it viewed as its conflicting obligations to peace-making and the Rome Statute (see DIRCO, 2016):

> In complex and multi-faceted peace negotiations and sensitive post-conflict situations, peace and justice must be viewed as complementary and not mutually exclusive. The reality is that in an imperfect world we cannot apply international law in an idealistic view that strives for justice and accountability and thus competing with the immediate objectives peace, security and stability. . . . Under these circumstances South Africa is of the view that to continue to be a State Party to the Rome Statute will not be helpful to achieve its foreign policy objectives for the following reasons: It will compromise South Africa's efforts to promote peace and security on the African Continent and to play an essential part in international peacekeeping missions in Africa and in related peace processes.

At the same time as it faces criticisms over its impacts on peace, the ICC's interventions into active conflicts have not, in many cases, resulted in its targeted perpetrators being brought to justice. Such are its shortcomings in bringing targeted perpetrators to account at the Court that it has now become commonplace for the ICC's proponents to claim that its ultimate success will be its impact on local justice – and not the number of individuals *it* prosecutes. In Libya, for example, where none of the five individuals indicted by the ICC have been surrendered to the Court since it opened an investigation there in 2011, the ICC's Office of the Prosecutor has focused primarily on how the Court's actions have galvanised domestic accountability via the principle of 'positive complementarity' (see Nouwen, 2013, pp. 13–14; Kersten, 2016a, pp. 182–83). More recently, Elizabeth Evenson (2015) of Human Rights Watch has written that '[d]elivering justice for victims is the *raison d'être* of the ICC. But making justice count for victims requires much more than fair trials in a Hague courtroom. . . . The Hague is not where the ICC matters most.'

Together, these realities have contributed to undermining the perception of the ICC as a positive force in situations of active war as well as an effective judicial body. Perhaps no situation has adversely affected views regarding the ICC's impact on peace processes as significantly as northern Uganda where, in July 2004, the ICC opened its first-ever investigation. This followed lengthy negotiations between officials in the Office of the Prosecutor and the Government of Uganda, which had itself been involved in a war with the LRA since approximately 1987. The referral (*Situation in Uganda*, 2004) was a poorly masked attempt by the Government of Uganda to refer its adversaries, the LRA, to the ICC. The initial referral of the LRA (and *not* the situation in northern Uganda) to the Court, as well as the public announcement of the referral at a London press conference featuring Prosecutor Moreno-Ocampo and Ugandan President Yoweri Museveni, signalled to many in northern Uganda that the Court's intervention would inevitably be biased. A chorus of observers have insisted that the Government and its military forces, and not just the LRA, are responsible for mass atrocities (see Weeks, 2002; Dolan, 2009; Mwenda, 2010). Despite the amendment of the referral to concern 'the situation in northern Uganda' (see Decision Assigning the Situation in Uganda, 2004) and prevarications from then-chief Prosecutor Luis Moreno-Ocampo that LRA crimes would receive priority because they were graver, a widespread sense that the Prosecutor was biased has persisted (see Moreno-Ocampo, 2005, 2007). At the same time, and perhaps owing to a belief that Museveni sought an ICC intervention in order to achieve military aims rather than as a result of any commitment to justice, the ICC investigation and its subsequent issuance of arrest warrants for five senior members of the LRA drew the ire of citizens and civil society groups in the region. There was widespread sense among these actors that the Court's actions would undermine a fragile peace process, disregard traditional forms of justice, and dissuade combatants from defecting from the bush (see Branch, 2004, 2011; Allen, 2006; Apuuli, 2006).

As noted above, empirical research suggests that the ICC's intervention, among a number of other factors, played a positive role in encouraging the LRA senior command to engage in peace talks with the Government of Uganda in Juba, South Sudan, between 2006 and 2008. However, many believe that the ICC also helped to undermine prospects of the LRA leadership signing a Comprehensive Peace Agreement. At best, the Court was irrelevant in dissuading the LRA from signing the peace pact with the Government because the peace talks themselves were never truly about achieving a lasting peace and they were undermined by other factors, including a lack of trust between the sides and a strategic use by both sides of the talks as a means to prepare for continued warfare (Kersten, 2016a, pp. 101–8).

In short, the ICC's intervention in northern Uganda acted as a lightning rod for criticism of pursuing in-conflict justice. That perception has persisted and bled into perceptions of the ICC's impacts in other situations. The Court's intervention in Darfur in 2005 precipitated a new round of dramatic assertions and loud condemnations regarding ICC justice and its implications on conflict resolution (see Natsios, 2009; de Waal and Stanton, 2009; Wegner, 2015, pp. 126–44). So too did the Court's involvement in Libya (see Sands, 2011; Saunders, 2011; Vinjamuri and Snyder, 2011). This is not to say that these claims are correct. Indeed, research on the ICC's effects on peace processes too often views the Court's intervention in a vacuum without considering additional conflict dynamics (see Kersten, 2016a). But the intuitive nature of arguments such as Michael Scharf's claim (2000, p. 180) that no warring actor can be expected 'to agree to a peace agreement if, directly following the agreement, they would find themselves or their associates facing potential life imprisonment', remain persuasive to many. These assertions help to undermine a core, and continuing, claim of the Court's senior-most professionals, namely that peace must be pursued through justice and that the institution is a 'partner' of governments and peoples in the 'journey towards sustainable peace' (see Bensouda, 2017).

At the same time as it faces criticisms over its impacts on peace, the ICC is unable to directly investigate allegations of international crimes in the context of ongoing and active conflicts. This is a result of a combination of two factors: one, the stringent criteria regarding risk-assessment for Court staff conducting operations in situation countries and, two, the reality that some states in which the institution has ongoing investigations are outright hostile to the Court.

The inability of ICC investigators to investigate on the ground during active conflicts is particularly evident in the two cases of referrals from the UN Security Council: Darfur and Libya. Despite opening an investigation into crimes committed in the context of the war in Darfur in 2005, not a single ICC official or investigator has ever stepped foot on the Sudanese territory of Darfur.[5] Similarly, following its investigations into the 2011 uprising in Libya, ICC investigators issued three public arrest

[5] Confirmed to the author by ICC staff.

warrants in June of the same year – for Colonel Muammar Gaddafi, Saif al-Islam Gaddafi, and Abdullah al-Senussi. Those warrants were issued in June 2011. But investigators only arrived in Libya *after* the conclusion of the uprising in October of that year. Prohibited from on-the-ground, in-conflict investigations, in both the Darfur and Libya situations, ICC investigators have had to rely on other sources of evidence, including intermediaries on the ground and the testimony of displaced persons.

In other instances, where the ICC *can* have an on-ground presence, the Court is severely dependent on the government of the situation country. A telling statistic of this dependence is that the ICC has only ever targeted the adversaries of governments that have self-referred a conflict or situation on their territory to the Court (see Tiemessen, 2014). The reasons for this are relatively clear and have been described by senior staff at the institution as a matter of 'pragmatism' (see Kersten, 2013). But, as Kenneth Rodman (2014, p. 7) argues, this comes at some cost: in situations of self-referrals and where a state is 'co-operative', the self-referring government may seek to instrumentalise the Court's intervention in order to castigate, delegitimise, and marginalise their adversaries.

In short, the Court believes that it must target government enemies first in order to ensure that it can achieve *any* justice for crimes committed in that state. If the Prosecutor was to initiate criminal proceedings against government officials, all state co-operation for the gathering of evidence, for the provision of security for investigators and Court staff, and for the ability of the ICC to conduct on-the-ground outreach programs would evaporate. The approach of the Prosecutor can thus best be described as 'rebels first, government officials (maybe) later'. Many are still waiting on the possibility of the latter.

In both situations – where the ICC faces an 'adversarial' government and thus cannot put investigators on the ground, or where the Court faces less hostile governments but is dependent on them for co-operation – the institution's record in having its targets surrendered to the Court is poor (see Rodman, 2014). It has been well noted that the lack of any means, beyond state co-operation to enforce arrest warrants, is the ICC's 'Achilles' heel' (see Sewall, Kaysen and Scharf, 2000, p. 6; Dicker and Evenson, 2013). And the Court's record in having active belligerents surrendered to the ICC is particularly weak. None of the suspects targeted by the ICC as a result of Security Council referrals in Sudan or Libya have been prosecuted at the Court. In northern Uganda, only one of five targets – the former child soldier turner rebel leader of the LRA,

Dominic Ongwen – has faced judges in The Hague.[6] It is notable that Ongwen was only surrendered to the ICC after he defected from the LRA, disengaged from active participation in hostilities, and after the rebel group's power and salience had been largely exhausted.[7]

Both the widespread perception that the ICC can potentially undermine peace processes as well as its apparent inability to ensure that the conflict actors it targets are successfully surrendered to the ICC weaken the perception of its utility as a first responder to conflicts and its efficacy as a criminal court. It appears that the Court has internalised this reality and taken some pause in its efforts to intervene in ongoing and active conflicts.

11.1.3 Pumping the Breaks on In-conflict Justice?

In a 2016 *New York Times* commentary on the International Criminal Court's response to ongoing tensions between some African states and the ICC, Thierry Cruvellier (2016) made the following observation: 'Not only is the [ICC] beginning to move away from cases involving African states; it is also partly moving away from atrocities committed during war.' While the Court cannot avoid intervening in situations of ongoing conflict, as to do so would undermine its mission and the expectations of its work, it does appear that the Court is increasingly reluctant to target senior-level perpetrators actively involved in active violent political conflicts.

Under the tenure of Prosecutor Bensouda, the ICC issued three warrants of arrest for international crimes.[8] Only one – the warrant for Mahmoud al-Werfalli, a commander in the self-styled Libyan National Army – pertains to an alleged perpetrator engaged in ongoing hostilities (*Prosecutor v Mahmoud Mustafa Busayf Al-Werfalli*, 15 August 2017). Another warrant, for the former head of the International Security Agency under Gaddafi, Al-Tuhamy Mohamed Khaled, was initially

[6] Three of the other five – Vincent Otti, Raska Lukwiya, Okot Odhiambo – are deceased, although the ICC has only terminated proceedings against the former two. Only LRA leader Joseph Kony is believed to be alive.

[7] There is an ongoing debate as to the strength of the LRA. However, many observers of the rebellion have suggested that the group has diminished in size and strength. An African Union mission against the LRA and supported by the US military ended in 2017.

[8] Under Bensouda, five individuals were also charged, in relation to the case against Jean-Pierre Bemba Gombo, pertaining to offences against the administration of justice (see *Prosecutor v Bemba et al.*).

issued in 2013 but was only unsealed in 2017 *(Prosecutor v Al-Tuhamy Mohamed Khaled*, 24 April 2017). The unsealing of the warrant against Khaled appears to have been the result of exasperation in the Prosecutor's office; despite the warrant being under seal, no state with the ability – notably Egypt – was willing to co-operate with the Court to secure Khaled's surrender (see Cusack, 2017). It is believed that the former regime figure is in hiding and has not been engaged in hostilities since at least 2011. His case may, however, suggest a shift in the ICC's strategy in pursuing belligerents with sealed arrest warrants and only unsealing them after their engagement in active conflict has passed and the ICC either identifies an opportunity for surrender or becomes exasperated with a lack of state co-operation and interest in enforcing warrants.

There may be other reasons for the ICC's apparent patience. Under Prosecutor Bensouda, the Office of the Prosecutor (OTP) made subtle, but significant, changes to its overall prosecutorial strategy, embracing a more cautious and diligent approach to case-building. In contrast to the widely perceived rushed approach of former chief Prosecutor Luis Moreno-Ocampo, and as a result of concerns from ICC judges that cases brought to them were weak, the OTP under Bensouda declared that its cases at the confirmation stage would be 'as trial-ready as possible' (Office of the Prosecutor of the ICC, 2013, p. 6; see also Whiting, 2013). It is easy to read this as an attempt to avoid having cases collapse once suspects arrive at the ICC, as they have on a number of cases under Moreno-Ocampo, most famously with Kenyan President Uhuru Kenyatta and Deputy President William Ruto. But this approach may also be a logical response to how difficult it is to build strong cases while conflicts are ongoing and ICC investigators cannot gather evidence on the ground.

The third warrant of arrest issued under Bensouda, for Ahmad al-Faqi al-Mahdi, is further evidence of the ICC's reluctance to target actors involved in ongoing conflicts. In the early hours of Saturday, 26 September 2015, the ICC issued a press release announcing that al-Mahdi, a Malian national and member of the extremist Ansar Dine group, had been transferred into the Court's custody (International Criminal Court Press Release, 2017). Days earlier, the ICC had issued an arrest warrant, under seal, charging al-Mahdi with the war crime of destroying mausoleums, shrines, and other sites of antiquity in Timbuktu, Mali. His arrest came as a surprise to many observers. The conflict in northern Mali had been under investigation by the ICC for over two and a half years, and no arrest warrants had been issued prior to al-Mahdi's transfer to The Hague. In the coming days, it became evident that al-Mahdi had been in prison in neighbouring Niger for months before the Court moved to indict and have him surrendered. In other words, al-Mahdi had been *hors de combat* for around a year prior to the ICC's warrant of arrest being issued. The OTP moved with haste to gain custody of al-Mahdi as a consequence of concerns that al-Mahdi might have been released from prison. Later, in the course of his trial at the ICC, it was revealed that al-Mahdi was willing to co-operate with the Court's investigators *prior* to being surrendered (see Judgement and Sentence, 2016, p. 45; see also Whiting, 2016). The result of his trial was the first-ever guilty plea at the ICC and a nine-year conviction for his crimes. His sentence was handed down a year and one day after al-Mahdi was surrendered to the Court – a remarkably quick turnaround for any international criminal tribunal, let alone the ICC. The institution's patient approach as well as the opportunity it identified in targeting a figure already in detention, who had long ceased being involved in active political violence, and who promised to co-operate in building cases against potential perpetrators involved in active conflict, paid off.

The cases of al-Mahdi and al-Tuhamy, in particular, indicate an increasing propensity for the ICC to pursue belligerents who were, but are no longer, engaged in active conflict. At this juncture, it seems unimaginable for the ICC to intervene in an active conflict and issue five arrest warrants for senior-level and active belligerents, as it did with the high-command of the LRA. Yet the ICC will continue to intervene in active conflicts – and it cannot simply wait until they conclude to issue warrants of arrest. So what can be done to ameliorate the reputation of the ICC as an in-conflict actor and to build stronger cases against active combatants? The next section turns to answering these questions.

11.2 Investigating International Crimes in Ongoing and Active Conflicts: Towards a New Model?

The ICC faces a dilemma. It cannot simply transform itself into a Court that intervenes after the conclusion of war. If it chose to do so, the criticism that the ICC risks thwarting the efforts to end wars would simply be translated into a criticism that the Court undercuts the maintenance of peace and its rebuke. There is no timing for ICC interventions that would insulate the institution from criticism. But the Court also can't proceed with business as usual and expect that it won't continue to be criticised for its effects on peace processes or improve its record in building strong cases and bringing belligerents to account. So what can the ICC do?

11.2.1 A Call for Sobriety

To date, and with some notable exceptions (e.g. de Gurmendi, 2015), the ICC's senior staff have responded to criticisms of its impacts by recycling the claims such as 'Peace and justice are two sides of the same coin' (Bensouda, 2013). On occasion, Court officials have also argued that the ICC has 'kick-started' peace negotiations (Bensouda, 2013). However, given that no organ of the court does any stock-taking on the institution's effects on conflict resolution or peace-making, these arguments represent a largely rhetorical, rather than empirically verified, position.[9]

ICC officials have also periodically offered an alternative view, namely that the institution has no responsibility over peace and that there is a division of labour between 'the interests of peace' and 'the interests of justice', with the former being the prerogative of other institutions such as the Security Council (see Office of the Prosecutor of the ICC, 2007). This echoes a question the author was once asked by an astute student at a conference as to whether it was fair to judge the ICC for its effects on peace when the institution is a criminal court and not itself involved in-conflict resolution and peace processes.

A problem is that the two above positions – that there is no peace without ICC justice and that the endeavour to achieve peace and the pursuit of justice are separate goals – reside in logical contradiction. Either the ICC is an institution through which peace can be achieved, as Prosecutor Bensouda has insisted, or peace is the responsibility of other actors, and the ICC cannot be judged for its impacts on it. The ICC is not merely judged because it intervenes in ongoing conflicts – but because its proponents and its senior staff continuously claim that the institution has positive impacts on peace.

One way out of this dilemma is for the ICC to embrace more sober assessments with regard to its effects. This would decrease the expectations that it must, without exception, have positive impacts on conflict resolution and peace. While it would be difficult to undo twenty years of lofty rhetoric, the Court would be less likely to be criticised if its senior

[9] This was confirmed to the author in a conversation with an OTP official.

staff discontinued the pretension that their impacts are all and invariably positive. Instead, the ICC could learn from research which illustrates the institution's mixed empirical record of its interventions and take the critical observations and concerns of diplomats, states, and researchers more seriously by endorsing the value of their work and embracing empirical research into the Court's impacts. There are signs that some senior ICC figures are willing to put forward a more balanced view of what the ICC can and can't achieve. In the same speech noted above, ICC President Fernández de Gurmendi (2015), for example, candidly declared:

> The positive impact [of the ICC on peace], I would say, is difficult to assess … but also there has been … a lot of arguing about the negative impact that justice can have [on], for instance, peace negotiations. So this has been a dilemma and a tension that has also been a part for the first ten years of the Court … and is extremely important discussion that is going to be continued because the Court has moved … squarely into [intervening in] ongoing conflicts. So this tension between peace and justice becomes more and more important and there is no real answer to this.

By embracing more balanced rhetoric, the Court could pivot in how it communicates its effects by stating that it is willing to work and engage with all relevant actors to minimise any unintended negative effects of its interventions and maximise its positive impacts. This would put forward an image of an ICC that was interested in setting realistic expectations and being honest not only in what it can achieve but the impacts that it has control over.

11.2.2 Alternative Forms of Investigating In-conflict Crimes

As noted above, due to security concerns and the risk thresholds for staff, the ICC simply cannot place its investigators on the ground in conflict situations. As a consequence, the OTP has relied on gathering evidence outside of the conflict zone or via intermediaries. Yet, while it would not solve the Court's Sisyphean struggle for effective state co-operation and the enforcement of its arrest warrants, the Court could build stronger cases by partly outsourcing investigations to a new breed of organisations specifically created to investigate crimes committed in the midst of active conflicts.

It is not unheard of to outsource elements of a tribunal's mandate to external entities that may have strategic advantages over the tribunal in question. On the contrary, it appears increasingly acceptable to do so. For example, outreach efforts during the trial of former Chadian President Hissène Habré in the Extraordinary African Chambers (EAC) in Dakar, Senegal, were fully outsourced to a group of communications organisations.[10] Franck Petit, team leader of the Outreach Consortium, maintains that the externalisation of outreach activities was the 'main innovation' of the EAC (see Justice Hub, 2017). These organisations had strategic advantages over any outreach efforts, which had to take place not only in Senegal but in Chad and internationally. In a similar vein, outsourcing investigatorial efforts to entities outside of the ICC Prosecutor's office could bear fruit.

One such group is the Commission for International Justice and Accountability (CIJA).[11] Established in 2012, the CIJA is private, non-profit non-governmental organisation (NGO) led by a team of former investigators from internationalised and hybrid tribunals, as well as domestic war crimes units. The organisation has approximately 150 personnel. Its staff train, mentor, and support over fifty investigators in Iraq and Syria, who investigate ongoing crimes by the regime in Syria as well as Da'esh in Iraq. The result of the CIJA's work is a repository of evidence that has been smuggled out of Syria and Iraq for safe-keeping and analysis in secure and specialised archives in Europe. These can be accessed by investigators from states as well as international institutions and civil society groups. The ultimate aim, according to its Executive Director, William Wiley, is to create 'dossiers inculpating ranking individuals for present-day and future criminal prosecution in domestic as well as international jurisdictions' (Subcommittee on International Human Rights, 2016). Importantly, unlike the UN Commission of Inquiry on Syria or other bodies and organisations documenting crimes in Syria and elsewhere, 'the CIJA is far more akin to the investigative division of an international prosecutor's office than it is to a human rights organization', whose investigations and analyses 'conform to the evidentiary standards applied within any international and western domestic criminal law jurisdiction' (Subcommittee on International Human Rights, 2016). The evidence collected by CIJA is precisely that

[10] The three organisations comprising the Consortium were: Belgium-based RCN Justice & Démocratie, Chad-based Magi Communication, and Dakar-based Primum Africa Consulting.

[11] While the CIJA does not have a website (for security reasons), detailed information and analysis regarding the organisation has been published widely (see Kersten, 2014; Borger, 2015; Taub, 2016; Wiens, 2016).

sought by institutions with criminal jurisdiction such as the ICC: linkage evidence which, as its name suggests, *links* evidence of atrocities to specific high-level and senior-ranking officials or, in the ICC's *lingua franca*, to those bearing the 'greatest responsibility' for international crimes.

According to its own internal numbers, in 2016, the CIJA received thirty-four requests for assistance from eleven countries, three NGOs, and one international organisation.[12] It has collected over '700,000 original pages of Syrian regime documentation; conducted hundreds of victim, and most especially insider, witness interviews; and collected other forms of physical and electronic evidence' (Subcommittee on International Human Rights, 2016). Stephen Rapp, the former chief Prosecutor of the Special Court for Sierra Leone and former US Ambassador-at-large for War Crimes Issues, has declared that the collected evidence against the Assad regime 'is massive and overwhelming, far better than we had, frankly at Nuremberg' or any other international criminal tribunal (CNN Amanpour, 2017). While it continues to be unlikely that the UN Security Council will refer the situation in Syria to the ICC, should that eventuality transpire, the evidence collected by the CIJA would assuredly inform any indictments and prosecutions brought by the Court's prosecutors.

While the evidence collected by investigators from the CIJA, especially evidence implicating senior-level figures, has not been thoroughly tested in either domestic or international courts, the strategic advantages of groups like the CIJA are evident. First and most obviously, precisely because the ICC does not have territorial jurisdiction over alleged crimes committed in Syria, it has never been mandated to collect evidence of atrocities committed there. This is particularly relevant, given that the war in Syria has, as of writing, been ongoing for over eleven years. Given the likelihood of regimes, like that of Assad, destroying evidence of criminality and atrocity, if the ICC was eventually to be requested to investigate crimes in Syria, it would be severely handicapped. The CIJA's archives thus act as something of an evidence bank in that the evidentiary investments and deposits made by its investigators can be redeemed and pay-off in the future – for the ICC or some other tribunal mandated to investigate and prosecute crimes in Syria. Second, the model of investigation offered by the CIJA should be of interest to the ICC even where it

[12] These statistics were presented by CIJA staff member at 2016 Assembly of States Parties of the ICC. A copy of these statistics is on file with author.

already has jurisdiction. Where the ICC cannot investigate on the ground due to security and personal risk thresholds, the CIJA can help 'fill the gap', producing quality evidence of ongoing atrocities that can be used to issue arrest warrants or build subsequent cases.

Of course, the work of groups such as the CIJA is not foolproof in producing impartial justice. Indeed, the CIJA faces the same reliance on opposition forces in Syria as the ICC has with self-referring governments. Both need to pick a 'devil' to work with in order to access crime scenes or areas where evidence may be stored as well as for reasons of personnel security. The result is the possible entrenchment of asymmetrical justice and accountability. For the CIJA, the work of its investigators in collecting evidence against the Assad regime and Da'esh requires the co-operation of opposition forces, thus leaving their alleged atrocities outside the scope of investigation. While it requires greater attention and scrutiny, this shortcoming of non-profit organisations investigating in-conflict crimes could potentially be alleviated by employing multiple investigatorial groups within the same conflict – something that the ICC, as a singular institution, could never achieve.

Conclusion: Towards a Future for Justice in Conflict

Sometimes it is necessary to take a step back in order to press forward. This is not news to the ICC. The Court's prosecutors under the tenure of Fatou Bensouda evidently re-evaluated their case-building models and preferred a more diligent, patient, and comprehensive approach to pursuing arrest warrants for perpetrators of atrocity crimes. The institution appears to be doing much the same with its penchant for pursuing perpetrators involved in ongoing violent political conflicts.

It is worth reiterating: the ICC will not cease its interventions into active and ongoing conflicts. To do so would undermine its *raison d'être*. If, after all, the world's only *permanent* international criminal court cannot intervene to address mass atrocities perpetrated when they erupt, then what is the ICC for?

Prosecutorial opportunities that compel the Prosecutor to act may arise in times of peace and in times of conflict. Moreover, while the practice of accepting politically tailored referrals from the UN Security Council remains controversial, it would be virtually unfathomable for the Court to reject such referrals. The aforementioned expectations that the ICC act as a first responder to political violence and mass atrocity would simply not permit the Court to reject a request to intervene in an ongoing and active conflict by the Security Council or by a state exercising its powers of self-referral. While such interventions, particularly those stemming from the Security Council, seem unlikely to yield positive impacts for the Court, the institution is stuck somewhere between a rock and a hard place; not intervening would only undermine the Court's reputation further. In both scenarios, the ICC would be severely criticised for exercising 'politics'. There is, as Darryl Robinson cogently observes, no 'Goldilocks zone' for the ICC (see Robinson, 2015).

But this does not mean that the ICC should yield to the status quo when it comes to interventions in ongoing and active conflicts. This chapter has argued that ICC staff should refrain from preaching that the effects of the ICC on peace-making and conflict resolution are always and invariably positive. A more balanced and sober assessment of what the ICC's effects have been, and indeed *can* be, would not undercut the Court's reputation. On the contrary, it would more effectively set expectations of the institution and present a more honest appraisal of what the institution can and cannot achieve when it comes to making justice and peace work symbiotically. It would also signal an interest to peacemakers, diplomats, negotiators, mediators, and experts in conflict and peace studies that the Court itself understands the concerns that have been raised and is interested in working to emphasise its positive impacts and minimise its negative effects.

The chapter has also argued that in order to build stronger cases against belligerents involved in active conflict, the ICC should consider outsourcing its investigatorial operations to non-profit organisations that have strategic advantages over the Court's investigation capacities due to their ability to investigate on the ground in in-conflict situations. Of course, to do so a clear memorandum of understanding and professional relationship between the two would have to be established. But the benefits of such a relationship, as described in Section 11.3, are evident.

It has now been over twenty years since the ICC was established. Its promise was to bring law to bear on situations of active conflict and atrocity; to bring the 'civility' of international criminal justice to the 'barbarity' of modern violent political conflicts. To fulfil that promise, the ICC must learn from its own past, accept its limitations, and forge creative means to overcome its own structural shortcomings. Doing so holds the possibility of one day finding the means of pursuing justice in order to truly bolster peace.

References

Allen, E. (2009). Seven questions: prosecuting Sudan. *Foreign Policy* (online), https://foreignpolicy.com/2009/02/12/seven-questions-prosecuting-sudan/.

Allen, T. (2006). *Trial Justice: The International Criminal Court and the Lord's Resistance Army*, London: Zed Books.

Amnesty International (2013). Dozens of countries call on UN to refer Syria to International Criminal Court (online), www.amnesty.org.uk/press-releases/dozens-countries-call-un-refer-syria-international-criminal-court.

Apuuli, K. P. (2006). The ICC arrest warrants for the Lord's Resistance Army leaders and peace prospects for Northern Uganda. *Journal of International Criminal Justice* 4(1), 179–87.

Arsanjani, M. H., and Reisman, W. M. (2005). Law-in-action of the International Criminal Court. *American Journal of International Law* 99, 385–403.

Barnett, M. N., and Finnemore, M. (2004). *Rules For the World: International Organizations in Global Politics*, Ithaca, NY: Cornell University Press.

Bensouda, F. (2013). International justice and diplomacy. *New York Times*, 20 March 2013 (online), www.nytimes.com/2013/03/20/opinion/global/the-role-of-the-icc-in-international-justice-and-diplomacy.html.

(2017) Statement of the Prosecutor of the International Criminal Court, Fatou Bensouda, on the conclusion of her visit to Colombia. International Criminal Court, 10–13 September 2017.

Borger, J. (2015). Syria's truth smugglers. *The Guardian*, 12 May 2015 (online).

Bosco, D. (2014). *Rough Justice: The International Criminal Court in a World of Power Politics*, Oxford: Oxford University Press.

Branch, A. (2004). International justice, local injustice. *Dissent Magazine*, 2004.

(2011). *Displacing Human Rights: War and Intervention in Northern Uganda*, Oxford: Oxford University Press.

Clark, J. N. (2011). Peace, justice and the International Criminal Court. *Journal of International Criminal Justice* 9, 521–45.

CNN Amanpour (2017). Assad war crimes proof 'better' than Nuremberg, available online at www.cnn.com/videos/world/2017/02/07/intv-amanpour-stephen-rapp.cnn.

Cronin-Furman, K. (2013). Managing expectations: international criminal trials and the prospects for deterrence of mass atrocity. *The International Journal of Transitional Justice* 8(4), 434–54.

Cruvellier, T. (2016). The ICC, out of Africa. *New York Times*, 7 November 2016 (online).

Cusack, R. (2017). Egypt refuses to send Gaddafi chief to the ICC. *The New Arab*, 28 April 2017 (online).

Dicker, R., and Evenson, L. (2013). ICC suspects can hide: and that is the problem. *Human Rights Watch*, 24 January 2013.

DIRCO (2016). South Africa's withdrawal from the Rome Statute of the International Criminal Court, available online at www.dirco.gov.za/milan_italy/newsandevents/rome_statute.pdf.

Dolan, C. (2009). *Social Torture: The Case of Northern Uganda 1986–2006*, New York: Berghahn Books.

Dworkin, A. (2013). Dilemmas of justice, accountability and peace in Syria. European Council on Foreign Relations, ECFR Background Paper.

Evenson, L. (2015). ICC success depends on its impact locally. *Human Rights Watch*, 26 August 2015.

Flint, J., and de Waal, A. (2009). To put justice before peace spells disaster for Sudan. *The Guardian*, 6 March 2009 (online).

de Gurmendi, S. F. (2015). Judge Silvia Fernández de Gurmendi on *The Law and Practice of the International Criminal Court*, The Hague, 28 September 2015.

Hayner, Priscilla B. (2011). *Unspeakable Truths – Transitional Justice and the Challenge of Truth Commission*, New York: Routledge.

Human Rights Watch (2016). Palestine: ICC should open formal probe. *Human Rights Watch*, 5 June 2016 (online).

Hunt, L. (2017). Myanmar's Rohingya crackdown 'Crimes Against Humanity': top UN official. *The Diplomat*, March 2017 (online).

International Center for Transitional Justice (2009). What is Transitional Justice? (online), www.ictj.org/what-transitional-justice.

International Criminal Court (2017). Situation in Mali: Ahmad Al Faqi Al Mahdi surrendered to the ICC on charges of war crimes regarding the destruction of historical and religious monuments in Timbuktu. *International Criminal Court Press Release.*

International Crisis Group (2011). *Popular Protest in North Africa and the Middle East (V): Making Sense of Libya*, Middle East/North Africa Report No. 107.

Justice Hub (2017). Outreach in the Hissène Habré Trial was an Exercise in Winning Hearts and Minds. *Justice Hub* (online).

Kersten, M. (2011). The fallacy of sequencing peace and justice. *Opinio Juris* (online).

Kersten, M. (2013). In the ICC's interest: between 'pragmatism' and 'idealism'?. *Justice in Conflict* (online).

(2014). What counts as evidence of Syria's war crimes. *The Washington Post*, 28 October 2014 (online).

(2016a). *Justice in Conflict: The Effects of the International Criminal Court's Interventions on Ending Wars and Building Peace*, Oxford: Oxford University Press.

(2016b). Seeing the forest for the trees: The International Criminal Court and the peace-justice debate. *International Criminal Justice Today*, 20 July 2016.

(2017). Targeting justice: targets, non-targets and the prospects for peace with justice. *Canadian Foreign Policy Journal* 23(3), 246–59.

Kiir, S., and Machar, R. (2016). South Sudan needs truth, not trials. *The New York Times*, 8 June 2016 (online).

Larcom, S., Sarr, M., and Willems, T. (2013). What shall we do with the Bad Dictator? VOX, available at http://voxeu.org/article/icc-justice-expense-peace.

Lie, T. G., Binningsbø, H. M., and Gates, S. (2006). 'Post-conflict justice and sustainable peace'. Centre for the Study of Civil War, PRIO and Norwegian University of Science and Technology.

Mbeki, T., and Mamdani, M. (2014). Courts can't end civil wars. *The New York Times*, 6 February 2014 (online).

Minow, M. (1998). *Between Vengeance and Forgiveness: Facing History after Genocide and Mass Violence*, Boston: Beacon Press.

Moreno-Ocampo, L. (2005). Statement by the Chief Prosecutor on the Uganda Arrest Warrants, 14 October 2005, The Hague: International Criminal Court, www.icc-cpi.int/sites/default/files/NR/rdonlyres/AF169689-AFC9-41B9-8A3E-222F07DA42AD/143834/LMO_20051014_English1.pdf.

(2007). Address to the Assembly of States Parties, 30 November 2007, The Hague: International Criminal Court, www.icc-cpi.int/sites/default/files/NR/rdonlyres/5E8FFFB4-89ED-4E3B-B7A3-37F77A8E3B26/278583/Statement_Prosecutor_en_30Nov2007.pdf.

Mwenda, A. (2010). Uganda's politics of foreign aid and violent conflict: the political uses of the LRA rebellion. In T. Allen and K. Vlassenroot, eds., *The Lord's Resistance Army: Myth and Reality*, London: Zed Books.

Natsios, A. (2009). Waltz with Bashir. *Foreign Affairs*, 23 March 2009.

Nouwen, S. M. H. (2013). *Complementarity in the Line of Fire: The Catalysing Effect of the International Criminal Court in Uganda and Sudan*, Cambridge: Cambridge University Press.

Office of the Prosecutor of the International Criminal Court (2007). Policy paper on the interests of justice, The Hague: International Criminal Court, www.icc-cpi.int/sites/default/files/ICCOTPInterestsOfJustice.pdf.

Office of the Prosecutor of the International Criminal Court (2013). Strategic plan June 2012–2015, The Hague: International Criminal Court, www.icc-cpi.int/sites/default/files/iccdocs/otp/OTP-Strategic-Plan-2013.pdf.

Olsen, T. D., Payne, L. A., and Reiter, A. G. (2010). *Transitional Justice in Balance: Comparing Processes, Weighing Efficacy*, Washington, DC: United States Institute of Peace.

Prosecutor v Ahmad al Faqi al Mahdi, Sentencing judgment, ICC-01/12-01/15, 27 September 2016.

Prosecutor v Al-Tuhamy Mohamed Khaled, Decision on Reclassification of the Warrant of Arrest, ICC-01/11-01/13-18, 24 April 2017.

Prosecutor v Mahmoud Mustafa Busayf Al-Werfalli, Warrant of Arrest, ICC-01/11-01/17-2, 15 August 2017.

Refugee Law Project (2005). Peace first, justice later: traditional justice in Northern Uganda, Refugee Law Project Working Paper No. 17.

Robinson, D. (2015). Inescapable dyads: why the International Criminal Court cannot win. *Leiden Journal of International Law* 28(2), 323–47.

Rodman, K. A. (2014). Justice as a dialogue between law and politics embedding the International Criminal Court within conflict management and peace-building. *Journal of International Criminal Justice* 12(3), 437–69.

Roht-Arriaza, N. (2000). Amnesty and the International Criminal Court. In D. Shelton, ed., *International Crimes, Peace and Human Rights: The Role of the International Criminal Court*, Ardsley, NY: Transnational Publishers.

Sands, P. (2011). The ICC arrest warrants will make Colonel Gaddafi dig in his heels. *The Guardian*, 4 May 2011 (online).

Saunders, D. (2011). When justice stands in the way of a dictator's departure. *Globe and Mail*, 2 April 2011.

Scharf, M. (2000). Justice versus peace. In S. B. Sewall and C. Kaysen, eds., *The United States and the International Criminal Court*, Oxford: Rowland & Littlefield Publishers.

Sewall, S. B., Kaysen, C., and Scharf, M. (2000). The United States and the International Criminal Court: an overview. In S. B. Sewall and C. Kaysen, eds., *The United States and the International Criminal Court*, Oxford: Rowland & Littlefield Publishers.

Situation in Uganda, Decision Assigning the Situation in Uganda to Pre-Trial Chamber II, ICC-02/04, 5 July 2004.

Snyder, J., and Vinjamuri, L. (2003/2004). Trials and errors – principle and pragmatism in strategies of international justice. *International Security* 28 (3), 5–44.

Spencer, R. (2012). Syria: Bashar al-Assad could be regarded as a war criminal, says Hillary Clinton. *The Telegraph*, 28 February 2012 (online).

Subcommittee on International Human Rights (2016). Mr. William Wiley (Executive Director, Commission for International Justice and Accountability) at the Subcommittee on International Human Rights, 22 November 2016.

Taub, B. (2016). Assad files. *The New Yorker*, 18 April 2016 (online).

Thoms, O. N. T., Ron, J., and Paris, R. (2010). State-level effects of transitional justice: what do we know? *The International Journal of Transitional Justice* 4(3), 1–26.

Tiemessen, A. (2014). The International Criminal Court and the politics of prosecutions. *The International Journal of Human Rights* 18(4–5), 444–61.

United Nations News Centre (2017). Burundi: UN independent panel calls for ICC probe into possible crimes against humanity, 5 September 2017, https://news.un.org/en/story/2017/09/564322.

Vinjamuri, L. (2015). The ICC and the politics of peace and justice. In C. Stahn, ed., *The Law and Practice of the International Criminal Court*, Oxford: Oxford University Press.

Vinjamuri, L., and Snyder J. (2011). ICC Sheriff too quick on the draw. *Duck of Minerva*, May 2011.

de Waal, A., and Stanton, G. H. (2009). Should President Omar al-Bashir of Sudan be charged and arrested by the International Criminal Court? An exchange of views. *Genocide Studies and Prevention* 4(3), 329–53.

Weeks, W. (2002). *Pushing the envelope: moving beyond 'protected villages' in Northern Uganda*, New York: United Nations Office for the Coordination of Humanitarian Affairs.

Wegner, P. (2012). Ambiguous impacts: the effects of the International Criminal Court investigations in Northern Uganda. Refugee Law Project Working Paper No. 2.

(2015). *The International Criminal Court in Ongoing Intrastate Conflicts*, Cambridge: Cambridge University Press.

Weissman, F. (2010). Humanitarian aid and the International Criminal Court: grounds for divorce (2), Social Science Research Council – Making Sense of Darfur, 22 April 2010.

Whiting, A. (2013). ICC Prosecutor announces important changes in new strategic plan. *Just Security* (online).

(2016). The significance of the ICC's first guilty plea. *Just Security* (online).

Wiens, M. (2016). Moving 600 K pieces of paper out of Syria: the Canadian effort to prosecute Syrian war crimes, *CBC*.

Wippman, D. (2006). Exaggerating the ICC. In J. Harrington, M. Milde and R. Vernon, eds., *Bringing Power to Justice?: The Prospects of the International Criminal Court*, Montreal: McGill-Queen's University Press.

INDEX

www.ingramcontent.com/pod-product-compliance
Lightning Source LLC
LaVergne TN
LVHW011811200926
848484LV00005B/1153
* 9 7 8 1 1 0 8 4 8 8 4 9 5 *